Kenzo Tange and the Metabolist Movement

Seven young Japanese architects and designers, pursuing a new approach to urbanism, founded an avant-garde group in 1960 and published its radical manifesto called *Metabolism: The Proposals for New Urbanism*. Numerous futuristic urban visions, along with experimental architectural practices, meant that the Metabolists became emblems of Japan's postwar cultural resurgence. At the root of the Metabolist urban utopias was a particular notion of the city as an organic process. It stood in opposition to the Modernist paradigm of urbanism and led to such ambitious design concepts as artificial land, marine civilization, metabolic cycle, megastructure, and group form, which embodied the Metabolists' ideals of social change.

The first full-length critical account of the Metabolist movement focusing on its urbanism and utopianism, this book situates Metabolism in the context of Japan's mass urban reconstruction, economic miracle, and socio-political reorientation. Zhongjie Lin argues that the Metabolists' fantastic urban ideas, which often envisioned the sea and the sky as human habitats of the future, were in fact the architects' response to the particular urban and cultural crises confronting postwar Japanese society.

Tracing the evolution of Metabolism from its inception at the 1960 World Design Conference to its grand swansong at Osaka's Expo '70, this study examines the works of Kenzo Tange, Kisho Kurokawa, Fumihiko Maki, Kiyonori Kikutake, and Arata Isozaki, among others, who have profoundly influenced contemporary architecture and urbanism in the world. This movement, characterized by diverse design and social ideas, will be of interest to architectural and urban historians, architects and anyone interested in avant-garde design or Japanese architecture.

Zhongjie Lin is Assistant Professor of Architecture and Urban Design at the University of North Carolina at Charlotte.

Kenzo Tange and the Metabolist Movement

Urban Utopias of Modern Japan

Zhongjie Lin

Routledge
Taylor & Francis Group

LONDON AND NEW YORK

First published 2010
by Routledge
2 Park Square, Milton Park, Abingdon, Oxon, OX14 4RN

Simultaneously published in the USA and Canada
by Routledge
270 Madison Avenue, New York, NY 10016

Routledge is an imprint of the Taylor & Francis Group, an informa business

© 2010 Zhongjie Lin

Typeset in Univers by
Keystroke, Tettenhall, Wolverhampton
Printed and bound in Great Britain by
TJ International Ltd., Padstow, Cornwall

British Library Cataloguing in Publication Data
A catalogue record for this book is available from the British Library

Library of Congress Cataloging-in-Publication Data
Lin, Zhongjie, 1973–
    Kenzo Tange and the Metabolist Movement : urban utopias of modern
    Japan / Zhongjie Lin.
        p. cm.
    Includes bibliographical references and index.
    1. Tange, Kenzo, 1913–2005—Criticism and interpretation.
    2. Metabolism in architecture (Movement)   3. Visionary architecture—
    Japan.   4. City planning—Japan—History—20th century.   I. Title.
    NA1559.T33L56 2010
    720.952′09046—dc22   2009029816

ISBN10: 0–415–77659–7 (hbk)
ISBN10: 0–415–77660–0 (pbk)
ISBN10: 0–203–86030–X (ebk)

ISBN13: 978–0–415–77659–2 (hbk)
ISBN13: 978–0–415–77660–8 (pbk)
ISBN13: 978–0–203–86030–4 (ebk)

To my wife Huilai and daughter Serena

Contents

Illustration credits

The author and publishers would like to thank the following individuals and institutions for giving permission to reproduce illustrations. We have made every effort to contact copyright holders, but if any errors or omissions have been made we would be happy to correct them at a later printing.

Akio Kawasumi: 0.1, 1.33, 3.08, 3.9, 3.13, 3.14, 3.17, 3.18, 3.21
Arata Isozaki Atelier: 1.24, 1.25, 2.2, 2.38, 2.39, 2.40, 2.41
© 2009 Artists Right Society (ARS), New York/VG Bild-Kunst, Bonn: 2.9
© 2009 Artists Right Society (ARS), New York/Frank Lloyd Wright Foundation, Scottsdale, AZ: 2.11
© 2009 Artists Right Society (ARS), New York/ADAGP, Paris/FLC: 2.25
© 2009 Artists Right Society (ARS), New York/Beeldrecht, Amsterdam: 2.29
CNAC/MNAM/Dist. Réunion des Musées Nationaux/Art Resource, New York: 5.15
Huilai Shi: 2.24
International Ocean Exposition Okinawa: 2.31
Jieun Kim: 2.4
Kisho Kurokawa Architect & Associates: 1.6, 1.10, 1.11, 1.12, 1.13, 1.14, 2.6, 2.7, 2.8, 2.12, 2.15, 2.16, 2.17, 2.20, 2.21, 2.22, 5.2, 5.3, 5.4, 5.5, 5.16, 5.20, 5.21, 5.22, 5.23, 6.1, 6.3, 6.4, 6.5, 6.6, 6.7, 6.8, 6.9, 6.10, 6.11
Kiyonori Kikutake: 1.1, 1.3, 1.4, 1.5, 1.7, 1.8, 1.9, 2.14, 2.18, 2.23, 3.7
Kiyoshi Awazu: 2.19
Koji Horiuchi: 3.24
Kokusai kenchiku: 1.26, 1.27
Lei Liu: 2.5
Louis I. Kahn Collection, University of Pennsylvania and the Pennsylvania Historic and Museum Commission: 3.11, 4.15
Maki & Associates: 1.15, 1.16, 2.32, 2.34, 2.36, 2.37
Masato Otaka Architect & Associates: 2.28, 3.6
Museum of Modern Art/Licensed by SCALA /Art Resource, New York: 5.18
Peter Wong: 2.3, 6.13
Shinkenchiku-sha: 5.12, 5.13
Shokokusha: 1.22, 1.32, 4.7, 6.14

Acknowledgements

My study of Kenzo Tange and the Metabolist movement began in 2002 as my dissertation project, which forms the basis of this book. I enjoyed wonderful advice from my mentors and professors at the University of Pennsylvania during the dissertation stage and beyond. Dr. Gary Hack and Dr. David Leatherbarrow deserve my deepest appreciation for their thoughtful guidance and continuing support. Their encouragement and faith, as well as their scholarly rigor have been a constant source of inspiration for me throughout this project. I also owe a great debt of gratitude to my committee members Jonathan Barnett and Annette Fierro for their insightful advice. Their respective expertises in urban design and technological avant-gardes have significantly enhanced the quality of this study.

I would like to express my sincere gratitude to all my colleagues at the School of Architecture of the University of North Carolina at Charlotte, and particularly Ken Lambla and Betsy West, for supporting my work in myriad ways. I enjoy the open and productive environment my colleagues create, and I thank Peter Wong, Lee Gray, and David Walters for their mentoring and friendship.

I have continued to travel to Japan for this project since the summer of 2004. During these sojourns, I received extraordinary support from several scholars in Tokyo. I am deeply grateful to Kinya Maruyama for guiding me on my initial trip around the country and introducing me to Japan's unique culture. His enthusiasm in vernacular architecture and his profound cultural consciousness inspired me with the connection between the traditional and the modern. Hajime Yatsuka not only kindly provided me a base of operations in Tokyo during 2005/06, but he also shared with me his research sources and made introductions to various people who assisted me in my research. The frequent conversations with him made my sojourns productive. David Stewart, too, offered constructive criticism that led my research into depth. His wonderful monograph of modern Japanese architecture provides a valuable context for this book.

Honor and respect go to all architects and designers involved in the Metabolist movement, and I congratulate them on the fiftieth year anniversary of the publication of *Metabolism: The Proposals for New Urbanism*. In particular I would like to thank Kisho Kurokawa, Arata Isozaki, Fumihiko Maki, and Kiyonori

Acknowledgements

Kikutake for their interviews with me, and for the images and other materials they provided. I am very pleased that Mr. Isozaki kindly accepted my invitation to write a Foreword for this book. I also appreciate the opportunities to meet with architects' descendants, including Mikio Kurokawa and Paul Tange, and I am grateful to them for providing me access to research materials belonging to the firms. I would like to thank Shigeru Matsumoto of Uzo Nishiyama Memorial Library, Misako Mataga of Kisho Kurokawa Architect & Associates, Yoshiko Amiya and Takako Fujimoto of Arata Isozaki Atelier, Yasuko Okuyama of Maki & Associates, Kaori Omura of Kikutake Architects, Yumiko Ichikawa of Tange Associates, and Mr. Horikoshi of Masato Otaka Architect & Associates for helping me collect images, and permissions, and for arranging site visits.

I want to thank a number of friends for their assistance at various stages. Toshio Ozaki helped with communications with architects' firms. Kiwa Matsushita assisted at interviews. Sarah Wilson provided excellent editorial assistance. Ken Tadashi Oshima translated Isozaki's essay into English. Peter Laurence offered valuable comments on my proposals. Peter Wong, Lei Liu, Jieun Kim, and Lan Wang provided their photographs. Heather Woofter, who is curating an exhibition on Metabolic Cities, kindly shared research sources and included me in interviews she arranged.

I have been privileged to work with the publishers, Routledge. I would like to thank editors Caroline Mallinder, Alex Hollingsworth, Francesca Ford, and Georgina Johnson for their impeccable work.

This project would not have been possible without generous financial support from several institutions. The publication grant from the Graham Foundation for Advanced Studies in the Fine Arts, the Japan Society for the Promotion of Science fellowship, a travel grant from the Association of Asian Studies, and UNC Charlotte faculty research grants assisted me in my travels, research, and completion of this book. Additional funds had been provided by the Japan Foundation and Asian Cultural Council in the early stages of this project.

This book is devoted, posthumously, to my grandfather Xianyong Kong who enlightened me in discovering the joys of reading and writing in my childhood, and guided me with his uprightness and wisdom as I grew up. I also dedicate it to my parents and in-laws in China for their unfailing faith, to my wife Huilai for always being a part of my life, and to my daughter Serena, whose growth and cheerful smile have been the best travel companion in my "journey" working toward this publication.

Foreword

Arata Isozaki

Those who set their aims at establishing future utopia, organize movements toward its realization, and put their ideas into practice as a guiding role in various artistic, social and political spheres are called the avant-gardes. One probably comes up with something like this in attempting to identify the historical characteristics of modern art movements from the beginning of the twentieth century. In the development of modern art and architecture in the twentieth century, especially the first half, first a movement was formed and then a manifesto put forth. A classic example was Futurism. Soon the forms of such movements expanded, and one could recognize the emergence of movements in the various "isms" in the informal appearance of Impressionism and Cubism, all the way to Symbolism. Furthermore, since around 1910, the various artistic factions like Futurism, Purism, Dadaism, Surrealism, and Existentialism proliferated and continued to create a greater current of the so-called modern artistic movement. The sphere of architectural design also completely overlapped with all of the artistic movements. Here one can see an institutionalizing tendency rather than a single movement. De Stijl, the Bauhaus, Russian Constructivism, etc. developed in tandem and grew into a movement in the form of a congress like the Congrès International d'Architecture Moderne (CIAM). As a result, the historic accounts of artistic and architectural movements in the twentieth century followed the format of a single chart of various groups. At the end, modern art and architecture is narrated according to the history of avant-garde movements.

In 1960 Metabolism was formed in Tokyo and became the final example of a modern architectural movement to raise a manifesto. I think the historical role of the avant-garde movement in a broader sense ended in the failure of the global cultural revolution in 1968. Of course, after 1968 expressions of the avant-garde and avant-gardism were still often used, but they were more like a metaphor or rhetoric, and did not have the historic meaning associated with the earlier avant-garde movements. Radical movements and ideas, free of ideology, were pushed forward. However, the original avant-garde form that organized the movement for realizing a single ideology by raising a manifesto can no longer be seen. Its historical role ended in the 1960s.

Today, if one looks back at the Metabolist movement that took place in Tokyo half a century ago, one should look at the two contexts that are layered upon it. One is the global development of the Modern Movement of architecture. Another is the particular context of Japan as an island nation on the edge of the Far East. Regarding the process of global development, it is sufficient to say that Metabolism was the last example of a modern art and architectural movement seeking utopia as an aim to raise an avant-garde manifesto. It provided a foothold connecting Japanese modern architecture to the global development of modern architecture.

Around 1960, the masters of modern architecture all reached the age of retirement and a generational change took place. At the same time, the architectural situation within the society shifted. In other words, there were several signs and preparations being made for realizing the condition of Postmodernism that became apparent in 1968. I believe that the Metabolist movement was not the beginning of the next period, rather it must be situated as the last modern architectural movement of the twentieth century that can be seen in the form of a movement.

The few comments that I would like to add here describe the special context that gave birth to the pure form of the technological utopia within Japan as a country on the edge of the Far East vis-à-vis the center of the West. The land throughout the nation received a devastating blow during the Second World War and was occupied militarily until the mid-1950s. The modern architectural movement, formerly developed at the center, was under a transition. In other words, if we also add the special conditions of the acceptance of modern architecture in Japan since 1930, this was Japanese domestication that can be seen as a unique transformation that I call the Japanization.

If we switch to the point of 1930 in Russia and Germany, which were at the center of the avant-garde movement of modern architecture at that time, we can see the movement itself was at a critical stage open to political criticism. Because of the counter-modernism of Stalinism and Nazism, the activities of modernism in these countries were stopped. In exactly the same period, China, the United States, and Japan, which had been on the fringe of the modern movement, began to receive influences of modern architecture from the West. These countries had already been on their way to modernization but, rather than spontaneously creating a progressive movement, they began to transplant modernism from the center of its birth. The proponents of the progressive movement of modernism were people in a position to determine its contents like critics, architects, and artists. Because what was transplanted and received as pre-made form was selectively transferred, these impresarios played a tremendous role as the driving force and connoisseur. Around 1930, one should probably pay attention to the activities of the intellectuals in charge of making the cultural policy for the Chinese Nationalist Party in Nanjing (China), of the first design curator of the Museum of Modern Art (MoMA) in New York, Philip Johnson (the US), and of the Tokyo Imperial University professor Hideto Kishida (Japan).

The Chinese Nationalist Party built a few national memorials such as the modern design of Sun Yat Sen's Mausoleum, through which they institutionalized a style that fused the traditional Chinese roof with Art Deco. During this process, Liang Sicheng who returned from studying with Paul Cret at the University of Pennsylvania stood out. The importance of his activities came to be seen after 1950 in the intellectual discourse of architectural styles and city building in the People's Republic of China.

Philip Johnson organized "Modern Architecture: An International Exhibition" (1932) at MoMA, and published *The International Style,* written together with Henry-Russell Hitchcock. The book was based on a survey of avant-garde architectural movements born in Europe, but his personal preference was for Mies van der Rohe. Guided by the emerging force of late Bauhaus post-humanism, Mies led the main stream of modern architectural interpretations in the United States in the 1930s. Such interpretation shaped the ideological current, fusing functionalism, industrialism, and metropolization. It resulted in the common idea of modern architecture equaling the International Style, and was coupled with the United States' establishment of economic and political hegemony in the world during the 1950s. The acceptance of Mies van der Rohe in the 1930s marked the outset of this move.

Also around 1930, Hideto Kishida (the mentor of Kenzo Tange) as Japan's impresario selected Le Corbusier. Kunio Maekawa and Junzo Sakakura had already spent time at Le Corbusier's atelier in Paris, and of course there were many Japanese who studied at the Bauhaus, but Kishida picked from the group Kunio Maekawa, and later Kenzo Tange, and backed up their activities. The one who transplanted Le Corbusier in its pure form, by contrast, was Junzo Sakakura. Kishida tried to reinterpret traditional Japanese architecture from the constructive perspective of modernism, and searched for a model that integrated it with Corbusian elements. Tange was the one who clearly responded to this goal. Such reception and transformation already began as the process of domestication during the Second World War. The debate resurfaced in the 1950s as the confrontation between and integration of the "national element" and the "modern element."

During the 1930s, these peripheral countries selectively accepted various strands of modernist architecture that conformed to their respective national characteristics. Due to the Second World War, this process took a different form of domestication and each of these countries developed it independently. In the 1950s, these architectural forms became matured. Through its victory in the war, the United States became a hegemonic country, and it tried to disseminate the functionalist international-style architecture around the world. That was a global trend until it faltered during the Vietnam War.

Soon after the communist revolution, when China undertook building its own nation in conjunction with Soviet Russia, they could not avoid the artistic methods of socialist realism under Stalinism. This was an old style of form modeled for opposing the formalism of the former Russian avant-garde. Then in the mid-1950s, Khrushchev demythologized Stalinism. However in the sphere of architecture, the country did not move beyond simple industrialism and functionalism. This ideological debate cast a deep shadow on the debates of architectural styles of the new China in the 1950s. The political leaders of China invited many self-claimed socialist realist architects and artists to play a guiding role in architecture. At the same time, they politically rejected Liang Sicheng's attempt to realize methodological reform of appraising and preserving traditional Chinese architecture from a modernist standpoint. The new China, which once again initiated a revolution half a century after a modern nation had been made, adopted an eclectic style (as seen in the Metropolitan Plan of Beijing and the Ten Grand Architecture project) as a political mandate to create a national expression with a flavor of traditional style in the form of the nineteenth-century nation state. This fell into the dead-end trap of continued domestication that finally became the re-evaluation of the "domestic methods." Modern architecture could not help but be detoured until the political reform that began in the 1980s.

In the 1950s, Japan entered a period in which economic growth began to be possible, born out of the condition of the stabilized policy of the welfare nation called the "1955 System." It followed the institutional reform of agricultural liberation and the breaking up of *zaibatsu* (the financial clique) after the Second World War, along with the Korean War in the neighboring country that sustained Japan's economic prosperity. Notwithstanding the new system and the ongoing social reorganization, cultural and ideological debates still developed along the axis centered on the issues of modern/tradition and modernism/nationalism dating from the 1930s. Kenzo Tange was the one at the center of the debates, who continued them from the 1930s onward and developed an independent model. A simple dialectical problematic was established as Jomonesqe = populist = ethnic versus Yayoiesque = elitist = international. Tange and Taro Okamoto, who studied the Western avant-gardes, advocated such dialecticism created through the tension of coexistence of both extremities. Tange initiated the point of view of integrating such binomial coexistence. He articulated this characteristic in the Hiroshima Peace Memorial Building (1955) and the Tokyo Olympic Stadium (1964). What made that possible was the fact that both buildings are national projects. In other words, although "Japan" as a modern nation state had been downplayed since the end of the Second World War, even with its meager national power, its strength as a unified nation still existed. This type of relationships continued until the Osaka World Exposition in 1970.

To summarize, the center of modernism, guided by the founding avant-gardes up to 1930 in Europe, shifted to peripheral countries – China, America, and Japan – where it started to be accepted selectively according to national conditions. Some twenty years of reception based on national conditions took place as a form of domestication. Liang Sicheng (China), Philip Johnson (who played both roles as impresario and architect in the United States), and Kenzo Tange (Japan) were those of the same generation who propelled this process. Their work represented the final form of transposed modernism. There were architects who continued as modernists afterwards, but the period as a whole began to show aspects that differed from the linear development or simple progress of political and social modernization. The avant-garde as an intellectual movement welcomed the end of the frustration from the cultural revolution of 1968. One can consider this phenomenon from the relationship between the nation state and capitalism, which coexisted basically from the beginning. In Japan up until around 1970, they were amalgamated, but after that capitalism began to take over the nation. Relatively speaking, the national image declined. The image of the nineteenth century nation state was expressed by the "architecture" of its capital. In the twentieth century, the metropolis itself becomes the lead actor, and architecture began to be absorbed by the metropolis. In short, the "city" became the image. This situation had been foreseen from the start of the modern movement. However, these issues went beyond the nation as an institution and dominant ideology, and became the comprehensive social problem in the mid-twentieth century. The Metabolist movement arose exactly from this situation.

Kenzo Tange recognized the problem of going beyond the "city" and "architecture." He was an assistant professor in the city planning orientation, newly formed after the war within the division of architectural engineering at the University of Tokyo. However what he lectured and researched was not related to the technical necessities controlling the city concretely through legislation and city planning. Rather it was related to the historical development of urban morphology that should be called Urbanism/Urban Design. Tange studied the movement of CIAM led by Le Corbusier focusing on the topic of the city. This differed from the concrete approach of city planning adopted by the bureaucracy to establish legal regulations generated by and based on reality; rather, it was examined from the perspective of the modernist planning aiming at social reform that moved toward utopia. Modernism was a utopian movement in a broader sense. The issue of "city" had remained the theme throughout the development of Tange's career since his Greater East Asia Co-Prosperity Sphere Memorial Plan (1942) during the Second World War. A materialization of this concept was the Hiroshima Peace Park Memorial Plan (1949–1955). This plan was applauded at the 1951 CIAM meeting organized around the theme of the Core of the City. As a memorial for the revitalization of Hiroshima's atomic bombing site, it provided a concrete form representing the method of modernism's utopian planning on its pure level.

As stated above, in contrast to the nineteenth-century nation state's capital city that prioritized architecture, the twentieth-century metropolis focused on the city. The postwar reconstruction plans in the 1950s heralded the theme of city: the reactionary restoration plans became the mainstream, as seen in the plans of reconstruction across Europe except for cases like the "Berlin Reconstruction Plan competition" (1955) that illustrated the impossibility of simply reproducing the city. For example, the reconstructions of the centers of Warsaw and Frankfurt simply became rehabilitations. The same thing happened in Japan, although most wooden buildings had been burned to the ground. What was implemented on these ruins was based on the prevalent method of city planning that had been institutionalized and commonly acknowledged throughout the world; therefore there was no room for a utopian proposal based on CIAM's modernist principles to intervene in the reconstruction. Through the 1950s, only cities like Chandigarh and Brasilia were left with the mark of utopian plans. Moreover, when criticisms were raised with regards to the contradictions inherent in the implementation of modernist methods, both these projects fell into a state of failure.

In the 1950s, Japan entered the extended period of economic growth, and after the conservative party's policy for the stabilization of social welfare (the 1955 System), population began to concentrate in big cities. In other words, cities like Tokyo had to undergo a transformation of their urban form. The metropolis characteristically dissolved its previous boundary (for example, the city wall) and expanded to the surrounding area (mostly farmland). However, the environs of Tokyo had already been urbanized and there was no room for expansion. Overcrowding occurred within the city in which land ownership was subdivided to cope with urban growth. At this point the plan to extend urban areas over Tokyo Bay emerged. Such a concept was initiated by bureaucrats who held the responsibility for city policy as well as the financial sector. Kenzo Tange cautiously moved toward this direction. He started with his research through a studio project that studied a marine city plan on Boston Bay on the occasion of being invited to lecture at the Massachusetts Institute of Technology. Tange presented the model at the 1960s Tokyo World Design Conference, in which the Metabolist Manifesto was distributed as a small pamphlet, and then he began to work on the Plan for Tokyo 1960. This project continued through 1960, and he officially presented it in a NHK (Japan Broadcasting Co.) special program during the New Year's day of the following year. Special mention must be made that its public debut was through the medium of television.

This utopian project literally began on a virtual place. If we assumed that the utopia is nowhere, then the Plan for Tokyo 1960 is truly a utopian plan.

(Translated by Ken Tadashi Oshima)

Introduction

City as process

A map of the world that does not include utopia is not worth even glancing at, for it leaves out the country at which Humanity is always landing.

Oscar Wilde, "The Soul of Man Under Socialism" (1891)

Visionary urban plans often serve as utopian projects to formulate certain social ideals. This phenomenon is more conspicuous in societies that are undergoing dramatic transitions politically, economically, or aesthetically. Italy in the early Renaissance, France during the period of great revolution, and Europe as a whole at the dawn of the twentieth century have provided some of the best examples of such utopian projects. Japanese society in the late 1950s and the 1960s turned out to be another fertile ground that nourished visionary urban designs. These Japanese utopian projects were closely associated with the avant-garde movement called Metabolism, which was launched in 1960, when a group of young architects and designers published their manifesto – *Metabolism: The Proposals for New Urbanism* – at the World Design Conference in Tokyo.[1] The manifesto called for radically reconfiguring the modern city, a process the Metabolists believed would lead to a new order critical for a society entering the post-industrial age. They developed and enriched their urban design concepts throughout the 1960s. Their schemes often envisioned sea and sky as future sites for human habitats, and they suggested the city would grow and transform in a manner like the evolution and metamorphosis of an organism. The time was right for such a futuristic tone and technological optimism: the decade of the 1960s was not only known as an epoch of ground-breaking technological discoveries, it also witnessed the most significant economic growth in Japanese history, later known as the "Japanese Miracle." Metabolists' utopian attempts to introduce a new urbanism were responses to the dynamic urbanization and transformation of Japanese cities during this period, and, on a more profound level, their plans addressed the nation's political transition and cultural reinvigoration after the end of the Second World War.

At the root of Metabolist urban utopias was a particular notion of "city as process." This idea stood in opposition to the modernist paradigm of city design and led to such radical design concepts as artificial land, urban structuring, marine civilization, and metabolic cycle, all of which embodied the Metabolists' ideals of social change. Inspired by rapid expansion and unpredictable change characteristic of contemporary cities, the Metabolists envisioned no physical destination of the city's development, but rather created patterns "which can be followed consistently from present into the distant future."[2] They approached the city as a living organism consisting of elements with different metabolic cycles: some are persistent while others tend to be ephemeral. To accommodate a city's growth and regeneration, Metabolists advanced transformable technologies based on prefabricated components and the replacement of obsolete parts according to varying life cycles. This notion of growth and change at the scale of a city ultimately overthrew traditional theories of city planning and demanded a redefinition of several critical relationships in design: order/chaos, permanence/transience, collective/individual, and planning/spontaneity.

Kenzo Tange and the Metabolist Movement: Urban Utopias of Modern Japan focuses on Metabolist architects' visionary concepts of the city and investigates their design and political implications for postwar Japanese society. Tracing the evolution of Metabolism from its inception at the 1960 World Design Conference in Tokyo to its grand swansong at the Osaka World Expositions in 1970, this book examines a formative period of postwar Japanese architecture. Metabolism not only involved its initial members, including Kiyonori Kikutake (1928–), Kisho Kurokawa (1934–2007), Fumihiko Maki (1928–), Masato Otaka (1923–), and Noboru Kawazoe (1926–), but also a few like-minded architect-urbanists, prominently Kenzo Tange (1913–2005) and Arata Isozaki (1931–). Tange played a particularly significant role in the Metabolist movement. Though never a formal member of Metabolism, he mentored the younger architects and virtually created the group by chairing the program committee of the 1960 World Design Conference. Tange's rationalist visions and monumental approach to architecture and urbanism influenced the Metabolists; in turn, his collaborations (and occasionally competitions) with Metabolists impacted the development of Tange's own design concepts. Tange's 1960 Plan for Tokyo, also known as the Tokyo Bay Plan, represented a sophisticated synthesis of Metabolist urban concepts, expanding their utopian themes to an unprecedented scale. Serving as a polemical alternative to the official plans for Tokyo, Tange's plan posed itself to fundamentally transform the urban structure of this mega-city for the imminent arrival of the post-industrial age. It thus illuminated the complex relationship between utopianism and urbanism, which is the theme of exploration in this book.

1
enzo Tange,
lan for Tokyo
960. Model view

Utopianism and urbanism

Tange and the Metabolists were not planners by training. Nor did they have the administrative power to implement their planning concepts. A critical distinction between utopian planners and professional planners, according to Robert Fishman, lies in their attitudes toward social change. While the former tend to advocate radical reaction to the status quo, the latter confine themselves to "technical problems" and are particularly intent on discouraging any suggestion that urban planning might serve the cause of social change.[3] This utopian nature was evident in Metabolists' works. They searched for emerging future-directed tendencies, "struggling to find expression against the opposition of established elites."[4] These young architects believed that a revolution in architecture and city design, more than anything else, would lead to a new order for modern society. They were both dismayed by the chaos in Japanese big cities during rapid urban growth and economic restructuring and frustrated by the impotence of the authorities to cope with these challenges. They thus countered mainstream planning with radical schemes, offering alternative images of modern society.

Metabolists' urban visions followed a longstanding tradition of utopian planning, in which speculations of future environment were combined with ideals of social progress. Since ancient times, conceptions of the good life or a perfect commonwealth have been firmly anchored to the form of the city. It was in this sense that Lewis Mumford claimed that "the first utopia was the city itself."[5] Conscious invention of utopias began in the modern times, when the idea received new considerations. Since Thomas More coined the term "utopia" in 1516, giving it an ambiguous meaning mixing "eu-topia" (good place) and "ou-topia" (no place), the word has been used to describe both the pursuit of an ideal state and the criticism of the reality.[6] The relationship of these two agendas was articulated in Karl Mannheim's definition, in which utopia was referred to as a "state of mind" that attempts to transcend the reality of its origin. In 1960 he wrote:

> A state of mind is utopian when it is incongruous with the state of reality within which it occurs. . . . This incongruence is always evident in the fact that such a state of mind in experience, in thought, and in practice, is oriented towards objectives which do not exist in the actual situation. However, we should not regard utopia as every state of mind which is incongruous with and transcends the immediate situation. Only those orientations transcending reality will be referred to by us as utopian which, when they pass over into product, tend to shatter, either partially or wholly, the order of things prevailing at the time. . . . In limiting the meaning of the term "utopia" to that type of orientation which transcends reality and which at the same time breaks the bonds of the existing order, a distinction is set up between the utopian and the ideological states of mind.[7]

Although Mannheim emphasized the "transcendence" of utopia, he never-theless recognized the relationship between utopia and the real world "within which it occurs."[8] Clearly, utopias always have a foot in reality. It is thus no surprise that utopian urban projects often emerged in periods of social transitions when a new social order challenged the old, such as the early Renaissance and during the Industrial Revolution. The early Renaissance witnessed Alberti and Filarete's conceptions of humanistic ideal cities in their respective treatises, as well as various artists' representations of utopian societies.[9] The deteriorating urban conditions and intensified social conflicts during the Industrial Revolution, accompanying the dramatic growth of productive power and great technological innovations, set the stage for a series of escapist utopian speculations by Robert Owen, Charles Fourier, and Claude-Nicolas Ledoux.[10] Similarly, the emergence of Metabolists' technological utopias was not incidental; rather, the dynamic yet chaotic social conditions and politico-economic turbulence in Japan after the Second World War nourished the architects' radical ideas of urban restructuring.

To a great extent, utopia projects addressed the central dilemmas of modern society and involved debates about different social ideas. From the root in modernity emerged two competing ideologies, rationalism and libertarianism, each influencing a series of utopian ideas. A rationalist utopia frequently had a predilection for highly centralized and regulated, if not regimented, social systems. A libertarian-oriented utopia countered rationalism by stressing decentralized power and local solidarities. These two types of utopias reflected the contradictions between a call for order and a desire for freedom, as well as the tension between a reliance on centralized, large-scale organization and a claim of local autonomy and individual creativity. This relationship between order and freedom basically dominated the development of modern utopias, making an imprint on the Metabolist movement as well.

Rationalist utopians held that a society was an object amendable to scientific study and rational construction. Mumford has, quite appropriately, given a name to such rationalist notion: the machine. He observed:

> It is at the very beginning of urban civilization that one encounters not only the archetypal form of the city as utopia but also another coordinate utopian institution essential to any system of communal regimentation: the machine. In that archaic constellation the notion of a world completely under scientific and technological *control*, the dominant utopian fantasy of our present age, first become evident.[11]

This notion of machine gained more significance in the twentieth century. In its extreme it resulted in the European totalitarian regimes in the interwar period, but it also influenced many other aspects of modern society in less drastic manifestations. In America, Frederick Taylor's theory of scientific management, originally conceptualized for industrial production, fundamentally changed ideas about the organization of modern society.[12] Soon Henry Ford pushed this notion of machine further by introducing the moving assembly line into his Model T factory. At almost the same time, American economist Thorstein Veblen wrote an essay attacking the disorderly and avaricious way the country was being run, and he called for a rational reorganization by professional engineers.[13] His proposal received more considerations during the Great Depression when Franklin Roosevelt incorporated it into his New Deal. Similar thoughts influenced France in the nineteenth century in the form of Saint-Simonianism, which suggested that the organization of industries should form the basis of an emerging new order run not by the state but by social elites, including industrialists, scientists, and artists. This view was taken up again in the early twentieth century by Neo-Saint-Simonians, also known as "technocrats," who similarly called for a rational organization of production and distribution led by technically trained managers.

Such technocratic ideas were obviously tempting to visionary architects who dreamed of a new order for the physical environment and a social system in accordance with their urban ideals. Though their political stances might have varied, these architects "shared a view of the machine as a social liberator, capable of provoking equality between men, not only by relieving them of physical toil but above all by engendering a universal art and a truly collective society."[14] For them, a city is a rational entity of systematic organization. Though there would be room for private speculations, they should only take place within a framework of public management and control, which often assumed the form of an articulated social hierarchy. This rational view of city was most evident in several planning schemes by Le Corbusier, who was influenced by Neo-Saint-Simonianism. His *Ville Contemporaine* (1922), a "city of towers," represented an ideal form dedicated to the industrial age with its efficiency, centralization, and uncompromised geometrical order.[15] A cluster of sixty-story office towers occupied the center of this "Contemporary City for Three Million People," providing space for technical, professional, and intellectual leaders in charge of the management of the nation. The architect's concern was with the world of distribution and administration, which he believed would determine the future of industrial civilization. His rigorous urban form went back to a Renaissance rationalist tradition as the architect insisted that geometrical regularity was "the symbol of expression of man's freedom from the contingent, his triumphant rationality and his point of contact with the deepest forces of the universe."[16]

The libertarian utopian impulse also stemmed from the Renaissance, but found its representations more explicitly in More's *Utopia*, which addressed the egalitarian and democratic spirit of modernity. Kristan Kumar observes:

> In its universality and fundamental egalitarianism, in its recognition of the necessity and dignity of labor, *Utopia* reflects More's Christianity more than his Classicism, his commitment to the equality of souls over and above his admiration for Platonic rationalism. This is what also separates *Utopia* from all previous versions and visions of the good society. More's *Utopia* announced that the modern utopia would be democratic, not hierarchical.[17]

The ideals of an egalitarian and democratic society were further pursued in modern city planning, as indicated in the partial realization of such social experiments in the twentieth century as Ebenezer Howard's Garden City and Frank Lloyd Wright's Broadacre City. In Broadacre City, Wright envisioned an ideal society based on individual land ownership.[18] He advocated decentralization of cities, which would make it possible for everyone to live according to his chosen lifestyle on personal property – a minimum of an acre per person. The center of society would move to homesteads spreading throughout the Broadacre city. A network of highways would connect the scattered elements of society and bind all citizens in a common endeavor of equality and democracy, values that were essential to Wright's utopian society.

The concern about equality and democracy also existed in Le Corbusier's ideal cities, but they were subordinate to the need for planning, and thus resulted in different urban forms. Instead of decentralization, Le Corbusier chose to tie urban spaces and programs in a highly concentrated and regulated pattern by using advanced industrial technologies. He wished this reversion to Platonism would create a single society united in belief and action while accommodating democratic and populist needs. Such duality combining rational planning and social democracy also manifested itself in the Metabolists' urban utopias. These Japanese architects were influenced by both rational and democratic impulses but inspired particularly by Le Corbusier's grand visions.

Like the master, Metabolists held that future society should represent an assertion of human rationality over impersonal forces, with architects assuming responsibility as mediators of urban reconciliation and construction, translating core values into a workable plan. Placed within the historic context of Japan, such rationalism can be read as running counter to both the wartime destruction and the disorder of postwar reconstruction. At the same time, arising from the introspection of an authoritarian regime during the Second World War as well as postwar American occupation was a democratic and populist awareness among progressive intellectuals. The marriage of rationalist and democratic impulses led to the Metabolists' urban design solutions, which were characterized by a comprehensive urban framework within which "each man can build his own house."[19] Their utopian schemes again reflected the contradictions between the centralized rational planning and the desire for identity and individuality, issues tied to the cultural context in postwar Japan, as this book will reveal.

What the Metabolists contributed to the tradition of utopian thinking was a radical notion of technology unique to the 1960s. Architects and urbanists in the 1960s were inspired by dramatic technological advances, such as new developments in genetics and life sciences, explorations of the moon and space, the inventions of robots and computers, and communication technologies, and developed a can-do mentality in conceiving an urban future. The speed with which technology changed in the postwar decades and the degree to which it infiltrated human life made any established urban form look retrogressively nostalgic. As a result, the 1960s saw numerous bold technological utopian concepts such as walking city, plug-in city, nomad city, computer city, and endless city. The Metabolists were particularly keen in demonstrating the potential of technology to change social structure. Their projects took this issue to an unprecedented scale, often involving the massive remaking of landform that would enable control of social development while facilitating mobility and liberty of individuals.

Post-CIAM discourse of urbanism

The rise of Metabolism manifested a significant transformation of architectural culture in the postwar decades. The investigation of this utopian movement, therefore, must be situated in reference to the international architectural avant-gardes of the 1950s and 1960s that stimulated rethinking of urbanism. The dream of changing the world by means of comprehensive intervention in the physical environment was certainly not foreign to architects in the modernist era. Inspired by dramatic technological and social changes, avant-garde architects since the beginning of the twentieth century had been enthusiastic about creating a total human environment. Among these avant-garde schools were Italian Futurism, Russian Constructivism, and German Expressionism.[20] However, it was not until the founding of the *Congrès Internationaux d'Architecture Moderne* (CIAM) in 1928 that the various isolated efforts were directed into a unified venue. Under the strong influence of Le Corbusier, CIAM made no secret of its goal to pursue comprehensive approaches to human environment, placing a particular emphasis on urbanism.[21] The historic fourth CIAM meeting assumed "Functional City" as its theme, resulting in a commanding series of proposals on town planning, later published in *The Athens Charter* in 1942.[22] This document directed planning efforts toward a rigid alignment of functional zones in town layouts, including dwelling, work, recreation, and circulation. It became a dominant methodology in city design as CIAM rose to prominence after the Second World War.

The 1950s, however, witnessed increasing dissatisfaction with CIAM's mechanical design principles. Architects reacted by turning to either regional concerns or avant-garde attitudes to design, echoing a general opposition to CIAM's bureaucratization. Such reactions were intensified at the tenth meeting in Dubrovnik in 1956 with a theme, prepared by the group called "Team 10," calling for solutions for "Problems of Human Habitat." The Team 10 architects, led by Peter and Alison Smithson of England and Aldo van Eyck of Holland, challenged the modernist establishment in urbanism with more empirical patterns of "human association," seeking inspirations in anthropological studies and the spontaneity of popular culture.[23] Team 10's uncompromising stance ultimately led to the dissolution of CIAM at its last meeting in Otterlo, Holland, in 1959.[24]

This study views the dissolution of CIAM in 1959 as a symbolic and critical event. It signaled a transition from a period dominated by a unified paradigm in architecture and urbanism to a new era characterized by multiple visions and competing ideologies which opened up possibilities for exploring new approaches to urbanism. Since then, functionalism has continued to be challenged by various theories of structuralism, semiology, and sociology. Instead of presenting a monolithic, self-consistent program, architects in the 1960s explored new bases for "scientific" determination of form, considering differences as aspects of pluralism to be expressed in the creative process without inhibition. Their works exhibited an array of interests, with commitment to the search for a more democratic and intrinsic ordering of the built environment.[25]

Tange was among the forty architects in their "forties" invited to the Otterlo meeting.[26] In addition to his recent projects (Kagawa Prefectural Office and Tokyo City Hall), Tange introduced to this international audience Kikutake's visionary plans, including "Tower-shaped City" and "Sky House." He thus sowed the seeds of the emerging Metabolist movement. After the meeting, Tange traveled to Boston to teach at the Massachusetts Institute of Technology where he instructed students to design a "community of 25,000 residents" on the Boston Bay. The project was lauded as the "first real megastructure."[27] According to the architect himself, it also marked a decisive shift in his approach to urban design "from functionalism to structuralism," and thus anticipated his Tokyo Bay Plan completed barely a year later.[28]

This book situates the Metabolist movement within the post-CIAM architectural culture and follows its development through the 1960s. This period corresponds to the era of socio-political transformation under the Economic

Miracle in Japan, and witnessed a transition in architecture from "Modernism" to "Postmodernism" in general. Experimental architectures flourished in this transitional period. Visionary architects and urbanists throughout the world, including Team 10, Louis I. Kahn, Yona Friedman, Archigram, Situationist International, and Metabolists, concentrated on inventing instruments which, in an attempt to fully exploit the implicit possibilities in an integrated use of new technologies, revolutionized traditional urbanism. Therefore in their 1976 *Architettura contemporanea*, Manfredo Tafuri and Francesco Dal Co claimed the late 1950s and the 1960s as the era of the "international concept of utopia."[29] At the same time, however, there was another group of urbanists – prominently among them Jane Jacobs, Christopher Alexander, and Aldo Rossi – who disagreed with the utopian ideas of urbanism. They dismissed those techno-utopias as overlooking human nature, social complexity, and the symbolic dimension of the city.[30] The debate between the utopian and the anti-utopian schools constituted the theme of urbanism in the 1960s. Even within either camp, different and often contradictory impulses can be found. Each architect or urbanist approached the city from a different perspective, reflecting the influences of a variety of social ideologies and local inspirations and emphasizing different aspects of human environments. The debates on utopian urbanism set up the background for this study of the Metabolist movement, which in turn sheds new light on the inherent complexity of postwar architectural culture that arose from various visions of the modern society.

Megastructure

The year Tafuri and Dal Co's *Architettura contemporanea* was published, Reyner Banham also completed his monograph investigating the phenomenon of this "international concept of utopias."[31] His title *Megastructure* summed up numerous utopian attempts in the 1950s and 1960s, and the term was soon widely recognized and later adopted by other historical accounts such as Jonathan Barnett's *The Elusive City*.[32] Both Tafuri's and Banham's historical accounts portrayed these utopian movements as an international liaison of architectural avant-gardes representing shared reactions to the interwar modernism rather than scattered local interventions, and both books featured Tange and the Metabolists' works as an important part of this global landscape. Such a conception of megastructure, though overly generalized, indicates the multiple connections of the Metabolist movement with its Western counter-parts: the influence of ideologies concerning postindustrial space from the West, the shared concerns of massification, mobility, and transformation of the modern city, the common strategy of using super-scale spatial frameworks to accommodate such change, transformation, and movement.

There is evidence beyond these justifications that Metabolism is a legitimate megastructural movement: the word "megastructure" was in fact coined by a Metabolist – Fumihiko Maki.[33] According to Maki's definition in the 1964 *Investigations in Collective Form*, megastructure refers to a strategy in urban design that tends to house the programs of a whole city or part of a city in

0.2
Reyner Banham,
Megastructure,
1976. Cover page

a single structure. Although he traced its origin to ancient Italian hill-towns, Maki insisted that megastructure was "made possible by present technology."[34] Maki's incisive observation conceptualized the new methodology that had just emerged from urban design practices in the 1950s but soon turned into a strong force sweeping across the architectural world as rapid expansion of modern cities seemed to justify urban interventions of exceptional scale. By the time Banham's book was published, he was able to identify hundreds of projects, built and unbuilt, which he called "the dinosaurs of the modern movement."[35] Banham described megastructures as composed of elements in two extreme scales: a single structural framework and numerous modular units. They had different life cycles, thus making the system capable of unlimited extension both spatially and temporally.[36] In *The Elusive City*, Barnett gave a more concise definition to megastructure: the city as a building.[37] He observed: "From the mid-1950s, and for almost twenty years, the idea of an urban area as a large, interconnected building dominated much architectural thinking about cities."[38] All three authors captured the important characteristics of megastructure, that is, a gigantic urban framework integrated with infrastructure, accommodating numerous individual units and providing a self-contained environment.

Undoubtedly, most of the Metabolists' works were in conformity with this definition of megastructure both in terms of the exceptional scale of interventions and their utopian agendas. These Japanese architects shared with their European and American counterparts an enthusiasm in shaping a total environment with contemporary technology. However, examining the architectural avant-gardes of the 1950s and 1960s through the lens of megastructure has its limitations. With an emphasis on the international influence, it tends to obscure the subtle yet essential differences of these architects' design philosophies and social attitudes, and it omits the particular regional and local concerns embodied in their diverse urban visions. For a study of Metabolism, these are exactly some of the important issues that need to be articulated.

Archigram, for instance, was one of the European avant-garde movements frequently compared to Metabolism. Archigram and Metabolism indeed paralleled each other in many aspects. Both emerged in the imaginative and optimistic years in the early 1960s and disbanded in the early 1970s when postmodern culture was on the rise. They bore similarities in their futuristic impulses of design, a formal strategy comprising megastructure and cell, and a reliance on architectural imagery. However, the propositions their architectures and urbanisms made were different. Archigram drew its ideas primarily from a mechanistic metaphor while gradually softening it into urban experience anchored by information and electronic media.[39] The projects by its members were based on the notion of material impermanence, which could be placed within a British tectonic tradition founded by the Arts and Crafts movement and the Garden City movement. Metabolism, on the other hand, was essentially inspired by a biomorphic model of growth and transformation. The idea of organic expansion and replacement of elements had its roots in "a traditional understanding of the cyclical movement of death, decay and rebirth, one that is decidedly Japanese."[40] More importantly, Archigram's passion of technological future and megastructural strategy in design were largely devoid of the heroic yet naive engagement in revolutionizing the social structure, which characterized many Metabolists' early projects.[41] It is thus no surprise that, at the end of the 1960s when the Metabolists gradually accepted the ascendancy of technological fantasy and marketplace dynamics over social concerns, their proposals became more akin to Archigram's works. This change was manifest in their projects for the 1970 World Expositions in Osaka.

Comparison of Archigram's and Metabolism's manifestos also suggests their different approaches toward technology and social utopianism. While Archigram published a series of *Archigram* magazines through the 1960s, and continued to develop their ideas by introducing new themes like "zoom," "plug-in," and "living pod," the Metabolists published only one manifesto, but continuously elaborated on those concepts with numerous urban and building projects.[42] It is also evident that, even within the Metabolist group, the concept of megastructure was a subject of constant debate. In *Investigations in Collective Form*, Maki not only conceptualized the urban form of megastructure, but quickly turned to criticize this planning method for its rigidity and monumentality. He opposed it with the concept of group form. Instead of a static physical structure, Maki called for a more subtle internal order that underlay the natural evolution of cities. His argument that a real urban order should accommodate certain degrees of disorder and encourage spontaneity provided an alternative interpretation of "city as process" to the megastructural approach.

The book in brief

The focus of *Kenzo Tange and the Metabolist Movement* is to examine the Metabolists' visionary ideas of the city. Chapter 1 – Metabolism 1960 – situates the founding of Metabolism and its futuristic manifesto within the historical milieu of Japan's postwar social transformation and cultural reorientation. The year 1960 is highlighted as a crucial moment in which political unrest, cultural debates, and architectural experiments intersected. In particular, the renewal of the US–Japan Security Treaty stirred radical reactions in the country, indicating the long-term unrest latent in Japanese society. Among the outcomes of the mass demonstrations against the Security Treaty was a change in the governing cabinet and the announcement of the new prime minister's income-doubling program that triggered the economic miracle. The redefinition of Japan's cultural identity after the war also led to heated debates on tradition which, to a great extent, influenced Tange's and the Metabolists' urban concepts. Particularly, the periodic reconstruction of Ise Shrine every twenty years, celebrating the notion of transformation and regeneration, became a prototype for Metabolism's urban concepts. The new consciousness regarding tradition was paradoxically combined with the sustained influences of European avant-garde ideas of architecture and urbanism. As the chapter reveals, the urban conditions and social changes in the postwar decades provided an atmosphere that encouraged the Metabolists to integrate these stimuli and embrace new technologies for plans of a future city.

The second chapter – Metabolist utopias – focuses on the issue of utopianism and its representation in Metabolists' urban designs. It traces the influence of Marxist ideology among Japanese intellectuals in the postwar period and Japanese architects' interest in Soviet urban planning. Metabolists' plans engaged in the search for a new type of communal society, addressing Marxist ideals of public land ownership and integration of town and country. Such ideas raised fundamental questions concerning the relationship between the collective and the individual in a postindustrial society. The second half of the chapter discusses a series of urban concepts centered on a fundamental notion of the city as an organic process, which constituted Metabolism's primary contribution to the world of utopian planning. The examination of Metabolist projects reveals that the Metabolists shared the concerns of urban growth and transformation while presenting different design solutions and ideologies. The debates of a variety of urban concepts growing out of the notion of "metabolism" – such as Maki's group form versus Tange's megastructure, Kikutake and Kurokawa's progressive attitude toward technology versus Isozaki's idea of "ruins" and Kawazoe's attempt of reinterpreting tradition – indicate the nature of the Metabolist Movement that was characterized by diverse design and social ideas, rather than a monolithic concept of megastructure.

Tange's 1960 Plan for Tokyo constitutes the central piece of this study and is elaborated on in the third chapter – The myth of Tokyo Bay. This plan provides an opportunity to examine the issues arising when utopia meets reality. The way Tange translated his utopian concepts into concrete forms and programs as well as the impact of this extraordinary design approach to a mega-city are studied. The chapter begins with the urban problems facing Tokyo in the postwar decades and goes on to describe several unsuccessful attempts to transform the urban structure of Tokyo prior to 1960. It then analyzes Tange's plan from three perspectives: mobility as the fundamental character of what Tange called a "pivotal city," the linear axis as the symbol of an open urban structure as well as an open society, and the representation of different metabolic cycles in the city. Examination of this plan and discussion of controversies surrounding it reveal the utopian nature of Tange's urbanism.

Chapter 4 – Structure and symbol – continues to trace the development of Tange's design methodology in the 1960s, using concepts initiated in the Plan for Tokyo. Tange's urban design ideas stemmed from his technocratic notion of social progress. With a dialectic view of modern technology and its impact on modern society, the architect developed a systematic approach supported by the concepts of "structure" and "symbol." Analysis of two seminal projects, the Yamanashi Press and Broadcasting Center and the Plan for Reconstruction of Skopje, provides the opportunity to examine Tange's structuralist and symbolic strategies in urban design.

The subject of Chapter 5 – Expo '70 – is the 1970 World Exposition in Osaka, which represented Tange's and the Metabolists' collaborative effort to realize their vision of a future city. The event was a great success in advertising Japan's rapidly growing industrial power and displaying the spectacle of modern technologies. Ironically, rather than legitimizing the Metabolists' urban visions, Expo '70 proved the bankruptcy of their idealism, as the social agendas of their projects fell through and the technologies that their projects relied on turned out to be no more than instruments for entertainment and advertisement in an overwhelmingly consumerist culture. The loss of modernist heroics in Metabolist designs reflected the general decline of utopianism in the broader context since the 1968 student upheavals in Paris. The book concludes with an epilogue discussing the legacy of Metabolism and the meaning of urban utopias in the contemporary age, using Kurokawa's Nakagin Capsule Tower as a case study.

Notes

1 Kiyonori Kikutake et al., *Metabolism: The Proposals for New Urbanism* (Tokyo: Bijutsu shupansha, 1960).
2 Noboru Kawazoe, "City of the Future," *Zodiac* 9 (1961): 100.
3 Robert Fishman, *Urban Utopias in the Twentieth Century: Ebenezer Howard, Frank Lloyd Wright, and Le Corbusier* (Cambridge, MA: MIT Press, 1982), 15.
4 Krishan Kumar, *Utopianism* (Minneapolis: University of Minnesota Press, 1991), 92.
5 Lewis Mumford, "Utopia, the City and the Machine," in *Utopias and Utopian Thought*, Frank E. Manuel, ed., (London: Souvenir Press, 1973), 13.
6 Thomas More, *Utopia*, 1516, trans. Clarence H. Miller (New Haven: Yale University Press, 2001).
7 Karl Mannheim, *Ideology and Utopia* (London: Routledge & Kegan Paul, 1960), 173.
8 In fact, Mannheim's conception of utopia was criticized for over-emphasizing its "realizability." Krishan Kumar, *Utopianism* (Minneapolis: University of Minnesota Press, 1991), 92.
9 Leone Battista Alberti, *De re aedificatoria* (1450). Filarete, *Trattato di architettura* (1461–1464).

10 Robert Owen's "village of unity and mutual co-operation," Charles Fourier's thoughts about "phalanstery," and Claude-Nicolas Ledoux's ideal city of Chaux, though based on different premises, arrived at the same solution to the dilemmas of industrial societies: the marriage of town and country. Robert Fishman, "Utopia in Three Dimensions: the Ideal City and the origins of Modern Design," in Peter Alexander and Roger Gill eds, *Utopias* (London: Duckworth, 1984), 95–108.

11 Lewis Mumford, "Utopia: the City and the Machine," *Daedalus: Journal of the American Academy of Arts and Sciences* (Spring 1965, Special Issue on "Utopia"), 279.

12 Frederick Taylor, *The Principles of Scientific Management* (New York: Harper & Brothers, 1911). Taylor's idea also influenced socialism in the twentieth century. Vladmir Ilich Lenin insisted on the introduction of Taylorism into Soviet factories. J.G.. Scoville, "The Taylorization of Vladmir Ilich Lenin," *Industrial Relations* 40 (2001): 620–626.

13 Thorstein Veblen, *The Engineers and the Price System* (New York: Viking Press, 1921).

14 Ruth Eaton, *Ideal Cities: Utopianism and the (Un)built Environment* (London: Thames & Hudson, 2001), 157.

15 Le Corbusier, *The City of To-morrow and Its Planning*, 1922, trans. Frederick Etchells (New York: Dover, 1987).

16 Ibid, 163–178.

17 Kumar, 50 (see note 4).

18 Frank L. Wright elaborated on his ideas of Broadacre in a series of writings, including *The New Frontier: Broadacre City* (Spring Green: Taliesin Fellowship, 1940), *When Democracy Builds* (Chicago: University of Chicago Press, 1945), and *The Living City* (New York: Horizon Press, 1958). For discussions of this utopian concept, see David G. De Long, ed., *Frank Lloyd Wright and the Living City* (Weil am Rhein, Germany: Vitra Design Museum, 1998), and Robert Fishman, *Urban Utopias in the Twentieth Century: Ebenezer Howard, Frank Lloyd Wright, and Le Corbusier* (Cambridge, MA: MIT Press, 1982).

19 Peter Smithson, "Reflections on Kenzo Tange's Tokyo Bay Plan," *Architectural Design* 34 (1964): 479–480.

20 Although not all Expressionist architects can be called utopianists, Bruno Taut was certainly one. His ideal of a modern society is evident in his theoretical project "Alpine Architecture." For discussion on Taut, see Matthias Schirren, ed., *Bruno Taut: Alpine Architektur, eine Utopie* (Munich: Prestel, 2004).

21 For a historical account of CIAM's discourse of urbanism, see Eric Mumford, *The CIAM Discourse on Urbanism: 1928–1960* (Cambridge, MA: MIT Press, 2000). A useful summary of CIAM and its principles has also been written by Reyner Banham in *Encyclopaedia of Modern Architecture*, ed. Gerd Hatje (London: Thames & Hudson, 1963), 70–73.

22 The publication was a much edited version of proposals from the conference by Le Corbusier. Le Corbusier, *The Athens Charter* (New York: Grossman, 1973).

23 For Team 10's propositions in urbanism, see Alison Smithson, ed., *Team 10 Primer* (Cambridge, MA: MIT Press, 1968).

24 At the end of this meeting a resolution was passed in which the participants agreed to drop the name CIAM from their activities. So the Otterlo meeting became CIAM's final gathering. This historic meeting was documented in Oscar Newman, *New Frontiers in Architecture: CIAM'59 in Otterlo* (New York: Universal Books, 1961).

25 General discussions of the significant transition of architectural culture during the post-CIAM period can be found in Joan Ockman, *Architecture Culture 1943–1968: A Documentary Anthology* (New York: Rizzoli, 1993); Philip Drew, *Third Generation: The Changing Meaning of Architecture* (New York: Praeger, 1972); and Sarah W. Goldhagen and Réjean Legault, eds., *Anxious Modernisms: Experimentation in Postwar Architectural Culture* (Cambridge, MA: MIT Press, 2000).

26 Recognizing the inevitability of generational shifts and the certainty of his own passing, Le Corbusier wrote in an open letter to the tenth meeting of the CIAM in 1956: "It is those who are now forty years old, born around 1916 during wars and revolutions, and those then unborn, now twenty-five years old, born around 1930 during the preparation for a new war and amidst a profound economic, social, political crisis, who thus find themselves in the heart of the present period the only ones capable of feeling actual problems, personally, profoundly, the goals to

follow, the means to reach them, the pathetic urgency of the present situation. They are in the know. Their predecessors no longer are, they are out, they are no longer subject to the direct impact of the situation." Oscar Newman, *New Frontiers in Architecture: CIAM'59 in Otterlo* (New York: Universal Books, 1961), 16.

27 Reyner Banham, *Megastrucutre: Urban Futures of the Recent Past* (New York: Harper & Row, 1976), 47.

28 Kenzo Tange, "From Architecture to Urban Design," *Japan Architect*, May 1967: 23–27.

29 Manfedo Tafuri and Francesco Dal Co, *Architettura contemporanea* (1976), trans. Robert Erich Wolf, *Modern Architecture* (New York: H. N. Abrams, 1979), 357–363.

30 The seminal works of these urban theorists are: Jane Jacobs, *The Death and Life of Great American Cities* (New York: Random House, 1961); Christopher Alexander, "A City is not a Tree," in *Architectural Forum* 122(1) (1965): 58–62 and 122(2) (1965): 58–61; and Aldo Rossi, *L'architecture della cittá* (Padova: Marsilio, 1966).

31 Reyner Banham, *Megastructure: Urban Futures of the Recent Past* (New York: Harper & Row, 1976).

32 Jonathan Barnett, *The Elusive City: Five Centuries of Design, Ambition and Miscalculation* (New York: Harper & Row, 1986).

33 Fumihiko Maki, *Investigations in Collective Form* (St. Louis: Washington University, 1964).

34 Ibid, 8. Banham also cited the Ponte Vecchio in Florence and the old London Bridge as early examples of megastructures that integrated architecture with infrastructure. Banham, 14–15.

35 Banham, 7 (see note 31).

36 Banham, 8 (see note 31).

37 Barnett, 157 (see note 32).

38 Ibid.

39 For Archigram's architectural and urban ideas, see Hadas A Steiner, *Beyond Archigram: The Structure of Circulation* (New York: Routledge, 2009).

40 Jennifer Taylor, *The Architecture of Fumihiko Maki: Space, City, Order and Making* (Basel: Birkhäuser, 2003), 42.

41 Archigram's indifference to ideological commitment is articulated in Simon Sadler, *Archigram: Architecture without Architecture* (Cambridge, MA: MIT Press, 2005). The author says: "Political commitment to a firmly defined left was one of the things Archigram felt it could do without in pursuit of its goal, to make living new. Simultaneously, its passion for the future made it overwhelmingly avant-garde, while its abandonment of Marxism made it suspiciously reactionary – and a prime example of what would soon be described as a 'neo-avant-garde,' and the 'neo-' prefix designating ideological as well as temporal distance from the 'historical' avant-garde." Sadler, 6.

42 *Archigram* newsletters were published from London in nine issues between 1961 and 1970.

Chapter I

Metabolism 1960

In May 1960, Louis I. Kahn made his first and only journey to Japan to attend the World Design Conference in Tokyo. During his time in Japan, Kahn delivered the famous talk on "Form and Design" at one of the conference seminars.[1] He then presented a lecture at Waseda University entitled "City Planning and the Future of Architecture" that elaborated his concepts of urban design. Through activities in and outside the conference, he acquainted himself with Japanese architects and designers. Kahn's brief sojourn, together with the ideas of architecture and urbanism he conveyed to his Japanese audience, earned him the reputation as one of the most influential Western architects in postwar Japan.[2] One of the remarkable moments of Kahn's visit was his encounter with a group of young Japanese architects who called themselves the "Metabolists." The group, which formally announced itself at the World Design Conference, would soon lead Japanese architecture in a new direction.

Until 1969, overseas travel remained the privilege of limited few in Japan due to the governmental regulation restricting Japanese travel abroad after the Second World War. Visits by foreign architects to Japan were thus viewed as important events in the country where architects and designers were eager to learn about the latest developments of modern architecture from their Western guests. Prior to the World Design Conference, Walter Gropius traveled to the country in 1953 to help solve the postwar housing crisis; Le Corbusier visited Tokyo in 1955 to prepare his design for the National Museum of Western Arts; and Konrad Wachsmann offered a series of seminars at Tokyo Institute of Technology in 1956. The World Design Conference represented an even more promising opportunity for Japanese architects and designers to interact with their European and American peers. Held in Tokyo from May 11 to 16 in 1960, the conference was "the most ambitious event of its kind ever staged in Japan."[3] It assumed an important place in Japan's postwar history as the country recovered from the war and was eager to return to the international community. Since the Japanese economy had become increasingly export-oriented, the national government placed great importance on design in order to improve the competitiveness of Japanese products. Approximately 250 architects and designers participated in the meeting, representing 27 countries. Among the participants were a cluster of stellar architects, including Paul Rudolph, Minoru Yamasaki, Peter Smithson, Jacob Bakema, Ralph Erskine, Jean Prouvé, B.V. Doshi, Ralph Soriano, and Kahn. In the Japanese delegation, three master architects, Kunio Maekawa, Junzo Sakakura – both prominent pupils of Le Corbusier – and Kenzo Tange, gave key speeches at the conference.[4] They were joined by a number of prestigious Japanese industrialists and governmental officials. It was also at this occasion that the young generation of Japanese architects, represented by the Metabolists, came to the forefront of the dialogue with the Western masters.

On the evening of May 13 after his lecture at Waseda University, Kahn was invited to the home of Kiyonori Kikutake, one of the Metabolist architects. The "Sky House," as Kikutake's house is known, was designed by the architect himself and had become an iconic building by that time. The house is essentially a square box elevated by four tall concrete panels. Unlike conventional columns supporting a building at the corners, these wide columns stand in the middle of each side, lifting the house over the hillside. Inside, under a paraboloid shell roof, is a single space divided only by storage units. The kitchen and bathroom are located on the outer edge of the space. The building provides flexibility for space arrangement with the possibility of future addition and renovation. It was planned that children's rooms could be added underneath the platform and the utilized units could be updated periodically, both of which did actually happen. It was with this building that Kikutake first explored the idea of a building being able to respond organically to cycles of growth and decay.

1
Kiyonori Kikutake,
Sky House, 1958

In Sky House, Kahn had a long conversation with a number of Japanese architects, including the Metabolists.[5] He answered questions well after midnight, with Fumihiko Maki, another Metabolist architect and then assistant professor at Washington University in St. Louis, interpreting. Kahn further discussed the distinction between "form" and "design." Form, he explained, has no shape and no dimension; rather it represents a "sense of order" and a "harmony of systems." Design, on the other hand, is a circumstantial act evolving from the form.[6] He used a spoon as an example of this distinction. The design of a spoon can vary in terms of its material, mold, and size. That a spoon proves to be a spoon, however, is due to its form consisting of "a cup-like container and an arm," which serves as the basis of any design.[7] Kahn urged young architects to rethink the meaning of form and to base any design projects – from a spoon to an entire city – on this fundamental principle. He used his own projects, the Richards Medical Research Laboratories and the plans for Philadelphia, to explain how reorganization of spaces or movements could lead to new design solutions. Although Kahn spoke in his typically enigmatic manner, some of his ideas seemed well received by his audience. The architects, designers, and critics of Metabolism also believed in a universal language for design, whether applied to a vessel, a building, or a city. Therefore Kahn's concepts of form and design were particularly intriguing to them. Moreover, Kahn's megastructural approach to urbanism and the distinction of "served space" and "servant space" in architecture, as presented in his projects in Philadelphia, also inspired the Metabolists. Over the next decade, these young architects were to produce a stream of megastructural proposals. They used

1.2
**Louis I. Kahn,
Richards Medical
Research
Laboratories,
Philadelphia, 196**

Kahn's concepts for their own interpretation of a general model of architecture and urbanism.

The founding of Metabolism

The Metabolist group emerged from the preparation for the World Design Conference. The International Design Community (IDC), which arranged the conference every four years, decided that the 1960 meeting would be hosted by Tokyo.[8] Three Japanese institutional members — the Japan Institute of Architects, the Japan Association of Advertising Arts, and the Japan Industrial Design Association (JIDA) – would be responsible for its organization. Early in the planning process, however, JIDA withdrew from this conference. Since the Association of Advertising Arts was a relatively smaller group, contributing less to the IDC, the Japan Institute of Architects assumed chief responsibility for the preparation of the 1960 meeting.[9] A World Design Conference Preparation Bureau was formed in 1958 under an executive committee led by Sakakura, Maekawa, and Tange. Sakakura, well connected to the political and financial circles in Tokyo, was named its chair. Thanks to his rising international reputation after the completion of the Hiroshima Peace Memorial Park, Tange was made the director overseeing conference programs. Because Tange had accepted an invitation from Massachusetts Institute of Technology to be a visiting professor for the 1959/60 academic year, he recommended Takashi Asada, his junior colleague at the University of Tokyo, to take charge of preparing programs. Asada was appointed Secretary General of the preparation committee.[10]

Once in his new position, Asada formed a working team. Serving as Tange's major assistant at his architectural laboratory in the university, Asada was active among young architects in Tokyo.[11] He first called upon two of his architect friends, Noboru Kawazoe and Noriaki Kurokawa.[12] Kawazoe was an architectural critic and former chief editor of *Shinkenchiku* (New Architecture); he had recently been forced to resign from the magazine because of his criticism of Murano Togo, another Japanese master architect known for his eclectic design style and use of expressive surface texture on large-scale buildings. Architecturally Kawazoe was sympathetic to Tange's Corbusian modernism and wrote a few essays on his works.[13] Kurokawa was Tange's graduate student at the University of Tokyo, and he had recently traveled to the Soviet Union as the Japanese representative for an international conference of architectural students. Asada recruited Kawazoe and Kurokawa to the committee, asking them to look for additional talented architects and designers to help with the preparation of the conference.

Kawazoe and Kurokawa visited several architectural firms, design studios, and universities in Tokyo, and they engaged Masato Otaka, Kiyonori Kikutake, Kenji Ekuan, and Kiyoshi Awazu. Otaka and Kikutake were rising stars among young Japanese architects. Otaka was a chief architect at Maekawa's office. He had recently completed the design of the Harumi Apartment Building, a mass housing project located on a reclaimed site in Tokyo Bay.[14] Besides his Sky House, Kikutake was known for his series of futuristic urban projects, including "Tower-shaped City" and "Marine City," both published in the journal

Kokusai kenchiku (International Architecture) in 1959.[15] Ekuan and Awazu represented the other two professional groups that constituted the International Design Community, industrial designers and graphic designers. These six young men, under the leadership of Asada, developed the programs for the World Design Conference.

As 1960 began, the Conference Program Committee fulfilled its official mission, but another issue soon arose. The withdrawal of the Japan Industrial Design Association from the conference would create a void in the host country's presence. Hoping to create an avant-garde group to mount its own presence at the conference, Asada persuaded Kawazoe to take the lead. In Asada's mind, this group should represent a "grassroots movement of the younger generation."[16] Meanwhile, these young architects who had just completed formulating the conference programs began to think about how they could communicate Japanese architects' visions to their international peers. Kikutake proposed developing futuristic urban schemes like his "Tower-shaped City" and "Marine City." While others members supported Kikutake's idea, Kawazoe argued that, beyond the individual projects, there should be the message about a "theory originating from Japan but applicable to the world in general."[17]

During the preparation for the conference, Asada stayed at a Japanese-style inn called *Ryugetsu ryokan* in the Asakusa district of Tokyo. The young architects often gathered there, discussing their work over meals. Over time the inn became a meeting place for progressive scholars, architects, and artists. Asada, who was enthusiastic about modern science and concerned about human civilization in general, often invited people in fields other than architecture to speak at the gatherings, opening up discussions to broader issues of history, technology, and philosophy. Among the people who came to *Ryugetsu ryokan* was an atomic physicist Mitsuo Taketani.

Taketani was a Marxist scholar and co-founder of the leftist intellectual group *Riken*, meaning "scientific research group." *Riken* attracted a number of progressive scientists who were influenced by Marxism and advocated Marx's theory of scientific dialectics. In meetings with the architects and artists, Taketani not only presented new scientific discoveries, but also introduced the dialectic approach, which influenced the Metabolists' design methods. Kikutake later recalled that Taketani's three-stage methodology for scientific research – the progression from "essence" to "entity" then to "phenomenon" as articulated in his book *Questions Concerning Dialectics* – inspired Kikutake to invent his own three-stage methodology for design. Kikutake called his three stages *ka*, *kata*, and *takachi*, meaning order, type, and form, with *ka* being the general system, *kata* being the abstract image, and *katachi* being the solution as built. He argued that these

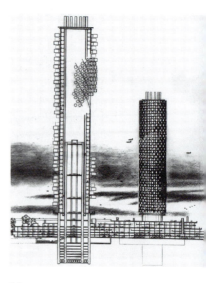

1.3
Kiyonori Kikutake, Tower-shaped City, 1958

steps summarized the evolution of design process from a broad vision to a concrete architectural form. Kikutake also acknowledged that Kahn's original distinction between form and design influenced his three-stage concept. His tripartite method, in effect, translated Kahn's poetic metaphor into a literal and systematic design process.[18]

Asada himself was an indispensable figure in the formation of Metabolism. Kawazoe later recalled the role Asada played in the movement:

> Our gathering and discussion at *Ryugetsu ryokan* often became his solo. He had incredible instinct and insight, and could speak from the everyday phenomena to the environmental issues of the earth. His intelligence and talent of speech was very charming to us. Even after forty years, his predictions are still valid to a great extent.[19]

After the end of the World Design Conference, the Metabolists still regarded Asada as the "honorary chairman" of the group. Together with Kawazoe, he provided the theoretical base from which the futurist design ideas of Metabolism were derived.

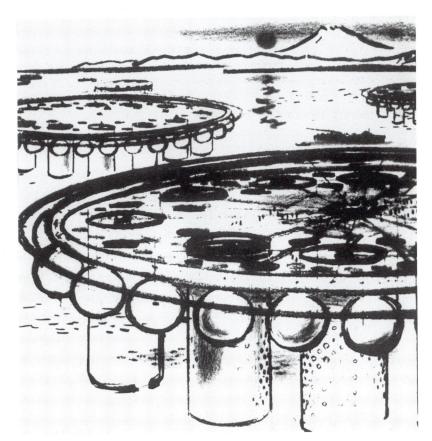

.4
Kiyonori Kikutake,
Marine City, 1958

Steered by Asada and Kawazoe, the architects and designers were forming a new group dedicated to the design of future cities. Gatherings at *Ryugetsu ryokan* were well under way when Fumihiko Maki joined the group in early 1960. He returned from the United States to work on a project for the redevelopment of the Shinjuku Station area. A former undergraduate student of Tange at the University of Tokyo, Maki was trained in the graduate programs of architecture at Cranbrook Academy of Art and Harvard University. He had taught at Washington University in St. Louis since 1956. When he returned to Tokyo, Maki was introduced to the Metabolists and decided to join the group. His participation enhanced the international presence within Metabolism.

At one of the meetings, these architects agreed on using a biological term as both the key concept of design and the name of the group. It was Kawazoe who suggested the term "Metabolism" when they examined Kikutake's Marine City project. Kawazoe recalled that he chose this name because metabolism, as the organic function of material and energy exchange between living organisms and the exterior world, is the essential process of life.[20] In addition to its biological meaning, the literal translation of metabolism in Japanese, *shinchin taisha*, also embodies the idiomatic meaning of "out with the old, in with the new." It thus came in line with the architects' notion that the city should be capable of continuous growth and renewal – a process, they believed, as important as an organism's natural metabolism. Kawazoe argued that *shinchin taisha* – interpreted either technically or colloquially – would change how people viewed the city.[21] Instead of the Japanese phrase, however, the architects decided to use the English translation to emphasize the concept's universality.

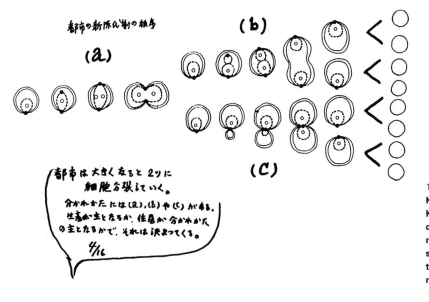

1.5
Kiyonori
Kikutake's
concept of urban
metabolism, a
sketch included in
the Metabolist
manifesto, 1960

The Metabolists were apparently inspired by new knowledge in biology and biological engineering when they chose the word. The 1950s witnessed important discoveries in life science, and was regarded as the "decade of genetic molecular biology." In 1953, James D. Watson and Francis Crick of Cambridge University identified the double-helix structure of the deoxyribonucleic acid (DNA), laying the foundations of modern molecular biology. A series of breakthroughs in genomics followed, including the successful duplication of various types of proteins. These discoveries deepened understandings of the science of life and in turn influenced people's worldviews. Not surprisingly, the young architect-planners, driven by the optimistic intellectual atmosphere of the time, employed a biological term to interpret their visions of the city and human society. Not only did they believe "metabolism" could best describe the nature of urban evolution and transformation, but more importantly, they insisted that the application of modern technology and design would promote social change, as suggested by metabolism's Japanese meaning – out with the old, in with the new. To a certain extent this confirmed the influence of Marxist ideology on their architectural philosophy. In the meantime, it also betrayed a somewhat naive technocratic notion that characterized all their urban proposals.

The group however did not reach a consensus on the meaning of "metabolism" in architecture. According to Kurokawa, who started his career as an architect in this movement, "each of the members joined the group with a different opinion about what the Metabolist movement was; there was no articulated theory on metabolism at the very beginning."[22] Rather, the architects were inspired by a vague connection between the city and the principle of life, exploring its meaning through various design approaches. This was reflected in the manifesto of the group, *Metabolism: The Proposals for New Urbanism*, published at the World Design Conference.[23] The manifesto opened with the following statement:

> "Metabolism" is the name of the group, in which each member proposes future designs of our coming world through his concrete

6
Title page of
Metabolism:
The Proposals for
New Urbanism

designs and illustrations. We regard human society as a vital process – a continuous development from atom to nebula. The reason why we use such a biological word, metabolism, is that we believe design and technology should be a denotation of human society. We are not going to accept metabolism as a natural historical process, but try to encourage active metabolic development of our society through our proposals.[24]

This statement articulated the group's fundamental idea that the city was an organic process instead of a static entity. It also revealed the architects' ambition for revolutionary approaches to urban design, further elaborated on in the individual essays in the pamphlet. Surprisingly, the word "metabolism" appeared only in Kawazoe's own essay. This may have been due to the limited time they had to prepare the pamphlet, which did not allow the authors to make their writings more coherent. However, this inconsistency may have also confirmed Kawazoe's confession that each member was presenting his own opinions under the term "metabolism" and his anticipation that "in the future, more will come to join 'Metabolism' while some will go; that means a metabolic process will also take place in its membership."[25] In fact, two factions of design ideas had appeared from the beginning: Kikutake, Kurokawa, and Kawazoe were particularly fascinated by the biological metaphor between the city and organism, while Otaka and Maki stuck to their method of "group form." Maki criticized Kikutake's series scheme of Marine City on some occasions. After the World Design Conference Maki seldom participated in the meetings, and gradually distanced himself from the group. Nevertheless, Maki's urban theory and his designs using the concept of group form proved to be a great asset to the Metabolist movement.

Unknown before the World Design Conference, the Metabolist group was undoubtedly a highlight of the event. Using this international conference to stage their debut, these young architects, critics, and designers announced their radical urban concepts through the publication of *Metabolism: The Proposals for New Urbanism*. This English and Japanese bilingual pamphlet is eight inches square and features four essays illustrated with speculative urban design schemes. The essays are Kikutake's "Ocean City," Kawazoe's "Material and Man," Otaka and Maki's "Towards the Group Form," and Kurokawa's "Space City." Ekuan and Awazu were also involved in the design and distribution of the pamphlet, although they did not contribute an essay. Maki provided English translation for the texts. Five hundred copies of the pamphlet were printed and sold at the conference for 500 Japanese yen each. It was the only publication ever produced by the Metabolists as a group.[26]

The bold ideas and radical projects in the Metabolist manifesto drew immediate attention at the World Design Conference, and soon earned the Metabolists international repute. As a result, Kikutake and Kurokawa were invited to participate in the exhibition entitled "Visionary Architecture" at the Museum of Modern Art (MoMA) in New York the following year. For the first time, the design works of Japanese architects were displayed side by side with those of the world-class masters, including Le Corbusier, Frank Lloyd Wright, and Antonio Sant'Elia. Thereafter the Metabolists was widely seen as spokespersons for a new generation of Japanese architects, who rendered their creativity with the most up-to-date technologies and developed design concepts on an unprecedented scale. In 1962, Maki and Kurokawa were invited to the meeting of Team 10, further consolidating their status as the vanguards of postwar Japanese architecture. Within the country, the success of the Metabolists was a great inspiration to their peers, who had been seeking a direction since the end of the Second World War. The influence of Metabolism was evident in the prize-winning schemes of a series of nationwide architectural competitions organized by the journal *Shinkenchiku* in the 1960s, dominated by Metabolism-inspired schemes. Some of these schemes were also published in the British journal *Architectural Design*.[27]

Kikutake and the Marine City

Kikutake's "Ocean City" is the first essay in *Metabolism: The Proposals for New Urbanism*, and comprises the first 36 pages of this 89-page pamphlet. It covered three urban projects: "Tower-shaped City," "Marine City," both completed in 1958, and "Ocean City *Unabara*" (Ocean City Sea-plain), a new scheme combining some characteristics of two earlier projects.

After graduating from Waseda University, Kikutake opened his architectural firm in 1953. He soon became famous in Japan for designing Sky House and the Museum of Shimane. Not contented with professional work, he became fascinated with speculative projects, using them to develop his architectural concepts as well as visions of the modern city. It was known that he and his staff worked on professional commissions during regular office hours, but, once the office was closed, they folded the drawings and turned to the theoretical projects. Kikutake published two urban projects in the first and second issues of *Kokusai kenchiku* in 1959; "Tower-shaped City" introduced a new concept of urban dwelling, and "Marine City" explored the possibility of floating and moveable cities on the sea. These projects soon became famous in Japan. When Tange attended the last meeting of the *Congrès International d'Architecture Moderne* (CIAM) at Otterlo in May 1959, he introduced these projects to the conference audience, among them Team 10 architects, Louis I. Kahn, and Ernesto Rogers. Even before the Metabolists formally announced themselves, Tange's presentation had become the first exposure of the Metabolists' work to an international audience.

Tower-shaped City and Marine City set the precedents for other Metabolist projects, based on the design concept of "artificial land" and the distinction between "major structure" and "minor structure." The major structure of Tower-shaped City was a concrete cylinder of 300 meters tall that would house the infrastructure of the entire city, including transportation infrastructure, utility pipelines, public services, and even a manufacturing plant for prefabricated houses. The concrete cylinder worked as a vertical artificial "land" upon which up to 1,250 dwelling units could be attached, thus creating a community for 5,000 people. The goal was not just to provide a solution to housing. Kikutake claimed: "Housing 5,000 is not the most important thing here. Instead, my goal is to solve the comprehensive problem through the three-dimensional dwelling."[28] He argued that the vertical megastructure would be free from the confusion and chaos characteristic of traditional cities consisting of streets and blocks; the megastructure could instead become an effective urban form for industry, living, and construction. The individual apartments, in the form of prefabricated modules built from steel, would be manufactured within the core and, once finished, plugged onto the exterior wall of the tower. Kikutake compared this process to a silkworm producing silk. The modules were replaceable units, scheduled to undergo self-renewal every fifty years. Kikutake expected the city to grow in the way a tree develops its branches and leaves. He thus defined the Tower-shaped City as "the combination of individual and society, architecture and city, as well as a new modern monument."[29] To show the viability of his concept, Kikutake included a model photo of Marina City, the twin towers then under construction in Chicago, along with his own sketches and diagrams.

Kikutake's second scheme, Marine City, was intended to transcend what he called "continental civilization." In current continental society, he argued, people were tied to the land, which was the origin of many evils and distortions of human society, such as wars. Marine City was intended to liberate people from their reliance on land and create a new type of society. It would take the form of a floating city on the sea. The ground of the artificial island would be reserved for agriculture, industry, and entertainment, while residential towers would grow downward beneath the water table, reaching as deep as 200 meters. Kikutake appropriated Le Corbusier's diagram of three fundamental elements of the city (sun, air, and green) and substituted his own three elements: sun, air, and water. Construction would take place at a floating manufacturing plant serving as the "mother body" to deliver Marine Cities. The cities would not be anchored

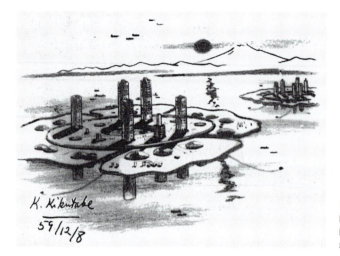

1.7
**Kiyonori Kikutake,
Marine City, 1959.
Sketch**

at a fixed point but could rather move anywhere. Like an organism, a Marine City would have its own life. When it was no longer suitable for living, it would move to the center of the ocean and sink itself. Its remains would become a fish bed on the bottom of the sea.

In *Metabolism*, Kikutake combined his Tower-shaped City and Marine City schemes to develop a new scheme called "Ocean City" or "Ocean City *Unabara*." This project took on an even greater scale planned as an industrial city for 500,000. The basic layout consisted of two rings: an inner ring for housing and an outer ring for production. The outer ring was tangent to the inner ring with

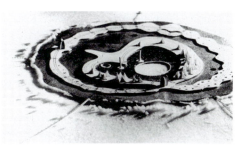

1.8
**Kiyonori Kikutake, Ocean City, 1960.
Model view**

.9
**iyonori Kikutake,
Mova-block, 1960.
Sketch**

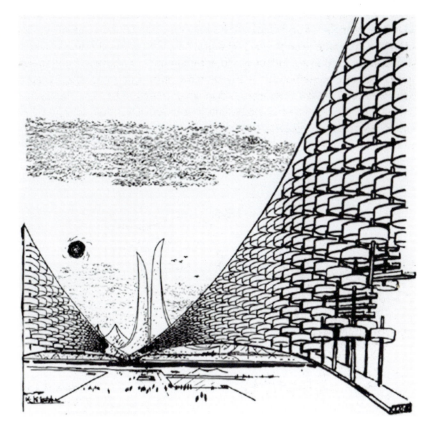

administrative buildings at the tangent point. The water body between the inner and outer rings would be used as fish farms, while the area within the inner ring itself was reserved for swimming and recreation. The population of Ocean City would be strictly controlled. Once it reached the limit, the city would multiply itself in a process similar to cells division. This concept, conceiving the growth of a city as a biological process, became the underlying notion of Metabolism. Kikutake envisioned that the process of proliferation would ultimately produce a series of ocean cities along the Pacific coast of the Japanese Archipelago, leading to a new age of "marine civilization."

Kikutake designed the Ocean City in details. Housing structures built on the residential ring took the form of triangular megastructures called "mova-blocks." Three mova-blocks formed a group, pivoting around a central "mast." Each mova-block carried numerous "movable houses." These residential units could move along a predetermined track and be replaced as needed. For each individual apartment, Kikutake adopted the idea of Sky House, providing a flexible arrangement of partitions and spaces. The production zone of the city was planned in a similar manner; it consisted of individual rectangular production spaces that formed a gridiron pattern, not unlike the layout of Kahn's Richards Medical Laboratories complex at the University of Pennsylvania. Kikutake declared: "It is most important that the space required for productive structure should be able to adapt itself to future expansion, reduction, and change."[30] Through the Ocean City project, Kikutake indicated his strong interest in establishing a system of replaceability and adaptability, a theme dominating many Metabolist proposals.

Kurokawa and Space City

Kurokawa was the youngest member in the Metabolist group, only 26 when the group was formed. Before entering the University of Tokyo for graduate study with Tange, he had been a student at Kyoto University and thus come under the influence of Uzo Nishiyama, a Marxist architectural theorist. In 1958, Kurokawa represented Japan at the International Architectural Student Conference in Leningrad. He spent three months in the Soviet Union, familiarizing himself with Socialist ideas of design and planning. These ideas inspired his own urban projects for the future society.[31] Although he had not realized any building project by 1960, his involvement in the Metabolist movement jump-started his career.

In his essay entitled "Space City," in *Metabolism*, Kurokawa introduced four projects: "Neo-Tokyo plan," "Wall City," "Agricultural City," and "Mushroom-shaped house." The Neo-Tokyo plan might be inspired by his mentor Kenzo Tange's 1960 Tokyo Bay project, in which Kurokawa participated. In contrast to Tange's model of a linear city, Kurokawa proposed that Tokyo be decentralized and rearranged into a cruciform pattern, stretching out from the existing city center. The series of "Bamboo-shaped Cities" would be dotted along the cruciform. A Bamboo-shaped City resembled Kikutake's idea of Tower-shaped City, but Kurokawa put his towers under the 31-meter

.10
Noriaki Kurokawa,
Neo-Tokyo plan,
1960

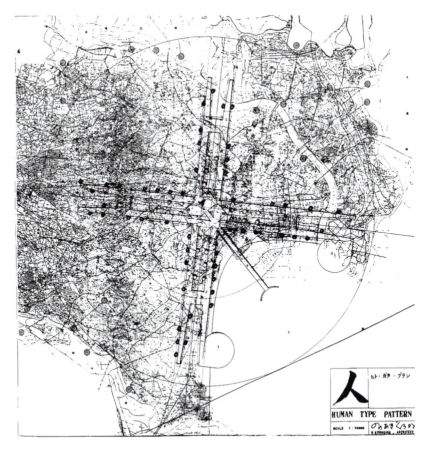

.11
Noriaki Kurokawa,
Wall City, 1960.
Sketch

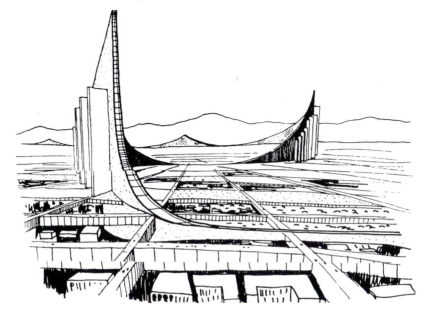

height limit prescribed by Tokyo's building code. Like Kikutake, Kurokawa stressed different durations of urban elements to keep the city moving forward:

> The city is eternally moving as a container of future life. There exists a changing cycle which differs according to each section of the city. There exists a difference in the durability and scale in the basic urban structure, urban connectors, living units and architectural equipment. One must, therefore, devise an urban design which will enable a flexible expansion between these differing elements.[32]

Kurokawa had observed how urban sprawl pushed housing and work place farther and farther away from each other. In "Wall City," he addressed the issue of strengthening the tie between these two domains of human society. His solution was a wall-shaped megastructure serving as the basic skeleton of the city, which could extend infinitely. The wall contained infrastructure for transportation, utility, and public services. Individual houses would be attached to one side of the "wall," and work spaces on the other. Thus, the distance between them would be as thin as the width of the "wall."

Based on the idea that agricultural production should be integrated into the organization of the modern city, Kurokawa's Agricultural City aimed to solve the classical contradiction between city and countryside, as Marxism advocated. Each community of the Agricultural City would be built upon a concrete slab of 500 meters by 500 meters, elevated four meters above the natural land by *pilotis*.[33] Infrastructure would be built into the concrete slab, thus reserving the entire land for agricultural production. Each community could accommodate 2,000 residents, with a gridiron street system dividing the slab into

1.12
Noriaki Kurokawa, Agricultural City, 1960. Model view

.13
Noriaki Kurokawa,
Agricultural City,
1960. Section

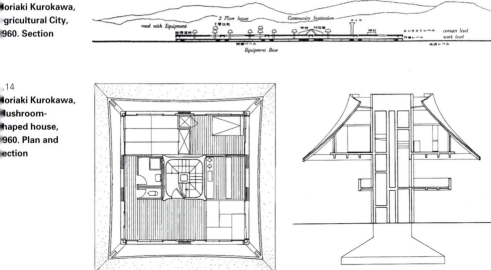

.13
Noriaki Kurokawa,
Agricultural City,
1960. Section

.14
Noriaki Kurokawa,
Mushroom-
shaped house,
1960. Plan and
section

25 blocks, 100 meters by 100 meters each. A central block was reserved for public facilities, including a shrine, an elementary school, and a temple. Individual houses would occupy the rest of the community. These one- or two-story houses were further elevated up above the slab, featuring the form of "Mushroom-shaped house." Mushroom-shaped house resembled Kikutake's Sky House to a certain extent; the space is closed in nature, isolated by concrete walls on four sides but open to the skylight at the center.

Kurokawa later developed the Agricultural City in greater detail and sent it to the Visionary Architecture exhibition at MoMA. He produced variations of the scheme in which the square slab – the artificial land – was broken down into strips, so the city could stretch out further. With these variations Kurokawa showed that the Agricultural City could adapt to different topographies.

Toward group form

Otaka and Maki approached urban design from a different perspective from other Metabolists. They did not produce an entirely speculative scheme, but rather used their proposal for a real urban site to reflect current issues of city planning and to formulate the concept of "group form." At the World Design Conference, they presented their plan for the redevelopment of the Shinjuku Station area in Tokyo.

The idea of group form was often attributed to Maki's book, *Investigations in Collective Form*, published in 1963. However, Otaka had begun to explore the same relationship between infrastructure and architecture in his graduation thesis in 1949. After joining Maekawa's firm, Otaka continued to develop his interest in the concept of "artificial ground," using a systems approach to study the organization of multiple building complexes. In contrast to other Metabolists' futuristic schemes in which buildings appeared to dance in the air, Otaka's projects stressed the notion of "ground" in architecture.[34] This concern was manifested in a few buildings he designed at Maekawa's firm, including the Harumi Apartment Building (1956–58) and the Tokyo Cultural Center (1957–61). Otaka's professional experience made him a leader of young architects in Tokyo, especially after he and Tanaka Sei won first place in the competition for the design of the National Diet Library in 1954.[35]

Maki's professional and academic experience in the United States brought the Metabolist group a desirable international perspective. During his years in America, Maki came under the influence of international Modernism through figures like Eliel Saarinen, then teaching at Cranbrook Academy of Art, and Walter Gropius and Jose Luis Sert, both professors at Harvard University's Graduate School of Design. His first apprenticeship was with Skidmore Owings & Merrill before he worked for Sert. Maki began to teach at Washington University in St. Louis in 1956 and moved back to Harvard GSD in 1962, where he taught until 1965 before returning to Japan to open his own practice. In 1958, Maki was awarded a Graham Foundation fellowship, which allowed him to spend the following two years traveling in Southeast Asia, India, the Middle East, and Europe. Through these trips he familiarized himself with a variety of vernacular human settlements and was particularly impressed by their repetitive patterns and the intricate order within the grouping of buildings. They became important inspirations of his concept of group form.[36]

In their essay, "Toward Group Form," Otaka and Maki argued that modern society was characterized by conflicts among numerous heterogeneous institutions and individuals. One of the major challenges facing design, planning, and development, they asserted, was creating and maintaining order without

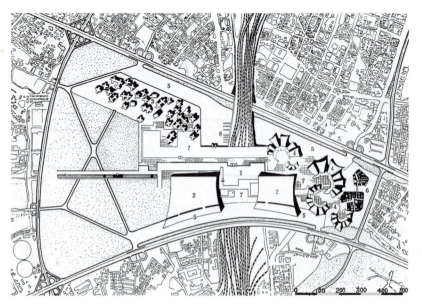

1.15
Masato Otaka and Fumihiko Maki, Shinjuku Station Project, 1960. Master plan

sacrificing the fundamental freedom of the individuals making up the society. They thus introduced the method of group form, hoping to achieve a total image through the repetitive form of its components. They expected that group form would create a new relationship between individual elements and the whole, a relationship fundamentally different from conventional building compositions. In the conventional compositional method, the totality is achieved through adding up all its components. When a single element is taken away from or added to the composition, the overall quality is altered. In contrast, group form derives from the abstraction of individual forms and presents itself as a typology governing the

.16
Masato Otaka and
Fumihiko Maki,
Shinjuku Station
Project, 1960.
Model view

individual elements. In this sense, group form is more than the sum of all the elements. Even if any individual component is changed, the total image will not be affected. In contrast to the singular monuments like the Parthenon, the Seagram Building, or Brasilia, group form leads to a more adaptable collective image. Therefore, Otaka and Maki contended that group form would be able to accommodate the unpredictable and rapid changes characteristic of contemporary society.[37]

The Shinjuku project aimed to develop a site – originally occupied by a water purification plant – on the west side of Shinjuku Station, into a business and entertainment district. The scheme envisioned a gigantic concrete slab over railway tracks, which became the artificial land that Otaka was very interested in. Upon this artificial ground, shopping centers, office towers, and amusement squares would grow in the manner of group form. Otaka designed the office tower cluster in the west, and Maki designed the amusement squares in the east. Otaka's office complexes were characterized by heavy structures and brutal sculptural forms, while Maki's buildings were dominated by lightweight large-span structures. Although they demonstrated the architects' different inclinations in form, both designs showed the character of group forms, each consisting of numerous homogeneous masses. For instance, the amusement square was conceived as "flowers." A major plaza occupied the center, around which opera houses, theaters, concert halls, and movie theatres radiated like petals of a flower. Even if certain petals were missing, the total image would remain. The same character existed in Otaka's group form.

"I want to be a shell"

As an architectural journalist, Kawazoe did not contribute a design project to the Metabolist manifesto. Instead, he wrote an article entitled "Material and Man" that was published along with the other Metabolist members' futuristic urban schemes. Unlike other essays in this pamphlet, his article addressed broader issues in modern society, reading more like a political manifesto. The author opened with a condemnation of nuclear weapons and the world's superpowers producing and controlling these weapons. Kawazoe's critique derived from Japan's anti-nuclear movement during the 1950s, and he linked this general concern to the prospect of architecture.[38] In this dangerous world, he declared, only architects and designers could bring optimism because they created works that would remain even though the world could be destroyed: "Even if all mankind is wiped out by radioactive shower, many cities and villages will be left as they are. . . . This fact makes architects and designers optimistic in a time of crisis."[39]

Like other Metabolists, Kawazoe went on to describe the world as engaged in a process of constant change and regeneration. He envisioned an age of "high metabolism" would arrive, and thus demanded that the development of cities be considered a natural process. He argued in a dialectical manner that "order is born from chaos, and chaos from order" and "extinction is at the same time creation."[40] Responsible for the physical forms of the cities, architects and planners should not conceive of them as static objects. Kawazoe declared: "We hoped to create something which, even in destruction, will cause a subsequent new creation. The 'something' must be found in the form of the cities we are going to make – cities constantly undergoing the process of metabolism."[41] To Kawazoe, metabolism was not just a concept of city design; it embodied the fundamental principles of human society that constantly transformed, and were subject to metamorphosis like destruction and regeneration. Such metamorphosis could be caused by nuclear weapons if a war broke out. Kawazoe's essay thus linked the theory of Metabolism to broader concerns of mankind in the modern time. Permeating the text was an anxiety about crises confronting modern cities and a sense of urgency of putting the urban metamorphosis under control.

Kawazoe closed the essay with a poem entitled "My Dream after 50 years." If the essay was explicit in its criticism, Kawazoe's poem turned toward ambiguity. In this poem, however, the author's complex feelings about the future of the world could be detected. The poem consists of three sections: "I want to be a *Kai* (seashell)," "I want to be a *Kami* (god)" and "I want to be a *Kabi* (bacterium)," respectively. The poem reads:

> I want to be a shell.
> I want to be a shell. In the peaceful world I do nothing but opening and closing my shell. Nothing can be better than this. This is the "heaven of lazy people." Soon the time will come that everything will be done by machine. The only thing we have to do will be dreaming.
> It seems that I have become a shell, deep into all kinds of illusions. Suddenly I think of a wonderful plan. Yes, let's do it! I get up.
>
> I want to be a god.
> I want to be a god. I hear the voice from the heaven. I am a prophet. Well, maybe I am a god myself. I order architects to build four-dimensional "universal architecture," so the plan must be drawn in three-dimensional geometry. Who will draw it? Masato Otaka? Kiyonori Kikutake? Or Noriaki Kurokawa? But the architects can only build three-dimensional space. I am the only one who can grasp the four-dimensional space. So I deserve to be a god.
>
> I want to be a bacterium.
> I want to be a bacterium. Mad, dogmatic, and fanatic are the negative words put on me. But being a god is too insipid. Perhaps I stick too much to the image of "myself." I must cast away my self-consciousness, and fuse myself into mankind and solely become part of it. I have to reach the state of selflessness.
> In the future, man will fill the whole earth, and fly into the sky. I am a cell of bacteria that is in constant propagation. After several decades, with the rapid progress of communication technology, every one will

have a "brain wave receiver" in his ear, which conveys directly and exactly what other people think about him and vice versa. What I think will be known by all the people. There is no more individual consciousness, only the will of mankind as a whole. It is not different from the will of the bacteria.[42]

Interpreting this poem, Cherie Wendelken links these analogies to the well-known design vocabularies of Metabolism, such as individual cell, structure, and capacity of growth. She claims: "The individual cell was self-enclosed and self-contained, like a sea shell or *kai*; the growth of cells was structured but flexible, like mold or *kabi*, which could conform to the surface of a rock; and finally, growth was motivated by a force or spirit, *kami*."[43] This interpretation is rather far-fetched, because the concept of "cell" was neither formalized in the early stage of the Metabolist movement; nor was it realized in design works until the 1970 World Exposition in Osaka and Kurokawa's Nakagin Capsule Tower in 1972. The translation of *kami* as "spirit" does not match the context of the poem either. Rather than suggesting practical design methods, the poem reflected on the future of the world and epitomized a complex sensation of melancholy and hope, anxiety and aspiration.

Nevertheless Wendelken accurately points out that the phrase "I want to be a shell" was already famous in the 1950s as the name of a popular Japanese TV drama. The show was about a Japanese soldier forced by his officer to kill a war prisoner during the Second World War. He was thus accused of a war crime and sentenced to death. The last words he said before his execution were: "I want to be a shell." This drama, revealing the conflict between war and human values, stirred tremendous responses and was widely regarded as a milestone in the anti-war and anti-nuclear weapon movements in postwar Japan.[44] Kawazoe must have been influenced by the drama's sophisticated theme. His poem reads like the confession of an architect wondering about his role in society: he wants to be a free artist (shell), expressing his imagination and creativity without any constraint; he wants to be a powerful planner (god), using his vision to direct other architects in building the world; the power of modernity, however, overwhelms individual consciousness and deprives architects of their individual identities.

Kawazoe was not alone in having such ambivalent feelings about the role of architects in the modern world. Arata Isozaki, who was close to Tange and the Metabolist architects, published a short essay in 1962 entitled "The City Demolisher, Inc."[45] It was written in the form of a conversation between two figures, Arata and Shin. Arata and Shin are in fact different pronunciations of the same Japanese character "shin," Isozaki's given name. In this bizarre story, Shin tried to persuade Arata to help him establish a business called The City Demolisher, Inc. to "completely destroy the big cities that have killed a large number of people with shabby means."[46] To achieve this end, Shin proposed several strategies to eliminate big cities, one of which was to foster utopian proposals. In fact, Isozaki published a few radical urban schemes in the early

1960s that in some way coincided with the theme of "The City Demolisher, Inc." One of these projects was called "Incubation." Featuring megastructures composed of joint-core systems emerging from the ruins of a classical city, Incubation was a cultural critique of the modern city and modern society, just like Kawazoe's essay.

Japanese tradition debate

The ambivalent sentiment in both Kawazoe's and Isozaki's writings betrayed an anxiety among Japanese intellectuals in search of a cultural identity in the postwar period. During the American occupation, Japan implemented a new constitution and a series of sweeping legal reforms affecting everything from land ownership to tax structures to building codes. These changes re-shaped Japan's postwar political system into a democratic one, fundamentally trans- forming Japanese society and every aspect of public life. For instance, the occupation staff determined that there was a close tie between Japanese Shintoism and the country's history of wartime ultra-nationalism, so they ordered a legal separation of Shinto from the state in December 1945, discontinuing state funding for Shinto institutions and forbidding the propagation of Shinto in public schools.[47] When the American occupation ended in 1952, the Japanese political system quickly adjusted to its newly regained independence, but conflicts also emerged. On the one hand, although Japan's political autonomy was asserted, the conservative Liberal Democratic Party government tended to follow the political framework established by the United States, sticking to the US–Japan Security Treaty and pursuing a pragmatic path of modernization. On the other hand, progressive intellectuals hoped to overcome the superfluous assimilation of Americanism, and called for complete political autonomy and a fresh national identity. The debates between both sides remained the theme of political and cultural conflicts through the 1950s and 1960s.[48]

Intimately associated with the issue of national identity was the question of tradition, widely debated in Japanese architectural circles and beyond during the 1950s. People agreed upon the urgency to mend the breaches in Japan's cultural fabric caused by the military defeat and occupation and to gain confidence of the nation, and the need of a new set of architectural vocabulary to represent Japan. To many Japanese, the once-popular form of the Imperial Crown Roof had unpleasant nationalist, even militarist, overtones in the new democratic and international climate. Architects thus reinvestigated Japan's cultural heritage in search of new architectural representations of the country while avoiding the pit of nationalism in a narrow sense. Under such circum- stances the *Nihon dento ronso* (Japanese tradition debate) swept through postwar Japanese architecture, involving many architects and architectural theorists, including the Metabolists.[49] To a certain extent, the foundation of the Metabolist movement had been laid in this great debate. Kawazoe, one of the advocates of the debate, regarded Metabolism as a movement that continued with the agenda of the tradition debate – searching for a new cultural role of architecture and urbanism in postwar Japan.

The effort to recapture tradition had a broader cultural background in postwar Japanese society. The tradition debate was initiated by a few leading intellectuals of the time, prominently Yoshimi Takeuchi, who called more generally for a national literature and a national culture.[50] Their ideas reflected the return of a nationalist ideology that resisted foreign influence, a characteristic of Japanese history since the Meiji Restoration (1862–69).[51] Debates over the meaning of Japanese tradition had plagued the architectural profession before the Second World War. In the design competition for the Imperial Museum of Tokyo in 1931, Maekawa's Modernist scheme was dismissed by the jury, stirring controversies not unlike the one caused by Le Corbusier's entry to the design competition for the League of Nations headquarters building in Geneva in 1927. The prize-winning scheme by Jin Watanabe featured an Imperial Crown Roof on top of a modern museum composition.[52] Architectural designs using such traditional Japanese vocabulary, sometimes referred to as *Nihon Shumi* (Japanese taste), became particularly favorable during the war. For instance, Tange's winning entry to the design competition for the National Memorial for the Greater East Asia Co-Prosperity Sphere in 1942 imitated the composition and architectural form of the Grand Shrine in Ise. Another winning scheme by Tange for the Japanese Cultural Center in Bangkok in 1943 employed the layout and elements of a Japanese *Shinden*-style complex.[53]

After the war, architects returned to the issue of tradition with a new sense of urgency. Ironically, whereas tradition had been deployed to preserve the status quo and bolster authority in the 1930s and 1940s, the reinterpretation of tradition in the postwar years challenged the conservative political order and promoted democratic social ideals. Authors argued for an alternative "tradition" centered on "the people," discrediting orthodox building forms representing authoritarian feudal regimes.

1.17
Jin Watanabe, Tokyo National Museum, formerly Imperial Museum of Tokyo, 1931

Ryuichi Hamaguchi, Tange's classmate at the University of Tokyo, wrote "Architecture of Humanism" in 1947, which became one of the first essays to deal with the issue of tradition and its relationship to modern architecture.[54] But it was Kawazoe who formally kindled the tradition debate in architecture in 1956 through an essay published in *Shinkenchiku* entitled "Toward the Discovery of Tradition and People."[55] In this essay, he called for "standing upon Japan's own tradition and absorbing the international method," and urged architects to participate in a debate that would "involve all levels of Japanese people in the discussion, and find the true people's artistic method of architectural creation."[56] Soon a steady stream of articles and panel discussions appeared in the major architectural periodicals, including *Shinkenchiku*, *Kenchiku bunka*, and *Kokusai kenchiku*, as well as popular periodicals and newspapers. These essays attempted from a variety of perspectives to situate contemporary architects' work in relation to pre-modern Japanese architecture, discussing both abstract ideas and physical designs.

Kawazoe identified two aesthetic strands in Japanese cultural history: *Jomon* and *Yayoi*. Jomon was the prehistoric culture that dominated the Japanese archipelago from approximately 10,000 BC to 300 BC. The Yayoi culture dated from the end of the Jomon culture until approximately 300 AD.[57] The distinct character of each cultural era is most clearly demonstrated in

18
mon Pottery,
th–3rd century

19
yoi Pottery,
d century BC–
h century AD

1.20
Katsura Imperial Villa, Kyoto, 17th century

its ceramic crafts. Kawazoe characterized Jomon as dynamic and plebeian, representing the spontaneous creative energy of people. In contrast, Yayoi was passive and ordered, indicating the highly sophisticated aesthetics of aristocracy. Kawazoe's Jomon/Yayoi argument originated from Taro Okamoto, a sculptor who had been exposed to European modernism during his extended stay in Paris and influenced by avant-garde artists including Pablo Picasso.[58] When he returned to Japan after the war, he became fascinated by the ancient earthenware of the Jomon era. In contrast to the elitist aesthetics of Yayoi then widely seen as representing the essence of Japanese arts, Okamoto stressed the older, and more dynamic native Jomon pattern, which he regarded as the seed of new arts based on general people's wisdom.[59] In architecture, a corresponding discourse also emerged, in which Yayoisque Japonism was deemed elitist while Jomonesque nativism was seen as populist and expressing the energy of the mass. Kawazoe followed Okamoto's dualism, and criticized Tange's recently completed Tokyo City Hall (1953–57) and Kagawa Prefectural Office (1955–58) as Yayoisque design and failing to present the "power of people." Tange responded by contending that Jomon and Yayoi, though originating from different stages in the history of Japanese architecture, had a dialectical relationship with each other. He cited evidence of coexistence of both aesthetics in some of the most successful pieces of architecture in history, such as Katsura Imperial Villa. The intersection of Jomon and Yayoi at Katsura indicated that there was no clear boundary between these forms.[60] Nevertheless, when Tange worked on his next civic project, Kurashiki City Hall (1958–60), he consciously moved away from his previous inclination to a serene and transparent style to employ the Brutalist elements of design, such as dynamic massing and rugged-concrete skin as seen in Le Corbusier's late works of *béton brut*.[61] The gesture was unmistakably Jomonsque.

When Metabolism was founded, the tradition debate was still going on and it influenced the Metabolists in several aspects. In terms of design

21
nzo Tange,
gawa
efectural Office,
58

language, the architects became fascinated by pre-modern arts and crafts, which encouraged the use of less refined materials and local building techniques. Otaka was involved in the debate when he worked for Maekawa and designed the Harumi Apartment Building. This housing project featured a structural system composed of massive reinforced concrete pillars that elevated multi-level flats above the ground. The flats were grouped every three levels in the manner of Le Corbusier's *Unité*. The gigantic structural elements and concrete building envelope indicated evidence of the Brutalist influence as well as the architect's inclination toward Jomon aesthetics. Its massive scale and structural hierarchy provided a prototype for ensuing megastructural designs in Japan. Kikutake

1.22
**Kenzo Tange,
Kurashiki City
Hall, 1960**

approached Japanese tradition from a different perspective. He researched traditional wood structures and developed a systems approach to design that could be applied with modern materials and techniques. One of the important things he learned from his experience of addition, modification, and relocation of traditional wood structures was to differentiate structural and non-structural elements and to assemble them into a "replaceable system." This principle of "replaceability" was applied to an urban scale, manifest in the architect's Tower-shaped City and Marine City schemes, and continued to appear as an important theme in many Metabolist designs.

The tradition debate was not simply an attempt to identify modern design with pre-modern Japanese architecture. More significantly, the debate served as a springboard, propelling Japanese architects and artists into the search for a new cultural identity in architecture and design. It enlightened the Metabolists, who took over the torch and set off for an architectural movement that would "send a message to the West."[62] Kawazoe later recalled:

> Nevertheless, at that time, I could hardly see any hope for the future.
> After the end of the war, the architects' dreams of rebuilding the c

ities up from the ruin and moor all fell apart, Kenzo Tange's Hiroshima Peace Memorial Park being the only exception. The city planning for rehabilitation and revitalization also encountered various frustrations. . . . The city planning method from the West was not effective at all in the face of Japan's reality. The tradition debate revealed the architects' dream for the city, and the desire of overcoming the poor industrialization of low-cost and low-tech patterns to catch up with the standard of America and Europe in terms of architecture. Metabolism in fact presented the true objective of the tradition debate in another form.[63]

In Kawazoe's mind, there was a fundamental distinction between Japanese conceptions of city building and the Western ideas. While the city was a monument in classical Western concepts, the Metabolists saw in Japanese tradition an image of the city as life and as nature. Kawazoe thus declared:

> The backbone of the Western civilization is a permanent and absolute idea, for which its architecture and city was the symbol. But in modern science, it becomes clear that a permanent and absolute existence does not exist. So in the future the society will keep changing too. . . . From the ancient times, Japanese have thought about the world as flowing and changing all the time. Based on this idea, the human being should not stand against the nature, nor should architecture and city. Rather they should become part of the nature. They should obey the theory of the life. What should be considered as the theory of life is metabolism.[64]

The reexamination of Japanese tradition provided the Metabolists with a philosophical foundation. Based on the fundamental relationship between architecture and nature, they began to pursue a new paradigm of architecture and city. Their ambition was manifested in Tange's book on Katsura and in Tange, Kawazoe and Yoshio Watanabe's book on Ise, both moving beyond the general aesthetic discussion to explore the philosophical roots and symbolism of architecture.[65] Other Metabolists also confirmed the impact of the tradition debate to their works. Kurokawa often recalled the inspiration that Buddhism had provided him since his early years, echoing Kawazoe's claim that East and West held different worldviews.[66]

However, while the tradition debate dealt with broader cultural meanings of arts and architecture, the impetus behind the Metabolist movement was to establish a concrete design methodology. It thus advanced from "image" to "form" and "structure." The objective was to build a general discourse on urbanism that architects would be able to follow. Isozaki's "Theory of Process Planning" was a manifestation of such an attempt.[67] This short essay was written in a format like a manual, providing instructions for an "architecture of growth" that could cope with the constant transformation over time. It was filled with keywords of Metabolism such as skeleton, group, growth, and system. Isozaki elaborated his processing planning method further in another essay, "Invisible City," written in 1966:

> We have before our eyes fragments of cities in the process of flux. The fragments constantly shift into succeeding phases. In a city of this kind, where exterior appearances move and change without cease, process alone is trustworthy. Design, or this genre of planning, can be called a theorized process. The making of decisions at any given point in time is tantamount to serving the total image of an object in motion. Even something fixed, like a work of architecture, when set down in the constantly metamorphosing city, is part of growth, change, and metabolism.[68]

The Metabolist image of city in constant mutation was explicit in this statement. Isozaki argued that designers must try to foresee from the present moment the ultimate form, but the ultimate form is not the end. Instead, it is the "point of origin to which all things return."[69]

Tange's wartime adventure

Isozaki's theoretical and design works in the 1960s demonstrated that Metabolism was not simply an avant-garde concept limited to a small group, but rather an idea shared by a number of visionary architects in postwar Japan.

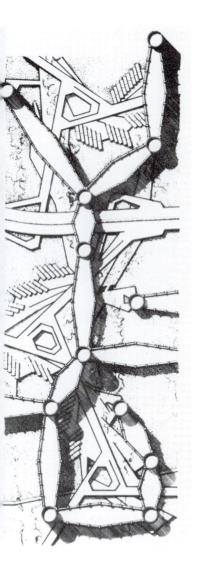

Isozaki entered Tange's architectural laboratory at the University of Tokyo as a fourth-year undergraduate in 1953, and later became his associate and was involved in many of Tange's projects. In Tange's laboratory, Isozaki was a close friend to Takashi Asada, whom Tange appointed to prepare for the World Design Conference. It is not totally clear why Asada did not include Isozaki in the preparation team for the conference programs, which eventually formed the core of the Metabolist group, but one possible reason was young Isozaki's political radicalism. As a student activist during his college years, he participated in the 1960 protests against the US–Japan Security Treaty. Although Asada appreciated Isozaki's genius as a designer, he might have regarded him as unsuitable for such an important governmental event as the World Design Conference.

Isozaki's radicalism was also evident in his urban concepts. In 1960, the very year Metabolism made its debut, Isozaki introduced his own vision of city design, the "Joint Core System," deriving from his scheme for the redevelopment of the Water Purification Plant site in Shinjuku. The plan was an assemblage of vertical elements joined horizontally by truss-like arms, each at the scale of an entire building and accommodating multi-floored living or workspace. The giant cores, conceived of as infrastructure serving vertical transportation and major structural elements, lifted the new city high in the air and divorced it from the existing urban fabric underneath. The concept of the joint core system was integrated into Tange's Plan for Tokyo later in the year, forming the office clusters on thecentral spine, and readopted in the 1964 plan for a business complex in the Tsukiji district of Tokyo commissioned by the Japan dentsu Corporation. Isozaki's megastructural scheme resembled Kikutake's

24
rata Isozaki, Joint Core System, 1960. Plan

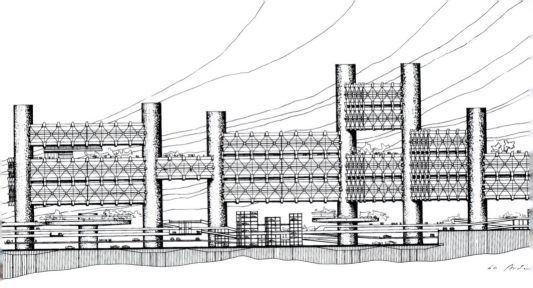

1.25
**Arata Isozaki,
Joint Core
System, 1960.
Elevation**

seaborne tower-shaped urban concepts in its scale of intervention and the mechanical imagery, manifesting the connection between Isozaki's urban concepts and those of the Metabolist members. In fact, the photomontage called "Incubation" that Isozaki created based on the joint core system project was displayed in the "City and Life of the Future" exhibition at Saibu Department Store in 1962, which featured Metabolism.

Tange's work was also included in the Saibu exhibition.[70] As David Stewart observes, Isozaki's thoughts on urbanism in the early 1960s, "for better or worse, bathed in the same emphasis on cybernetics and cybernation that has accompanied all Tange's pronouncements on matters touching the city."[71] This comment is applicable, moreover, to most Metabolist members. As the mentor of these young architects, Tange played a significant role in the Metabolist movement. His appointment of Asada to form the preparation team for the World Design Conference led to the emergence of Metabolism. More importantly, his thinking about architecture and urban design, characterized by a shrewd reinterpretation of tradition, a continuing pursuit of technological expression, and an articulated monumentality, strongly inspired the Metabolists in plotting the futures of the modern city.

Hajime Yatsuka also recognizes that Metabolism – from its inception at the 1960 World Design Conference until the 1970 Osaka World Expo – had always been under a sort of mutual influence with Tange. Yatsuka invokes an interesting analogy to describe such a relationship by comparing the five Metabolist architects and two "periphery figures" (Isozaki and Sachio Otani) to the seven stars of the Big Dippers surrounding the Pole Star (Tange).[72] This metaphor holds some truth. It is impossible to talk about any postwar Japanese architectural movement without mentioning Tange. However, a question must be raised: What particular aspects of the Metabolists' work — and the Metabolist movement as a whole — did Tange most significantly influence? A review of Tange's earlier architectural career during wartime is especially instructive in this regard.

Tange's first public statement was a ten-page article published in the journal of *Gendai Kenchiku* (Modern Architecture) in 1939 entitled "Ode to Michelangelo: As an Introduction to the Study of Le Corbusier."[73] It was a manifestation of Le Corbusier's influence on Tange, an influence that persisted throughout his entire career. Born in Imabari on the southern island of Shikoku, Tange spent part of his childhood in Shanghai before moving back to his native town.[74] He went to Hiroshima High School to study literature in 1930, where he happened to see Le Corbusier's competition entry for the Soviet Palace in a foreign art journal. This incidental encounter set the young Tange on the road to becoming an architect. After two unsuccessful attempts, he was finally accepted by the Architecture Department of the Imperial University in Tokyo in 1935.[75]

Tange's mentor at the Imperial University was Hideto Kishida, then one of the most influential professors at the Department of Architecture along with Yoshikazu Uchida and Aika Takayama.[76] These professors were founding members of the *Nihon kosaku bunka renmei* (Japanese Alignment of Cultural Work), an association of progressive intellectuals, architects, and artists, established in 1937. The mission of this organization was to foster collaborations among scholars in different disciplines and to engage them in research on contemporary issues of architecture, city planning, and social reform. Romantic and nationalist in nature, *Nihon kosaku bunka renmei* echoed the militarist government's political agenda of expanding Japan's influence in Asia, and its members were involved in the planning and development of Japanese-occupied Manchuria (*Manchukoku*), which Japan seized from China through a series of battles and conspiracies, as a comprehensive project of building a new frontier of Japan's "total empire."[77] For instance, Takayama and Uchida provided a master plan for the city of Datong in 1939, which not only became a model of town planning in Manchuria, but also influenced urban reconstruction in Japan after the Second World War. In June 1939, *Nihon kosaku bunka renmei* launched the magazine *Gendai Kenchiku*, publishing the group's architectural manifestos, research, and projects. Tange's "Ode to Michelangelo" appeared in its December 1939 issue, which, as he himself claimed, "stirred up considerable comment."[78]

Although the young architect's original intention had been to explain the principles of Le Corbusier through a study of Michelangelo, the prose was written in a gallant style, showing heavy influence of Yojiro Yasuda, the Romantic poet, literary critic, and leading figure of the *Nihon Romanha* (Japanese Romantic Movement). For Tange, Le Corbusier was the only modern Western architect taking a revolutionary approach toward architecture, one full of poetic inspiration. Tange was fascinated not only by the master architect's capacity as a sculptural form-giver in architecture, but also his grand visions for the modern city. What Tange saw in the scheme of the Soviet Palace was a powerful architectural image that combined technological progress and urban continuity, and represented a harmonious balance between social order and democracy. These qualities permeated the ensemble of Le Corbusier's works, which contrasted with the radically discontinuous urban environment during Japan's interwar period.

Tange also benefited from his relationships with two of Le Corbusier's former disciples: Maekawa and Sakakura. He knew Sakakura from the Imperial University and worked with him on projects in Manchuria. Sakakura's plan for *Nanko* (South Lake), a residential quarter in the capital of pseudo-Manchukoku, *Shinkyo*, was another monumental work of city planning in the late 1930s. Through the 1930s and early 1940s, the city building in Manchuria was carried out mainly by *Mantetsu* (the South Manchuria Railway Company), a powerful semi-governmental organization in charge of the development of infrastructure in this Japanese puppet state. Mantetsu also served the Japanese militarist government as a think tank, gathering a large number of intellectuals for research in various fields.[79] The planning projects in Manchuria in this period often became urban experiments, in which innovative design methods were employed. Sakakura's Nanko project followed Le Corbusier's idea of planning, and envisioned a modern city resembling a fragment of Le Corbusier's *Ville Radieuse*, organizing large-scale buildings and open greenery in a way that drastically contrasted with the dated urban framework of Shinkyo's historic center. Although this plan was not implemented, observation of Sakakura's works might have provided young Tange with primary knowledge of modern city design.

Upon his graduation in 1938, Tange chose to join Maekawa's firm, where he could remain in contact with Le Corbusier's work. Not content to emulate the master in silence, however, Tange determined that he should "try to uncover the secret of his appeal."[80] He decided to leave Maekawa's office in 1942 when, thanks to the war, "there was no building to design."[81] He reentered the Imperial University as a postgraduate student, and stayed until the end of the war. These additional school years proved crucial for Tange's career as he later recalled: "This was the time when I began considering the importance of urban design, not in the sense of mere city planning involving land-use and street-network composition, but three-dimensional urban design."[82] He studied with enthusiasm the folios containing engravings of Greek and Roman marketplaces he found in the library. Preoccupied by his romantic ideas, Tange translated the concepts of agora and forum into spatial orders that integrated architectural elements derived from Buddhist temples, Shinto shrines, and the Heian-period Shinden residences.

Tange was soon able to apply his study of these foreign and native sources in two national competitions: the Memorial for the Greater East Asia Co-Prosperity Sphere in 1942 and the Japanese Cultural Center in Bangkok in 1943. He won first place in both competitions, thrusting himself into the limelight in wartime Japanese architecture. The scheme of the Memorial for the Greater East Asia Co-Prosperity Sphere was particularly significant because it indicated the primary approach to urbanism that he would continue to develop in later works.[83] Tange intuitively sensed how to create a dramatic setting for a monumental architecture representing Japan. The competition rules specified neither a site for this memorial nor detail of its program, rather it allowed designers to select their own site and formulate the program. Tange chose to locate his project at the foot of Mt. Fuji, a site evocative of nationalistic associations, and dedicated the monument to fallen Japanese soldiers. Mt. Fuji had long been regarded as the symbol of Japanese culture and Japanese spirit, represented across a wide array of artistic works. However, it was not until the publication *Nihon Fukei-ron* (Theory of the Japanese Landscape), written by geologist Shigetaka Shiga in 1897, that Mt. Fuji was firmly established as the national icon of Japan.[84] As the country became increasingly dominated by nationalist ideology during the first half of the twentieth century when it was engaged in a few wars in the Far East, this symbolic association continued to be strengthened.[85] Tange's scheme echoed this nationalist sentiment by situating the memorial complex in a sacred, idyllic setting and incorporating the image of Mt. Fuji.

In his scheme for the memorial, Tange combined what he refers to as "the pure image of Ise Shrine" with the Western classical layout of monuments.[86] The complex was organized in a strictly hierarchical manner along a central axis that linked its major memorial structures. Tange placed two trapezoidal colonnades along the axis, with the second one enclosing the main memorial hall reminiscent of the plaza at Capitoline Hill in Rome, betraying the architect's familiarity with monumental architecture of Italian Renaissance and particularly Michelangelo's works. The forecourt of the complex recalled Gian Lorenzo Bernini's great colonnade at St. Peter's. The architectural form of the memorial hall that terminated the axis, however, appeared to descend directly from the grand sanctuary at the Ise Shrine. This reinforced-concrete building, which was to become the dominant element of the entire complex, had a broad podium and a massive gabled roof set perpendicular to the main axis. Its entrance was placed at the center under the eaves of the imposing roof, just like Ise Shrine.

Historian Jonathan M. Reynolds holds that Ise Shrine, after which Tange modeled his memorial, had always played an important role in legitimizing the imperial institution. This continued even after the Meiji Restoration, when the country transformed itself into a modern nation.[87] Architectural historians in the prewar period – prominently among them Chuta Ito (1867–1954) – tended to present Ise as the cornerstone of a national culture, lauding it as "architecture that manifests the spirit of simplicity that is characteristic of the Japanese people."[88] Such nationalist rhetoric was common in the interwar period when Ise became an important ideological tool for the government to mobilize the Japanese people for an all-out war and to defend its invasion of other countries. As a result, Ise Shrine emerged as a symbol of Japan's military aggression across Asia. It was thus not surprising that Tange employed this form in the design of a state memorial.

However, Tange's sacred site was not an isolated and inaccessible retreat like Ise. Instead, the architect conceived of his complex as the nerve center of the Greater East Asia Co-Prosperity Sphere at large, the nucleus of a new empire removed from congested Tokyo and historically rich Kyoto. The complete name of this project, "Plan for a Memorial Building Connecting the Greater East Asia Highway – Chief Motif: Plan for a War Memorial to the Construction of a Greater East Asia," already indicated his purpose that was to

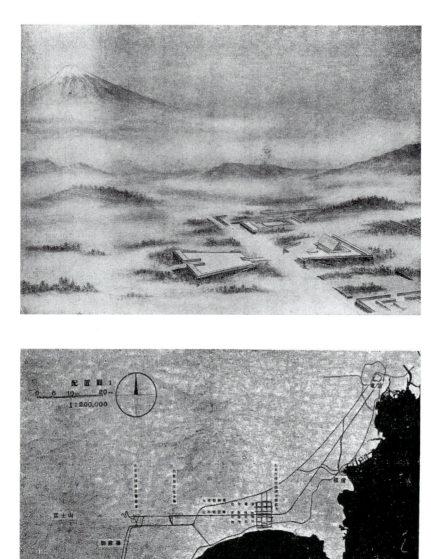

1.26
Kenzo Tange,
Memorial for the
Greater East Asi
Co-Prosperity
Sphere, 1942.
Competition ent

1.27
Kenzo Tange,
Memorial for the
Greater East Asia
Co-Prosperity
Sphere, 1942.
Concept of a
regional plan

base the memorial project on an ambitious city planning scheme. The city
memorial, which he conceived of as the nation's new cultural center, would be
connected to existing major cities, including Tokyo and Kyoto, through a linear
network of highways, which would form the nation's development spine. The
spine would start right at the Imperial Palace in Tokyo, run southward to the

east side of Mt. Fuji, where the sacred precinct was set perpendicularly to the highway, then continue all the way to Kyoto. No comparable attempt had ever been made on this scale in Japanese urbanism. The scheme demonstrated the vision of the young architect, who had since the start of his career dreamt of reforming the country's rampant urban growth. The idea of an extensive linear plan heralded his major urban speculations after the war, particularly the 1960 Plan for Tokyo. With his enthusiasm for futuristic urban mobility and concern for regional planning, Tange dealt with issues not yet articulated by other Japanese architects. The architect's inspiration might have come from the super-express train "Asia Express" in Japanese-occupied Manchuria, developed by the South Manchuria Railway Company.[89] The linear network of transportation connecting major urban centers that Tange called for actually anticipated the Tokaido Megalopolis, which was shaped by the Shinkansen super-express railroad barely two decades later.

Another historian, Jacqueline Kestenbaum, argues that Tange achieved architectural monumentality in the Memorial for the Greater East Asia Co-Prosperity Sphere project through three elements: an instantly identifiable Japanese focus; a classical, hierarchical, and essentially Western organization; and a link to an urban network.[90] I would add a fourth: the highly symbolic site of Mt. Fuji. There is no question that wartime attitudes and conditions affected Tange's architectural notions. His theoretical and practical ventures in this period prescribed the territories he would continue to explore in the following decades, and his eventual success was closely bound up with Japan's recovery from the war.

Hiroshima Peace Memorial Park

After Japan's defeat in 1945, the challenge of defining a modern architecture occurred in a completely new political context: a dramatic shift from a dominant ultra-nationalist ideology to the pursuit of democracy amid anti-war movements. Although the traditional vocabulary that Tange employed in the wartime design competitions were replaced by a Modernist architectural language as well as a pragmatic approach to urban reconstruction, the architect's central notion of "planning" continued.

Soon after the war ended, Tange became a member of the governmental agency for reconstruction and was put in charge of the survey team for rebuilding Hiroshima. In 1949, he entered the competition of designing the Hiroshima Peace Memorial Park, a site, it was hoped, that would both revitalize the city center and memorialize its victims. Tange won the competition, and his design was executed by 1955. This proposal was once again based on an axial configuration. The central area of the park followed the Capitoline layout previously employed in his project of the Memorial for the Greater East Asia Co-Prosperity Sphere. The Atomic Memorial Museum, resting on 6.5-meter *pilotis*, formed the centerpiece of the main architectural grouping. The building's extensive horizontality and the lattice pattern on the façade captured the proportions of Japanese traditional architecture. The museum was fronted by

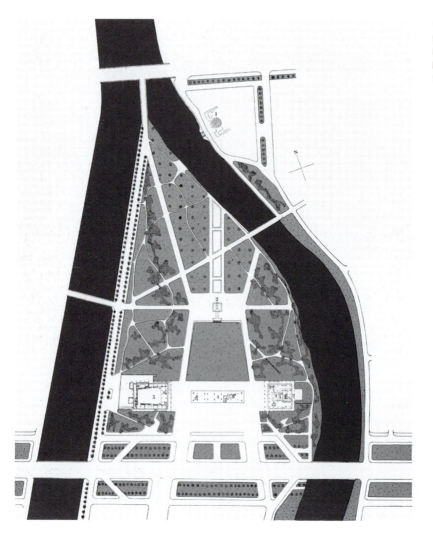

1.28
**Kenzo Tange,
Hiroshima Peace
Memorial Park,
1955. Plan**

the memorial's iconic figure, a fragment from a neoclassical dome that was the only structure to survive the bombing in this area of the city.

Tange, then in his late thirties, presented this project at the CIAM conference in Hoddesdon, England in 1951. This meeting was structured around the theme of "the urban core." The reconstruction of Hiroshima after the atomic bombing was pertinent to this discussion in unique and unprecedented ways. Tange's design successfully devised a new architectural language with a recognizable Japanese identity. It was modern in every sense, using concrete, a flat roof, and a rational frame structure, while combining classical arts in configuring urban space. Well received by Western architects, this combination of Modernism and tradition provided the city with a new sense of order out of the chaotic urban scene in the immediate postwar years. Afterwards, it turned out to be almost a cliché for Japan's postwar Modernism.

On the strength of the Hiroshima project as well as other civic projects in the 1950s including the Tokyo City Hall and the Kagawa Prefectural Building, Tange called for a "new tradition" for Japanese architecture.[91] With this "new tradition," he attempted to shift the character of Japanese architecture from its emphasis on traditional vocabulary in the prewar period to the search for more abstract aesthetics or "spirit," a word he repeatedly used in different occasions after the war. For instance, when Tange argued with Ernesto Rogers about the relationship between tradition and architectural creation at the CIAM meeting in Otterlo, he insisted that architects should "inherit spirit, not specific idioms."[92] This attitude toward using a new tradition to present Japan's national identity was demonstrated in his two monographs, one on Katsura and the other on Ise. *Katsura: Tradition and Creation in Japanese Architecture* was a collaborative work with the architectural photographer Yasuhiro Ishimoto, with an introduction by Walter Gropius, who visited Japan on a Rockefeller Foundation grant in 1954 and made a pilgrimage to Katsura Villa. The other monograph, *Ise: Prototype of Japanese Architecture*, was co-written with Kawazoe, with photograph by Yoshio Watanabe, and first published in Japanese in 1962.[93]

Tange's dialectic understanding of Katsura as inspiration of both Jomon and Yayoi traditions for modern design has been mentioned. More significant in his notion of tradition was the renewed tribute he paid to Ise and a subtle transition in interpreting its legacies. In his 1942 competition entry for the Memorial for the Greater East Asia Co-Prosperity Sphere, Tange appropriated the form of the main sanctuary of Ise Shrine and hybridized it with a Western composition of monument. In his postwar writing, however, he diluted Ise's close association to the imperial institution. Writing in a similar tone to his analysis of Jomon and Yayoi styles in the earlier book on Katsura, Tange presented Ise as the prototype for traditional Japanese architecture, and described in great detail the relationship between Shinto architecture and nature. In *Ise: Prototype of Japanese Architecture*, he declared: "The entire later course of Japanese architecture starts at Ise. The use of natural materials in a natural way, the sensitivity to structural proportion, the feeling for space arrangement, especially the tradition of harmony between architecture and nature, all originated here."[94] He thus shifted the emphasis of Japanese tradition from the concrete architectural form to the concern of "natural process" embodied in Ise.

His co-author Kawazoe went on to articulate this "natural process." He cited Ise as a prime example of a tendency in Japanese architecture to perpetuate architectural form without strictly preserving the actual building itself. For Kawazoe, this suggested an appreciation of the mutability of the nature and the recognition that the practice of building should be attuned to such natural process. He contended:

> The design, one might say, had its own *metabolism*, which allowed it to keep pace with the cycles of life in Nature and society. To paste new paper on the shoji, which set the basic tone of the Japanese room, was enough to create a startling effect of freshness and light. In the same way, to have the tatami re-covered was to fill the room with the faint, clean smell of rice straw. . . . The custom might even be described as an echo of the regular rebuilding of the Ise Shrine.[95]

Here Kawazoe used the concept of metabolism to interpret Ise and Japanese building tradition by linking them to the natural process. He then focused on the most remarkable feature of Ise: a historical continuity paradoxically achieved through the unusual practice of complete rebuilding over 1300 years. Every twenty years or so, the main shrine of Ise is torn down and a new one is built on an immediately adjacent site in an identical form except for some minor details. This symbolic rebuilding, known as *shikinen zokan*, expresses the deepest ideas of Shintoism, the belief in the necessity of periodic ritual renewal.[96] Such periodic rebuilding was regarded as obeying the "law of nature." In several writings this "natural" renewal has been seen to represent the cultural essence of Japan, including Chuta Ito's "Ise Daijingu" published in 1921.[97] Apparently aware of this unique process, Kawazoe and his Metabolist colleagues attempted to establish it as the core principle of the Metabolist theory. By equating Japanese architectural practice with natural processes, the Metabolists hoped to rediscover a true Japanese tradition that would not only transcend the naive imitation of form in the prewar period, but also trump the mechanical and unnatural methods that predominated in the West.

Tange and the Metabolists

To a significant degree, Tange's wartime and postwar experiences anticipated the role he played in the Metabolist movement. His influence on the Metabolists was evident in three aspects of his work: the definition of a "new tradition," the comprehensive approach to city planning, and the expressive use of technology. These issues were, of course, not phenomena seen only in the lineage of

Tange-Metabolism. Rather, they were the threads along which Japanese architecture had developed during the postwar decades, and they were closely associated with the social transformation and political climate in Japan during this period. Tange played a direct and decisive role in this enterprise through his theoretical articulations and design experiments, which influenced Metabolist members. As Hajime Yatsuka and Hideki Yoshimatsu describe, the Metabolist group was an extension of Tange's effort to find a new formal and spatial representation of Japanese culture.[98] The Metabolists continued with the exploration of the new concepts of architecture and urbanism that Tange had initiated while criticizing his conservatism. Through this process, they established their own identity, and in turn inspired the elder master. This reciprocal relationship, to a great extent, shaped the Metabolist movement.

The tradition debate sweeping the architectural circles in Japan in the 1950s had a profound impact on the Metabolist movement, involving its key members including Kawazoe, Otaka, and Kikutake. Moving away from the pursuit of *Nihon Shumi* in prewar and wartime architectural movements, the issue of tradition was spotlighted again in the postwar period, but new meanings were given to it. On one hand, an increasing concern for cultural roots demanded a re-evaluation of Japanese tradition; on the other hand, the new political environment called for an architectural language in accordance with a democratic society and serving "arts for people."[99] Similar phenomena were seen in Europe, demonstrated by the "urban core" theme at the eighth CIAM meeting which called for a return to traditional urban form centered on symbolic civic spaces such as piazzas. Responding to such new social contexts, Tange made a dramatic move by advocating a "new tradition." His design works, including the Hiroshima Peace Memorial Park, the Kagawa Prefecture Office Building, and Tokyo City Hall, went beyond the Functionalist approach to combine three distinct qualities: the dramatic expression of up-to-date technology, the incorporation of civic spaces, and the unmistakable revisions of traditional architectural vocabulary. These buildings featured public access and included public galleries and community meeting spaces, making a gesture for democracy. Tange exposed raw concrete on building surfaces, and used concrete structure to present an abstract order of classical composition. His proposal that architects should inherit spirit, not specific idioms, freed young architects from formal constraints and encouraged them to explore new paradigms of architecture.

Like many of their contemporaries, Tange and the Metabolists believed that thoughtful architectural forms embodied cultural meaning and national spirit and that they afforded the surest defense against the erosion of time. Timeless form manifested itself in continuities just like the punctual rebuilding of the Grand Shrine at Ise. With its emphasis on transformation and renewal, such radical thought returned to the ancient concept of the universe incorporated in traditional Japanese religious doctrines. It was significant that Tange and the Metabolists' reflections on such ideas, however naive, helped turn architectural thinking toward their own home ground, an effort that paradoxically had little to do with specific forms of traditional architecture.

Tange's profound interest in city and regional planning constituted another link to the young Metabolists. Through Tange's entire career, urbanism consistently grounded his architecture. Since the prewar years, Tange had dreamed of reforming the rampant urban growth which had already become a pressing issue in Japan. When the Architectural Institute of Japan requested architectural guidelines for the occupied areas in Asia during the war, Tange responded:

> It is urban planning that affords a context. In this way individual
> architectural creations will achieve a self-evident meaning endowed

with maximal freedom, without which such works would be unprincipled. Thus a vigorous form of southern urban planning and construction, motivated by a new Japanese spirit, will emerge.[100]

This notion of planning as the foundation of architecture and national development was manifest in his competition entry for the Greater East Asia Co-Prosperity Sphere Memorial. Immediately after the war, Tange published a paper entitled "Some Questions Related to Construction."[101] In this paper he called for a fundamental reform under a democratic system in order to break away from the influence of the dated feudal system, which still remained significant in Japan's city building. Tange's appeal had nothing to do with architectural style; rather he squarely addressed the significance of city and national planning, which he regarded as the foundation for economic and social stability. In this essay, Tange quoted André Siegfried to claim: "the world is standing in the cross-road, whether free or planned."[102] He continued to advocate systems approaches to planning in several other essays, including the pamphlet *Theory of Regional Planning*, published by the Bureau of National Resource Investigation in 1950, and his 1959 doctoral thesis entitled "The Regional Structure and Architectural Form of Modern Metropolis."[103] In 1965, he co-founded the Department of Urban Engineering at the University of Tokyo, where he taught for his lifetime.

Like Le Corbusier, Tange favored a comprehensive approach to city design. His visions of a new order for the city often involved challenging existing parameters. His wartime memorial project had demonstrated his ambition to intervene on a regional scale. This notion remained in his postwar projects and was continually reinforced by more sophisticated architectural language. The Metabolists shared his faith in planning, but pursued it with more radical design methodology, plotting an urban future based on super-scaled structures and a particular notion regarding life cycles in the urban environment. Their experimental projects, in turn, provided Tange with much-needed vitality and enhanced imagery, which he eventually incorporated into his more sophisticated undertakings.

Both Tange and the Metabolists based their urban visions upon the promise of technology. In the primary scheme for the Hiroshima Peace Memorial, Tange proposed a gigantic arch resembling the suspension structure of the auditorium in Le Corbusier's Soviet Palace project, which had inspired Tange since the very beginning of his career. The influence might have also come from Eero Saarinen's 1947 design of the Gateway Arch in St. Louis, though not built until 1965. Both Saarinen's and Tange's arches went beyond pragmatic necessity and current technical capacity to express an optimism in modern technology and redefine the concept of monument. However, because of economic constraints in postwar Japan and the need for prompt reconstruction in Hiroshima, Tange's arch was never built. It was nevertheless an important step for the architect, who continued to explore a new scale of design and new possibilities of technology in his postwar projects.

During his extended stay in the United States in 1959, Tange's development of a new methodology in urban design reached a milestone.

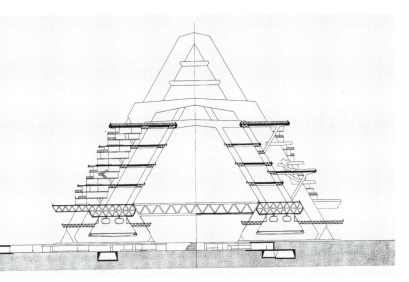

.34
enzo Tange,
ommunity for
5,000 over
oston Bay, 1959.
ection

He instructed fifth-year architectural students at MIT to design a residential community for 25,000 to be erected on Boston Bay. The visiting professor apparently had in mind Kikutake's Marine City, which he had presented at the CIAM meeting in Otterlo right before traveling to the US. However, Tange's specifications reversed Kikutake's formula by placing the residential function directly over the water – a much more dramatic idea. As it worked out, the Boston Bay project consisted of two gigantic linear constructions connected by a highway within the structures and connecting the community back to the land. The giant blocks were characterized by an A-frame section, and carried numerous dwelling units arranged upon layers of artificial grounds supported by the structure. Extraordinary both in scale and technology, the scheme became Tange's first attempt at what Fumihiko Maki and Reyner Banham later called megastructure.[104] As Banham pointed out, the Boston Bay project indicated the influence of Le Corbusier's 1931 plan for Algiers that featured a bookshelf-like megastructure along the seashore housing the infrastructure and residences of an entire city. Tange's A-frame structure, as a substantial improvement of Le Corbusier's concept, in fact derived from the massive public housing building in Harumi by Otaka, known for its enormous structural members and Corbusian *pilotis*.

The Boston Bay project thus turned out to be the meeting point between Tange's and the Metabolists' ideas of technology. Kawazoe was later to claim that the integration of megastructure and minor-structure characterizing this project was a particularly Japanese concept non-existent in Western culture. In 1960, Tange presented this project at the World Design Conference. His address, entitled "Technology and Humanity," further underscored the great importance he attributed to this domain.[105] He recognized both opportunities and challenges that technology offered human society, urging that its power be used for the benefit of human beings. He contended that this task could never be achieved without mediation by architects because "they are the only people standing in the middle ground between technology and humanity."[106] In his speech Tange employed such words as "metabolism" and "cell," betokening his familiarity with the ideas of the Metabolist group.

The Anti-Security Treaty Movement

It was not a coincidence that the radical Metabolist movement came into being in one of the most turbulent years in Japan's postwar history. When the World Design Conference convened in Tokyo in 1960, the city was overwhelmed by enormous social tensions caused by the renewal of the US–Japan Security Treaty, also known as *Anpo*.[107] A massive Anti-Security Treaty Movement was launched, culminating in mass demonstrations and bloody clashes in May and June involving more than five million students, intellectuals, and workers throughout the nation, making it the largest popular movement since the war. Many progressive architects, including the Metabolists, actively participated in the demonstrations. The Metabolists were particularly sympathetic to the Anti-Security Treaty Movement because this outburst of leftist intellectual resistance to the Japanese postwar political system, to a great extent, paralleled the political ideals embodied in most of their utopian urban projects.

The new treaty was drafted in January 1960 by the conservative Liberal Democratic Party (LDP) government under the leadership of Prime Minister Nobusuke Kishi. Although articles in the treaty were regarded as favorable to Japan, as compared to the one implemented after the American occupation ended in 1952, it was widely resisted by Japanese society. The opponents contended that the new treaty contradicted the notion of Japan's status as a pacifist nation – as prescribed by the constitution – by firmly allying Japan with the United States and placing Japan under America's nuclear umbrella. Since late 1959, numerous protests and political contentions had erupted to boycott the treaty. On May 19, 1960, only a few days after the close of the World Design Conference, Kishi and the LDP forcibly passed the treaty in the Congress, infuriating opposition parties as well as the general public, and triggered more severe protests and continuous strikes. On June 15, tens of thousands of angry student demonstrators led by the *Zengakuren* (National Federation of Students Self-Government Associations) stormed into the National Diet Building.[108] The clash with the police resulted in a numbers of casualties, including the death of a female student of the University of Tokyo.[109]

Nevertheless, the revised security treaty was approved by the National Diet. In July, after the treaty was ratified, the Kishi cabinet resigned as a whole in order to defuse the crisis. The former Minister of Finance, Hayato Ikeda, succeeded Kishi as the Prime Minister. In December, Ikeda announced his ambitious Income-Doubling Plan, making a dramatic shift in national policy to focus on the economy. This marked the beginning of Japan's continued double-digit economic growth in the following decade and a half, later known as the "Japanese Miracle." It is plausible that the new security treaty was an important factor leading to the ensuing economic miracle, as the nation retreated from political engagements to concentrate on economic development. Japan's conservative government triumphed, signaling the decline of the left-wing opposition movements in Japan. Struggles for modernity in political terms, with an emphasis on democracy, gradually gave way to the pursuit of stability, mass consumption, and material gain. A psychological divide, however, became more firmly established as Japan's power in the economic sphere grew and the political establishment of conservatism was openly accepted. Intellectuals, including progressive architects, thus had to seek different outlets for their ambitions and dreams as well as frustrations. This was the background against which Tange's and the Metabolists' urban utopias would continue to evolve.

The shift of direction in national policies in 1960 also influenced the development of the Metabolist movement from another aspect. Ironically, although the Metabolist architects opposed the political conservatism and the loss of the Anti-Security Treaty Movement dealt a blow to their social ideals, the outcome of political change in 1960 proved to be facilitating their visionary urban projects rather than hindering them. The economic miracle triggered an enormous construction boom and resulted in an unprecedented pace in urban development. The massive urban buildings provided the stage for the Metabolists' grand ideas of the city, and supported the realization of their designs. For instance, as an immediate response to Ikeda's Income-Doubling Objective, Tange published his ambitious Plan for Tokyo at the beginning of 1961. Since then, proposals of urbanization through reclamation and megastructural developments have been seriously studied as solutions for urban expansion and increased density. A number of mass housing projects and satellite cities were created. In 1963, the 31-meter building height limit in Tokyo was lifted, enabling the vertical growth of the city. The growing economic power also brought Japan the opportunities of hosting significant international events, including the Olympic Games in 1964 and the World Exposition in 1970, both featuring spectacular architectures by Tange and the Metabolists.

Notes

1 World Design Conference Organization, *World Design Conference 1960 in Tokyo* (Tokyo: Bijutsu Shūpansha, 1961), 217–219. The lecture is reprinted in Alessandra Latour ed., *Louis I. Kahn: Writings, Lectures, Interviews*, (New York: Rizzoli, 1991), 113–116.

2 For Kahn's influence on generations of postwar Japanese architects, see Hiroshi Watanabe, "Kahn and Japan," *Progressive Architecture* 65 (Dec. 1984): 78–81.

3 Ibid., 78.

4 For programs and papers of the conference, see *World Design Conference 1960 in Tokyo* (Tokyo: Bijutsu Shūpansha, 1961), published in English and Japanese by the World Design Conference Organization. For details of this conference see "Age of Metabolism" in *Kikan Obayashi* 48 (Special issue: Metabolism 2001): 96–99.

5 About fifteen to twenty people participated in this conversation, including Oshita Seinan, then president of the *Bijutsu Shūpansha* (Fine Arts Press), along with architects and designers. Watanabe, 78 (see note 2); and Fujisaki Keiichiro, "Kikutake sensei, ano yoru, Kahn to nanni ga attan desuka?" (Professor Kikutake, how was the meeting with Kahn in that evening?), *Casa* (July 2004): 75.

6 For a detailed explanation of Kahn's idea about the distinction between form and design, see Louis I. Kahn, "Form and Design," in World Design Conference Organization, *World Design Conference 1960 in Tokyo* (Tokyo: Bijutsu Shūpansha, 1961), 217–219.

7 Ibid.

8 Hajime Yatsuka and Hideki Yoshimatsu, *Metaborizumu: 1960 nendai no Nihon kenchiku avangaruto* (*Metabolism: Japanese Architectural Avant-garde of the 1960s*) (Tokyo: Inax Publishing Co., 1997), 10.

9 Noboru Kawazoe, "Metaborisuto tachi to gakunda toki to ima" (The Metabolists: From the Years of Learning till Present"), in Masato Otaka and Noboru Kawazoe, eds, *Metabolism and Metabolists* (Tokyo: Bijutsu Shūpansha, 2005), 14.

10 For a historical study of the preparation for the World Design Conference, see Yatsuka and Yoshimatsu, 10–18 (see note 8).

11 Architectural graduate programs in Japanese universities are organized around "laboratories," each centered on a professor. Tange's laboratory at the University of Tokyo was among the most prestigious ones, and it attracted many talented architects. In the late 1950s and early 1960s, two of Tange's major assistants in the lab were Takashi Asada and Sachio Otani. Otani was later known for his winning competition entry for the Kyoto International Forum. During the 1960s, Arata Isozaki, who himself had graduated from Tange's lab, succeeded as his major assistant. Most of Tange's urban design projects were carried out in this laboratory. It was not until the late 1960s, when the student strikes became more frequent that Tange had to move all design jobs to his private architectural firm.

12 Noriaki Kurokawa later changed his name to Kisho Kurokawa.

13 Noboru Kawazoe, "Kenzo Tange no Nihonteki seikaku" (Kenzo Tange's Japanese Personality),

Shinkenchiku 30, n.1 (Jan. 1955): 62–69; and "Kenzo Tange ron: sono sonzai no geidai no imi" (On Kenzo Tange: the Meaning of his Existing in the Contemporary), *Asashi jānaru* (Mar. 21, 1965): 89–97.

14 Kawazoe wrote an article on the Harumi Apartment Building, praising it as a direction of new architecture. Noboru Kawazoe, "A step toward the future," *Japan Architect* 34 (Mar 1959): 24–31.

15 Kiyonori Kikutake, "Tower-shaped City," *Kokusai Kenchiku* 26 (Jan. 1959): 12–19; and Kiyonori Kikutake, "Marine City," *Kokusai Kenchiku* 26 (Feb. 1959): 36–39.

16 Toren Berns, "Why Metabolism was Never Modern" *Architecture et idâees* (Summer/Fall 2000): 59.

17 "Age of Metabolism," in *Kikan Obayashi* 48 (Special issue: Metabolism 2001), 97.

18 For a period of time, Kikutake's firm was organized into three teams, each concentrating on one of the three stages of design that he defined, Watanabe, 79 (see note 2). For details of Kikutake's concept of *Ka*, *Kata*, and *Katachi*, see Kiyonori Kikutake, "On the Notion of Replaceability," *World Architecture* 32 (1995): 26–27.

19 Noboru Kawazoe, "Metaborizumu 1960–2001: 21 seiki he no zikken" (Metabolism 1960–2001: the Experiment of the 21st Century), in *Kikan Obayashi* 48 (Special Issue: Metabolism 2001): 3.

20 Yatsuka and Yoshimatsu, 28 (see note 8).

21 Noboru Kawazoe, "Thirty Years of Metabolism," *Thesis, Wissenschaftliche Zeitschrift der Bauhaus-Universität Weimar*, 44 (1998): 146–151. This article originally published in Japanese in *Approach* 116 (1991).

22 Kisho Kurokawa, *Kisho Kurokawa Nōto: Shisaku to sōzō no kiato* (*The Note of Kisho Kurokawa: The track of thinking and creation*) (Tokyo: Dōbunshoin, 1994).

23 Kiyonori Kikutake et al., *Metabolism: The Proposals for New Urbanism* (Tokyo: Bijutsu Shūpansha, 1960).

24 Ibid., 3.

25 Ibid.

26 The Metabolists published a retrospective book in 2005, which covered their recent design works. However, it is offered more as a recollection than new theoretical developments. Noboru Kawazoe and Masato Otaka, eds., *Metabolism and the Metabolists* (Tokyo: Bijutsu Shūpansha, 2005).

27 For details see the May 1965 issue of *Architectural Design*.

28 Kiyonori Kikutake, "Ocean City," in *Metabolism: The Proposals for New Urbanism* (Tokyo: Bijutsu Shūpansha, 1960), 12–13.

29 Ibid., 16–19.

30 Ibid., 38.

31 Kurokawa wrote an essay entitled "Report on the Town Planning of USSR" after he returned from the Soviet Union. It was published in *Kokusai Kenchiku* 26 (May 1959) as one of his essays on the theme of "Current Works of Urban Design in Countries through the World."

32 Noriaki Kurokawa, "Space City," in Kiyonori Kikutake et al., *Metabolism: The Proposals for New Urbanism* (Tokyo: Bijutsu Shūpansha, 1960), 80.

33 It was said that when designing this scheme, Kurokawa was influenced by his early experience in his hometown during a flood season, when his family had to stay on the second floor of the house for a few days. Noboru Kawazoe, *Kikan Obayashi* 48 (Special Issue: Metabolism 2001): 18. Yatsuka and Yoshimatsu found that Kurokawa's Agricultural City resembled a student project in the Soviet Union in the 1920s by the Bavirov Brothers, students of the urban theorist Ivan Leonidov, who advocated the dissolution of cities. They suspected that Kurokawa might have seen this scheme as he had recently made an extended stay in the Soviet Union. Yatsuka and Yoshimatsu, 17 (see note 8).

34 Otaka grew up in a farmer's family in Fukushima, a city in north Japan where people relied on agriculture. The awareness of land as the basis of agriculture might have influenced Otaka's thought since his childhood.

35 Kawazoe and Otaka, 12 (see note 26).

36 Fumihiko Maki, "Acceptance Speech at the 1993 Ceremony for Pritzker Architecture Prize," in the Hyatt Foundation, *The Pritzker Architecture Prize 1993, Presented to Fumihiko Maki* (Los Angeles: Jensen & Walker, 1993); and Fumihiko Maki, "Notes on Collective Form," *Japan Architect* 16 (Winter 1994): 247–297.

37   Otaka and Maki, "Toward Group Form," in Kiyonori Kikutake et al., *Metabolism: The Proposals for New Urbanism* (Tokyo: Bijutsu shūpansha, 1960), 56–59.

38   The anti-nuclear movement in Japan was triggered by an incident in 1954, in which Japanese fishermen working on the South Pacific Ocean were exposed to nuclear radiation caused by the US army's nuclear experiments. The anti-nuclear sentiment is the theme of a series of Godzilla movies produced between the 1950s and the 1970s. In these films, the monsters that destroyed one city after another were thought of as incarnations of nuclear power. See Hajime Yatsuka, "Godzilla versus the Metabolist Mega-monuments," in Botond Bognar, ed., *Tokyo: World Cities* (London: Academy Editions, 1997), 353–354.

39   Noboru Kawazoe, "Material and Man," in Kiyonori Kikutake et al., *Metabolism: The Proposals for New Urbanism* (Tokyo: Bijutsu shūpansha, 1960), 48.

40   Ibid.

41   Ibid., 49.

42   Ibid., 50–51. Translated from the Japanese text by the author.

43   Cherie Wendelken, "Putting Metabolism Back in Place: The Making of a Radically Decontextualized Architecture in Japan," in Sarah Williams Goldhagen and Réjean Legault, eds, *Anxious Modernisms: Experimentation in Postwar Architectural Culture* (Cambridge, MA: MIT Press, 2000), 286.

44   "I want to be a shell" was produced by Japan Broadcasting Corporation (NHK) in 1958.

45   "The City Demolisher, Inc." first appeared in *Shinkenchiku* in the November 1962 issue. It was published again in Arata Isozaki, *Kōkan he* (*Toward Space*) (Tokyo: Bijutsu Shuppansha, 1971), 11–20.

46   Ibid.

47   Jonathan M. Reynolds, "Ise Shrine and a Modernist Construction of Japanese Tradition," *Art Bulletin* 83 (June 2001): 324.

48   For a discussion of the debate of the modernization in Japan, see Harry Harootunian's essay "America's Japan/Japan's Japan" in Masao Miyashi and Harry Harootunian, eds, *Japan in the World* (Durham, NC: Duke University Press, 1993), 196–221.

49   For details of the *Nihon dento ronso*, see Hajime Yatsuka, *Shiso toshite no Nihon jindai kenchiku* (*The Intellectual History of Japanese Modern Architecture*) (Tokyo: Ishinami shoden, 2005), and Terunobu Fujimori, "Dento ronso" (*Tradition Debate*), in *Gendai kenchiku no kiseki* (*The Trace of Modern Architecture*) (Tokyo: Shinkenchiku, 1995), 16–30.

50   Takeuchi was an expert in Chinese modern literature. He translated and introduced to Japan the works of Lu Xun, one of the most important Chinese writers in the twentieth century.

51   The continuing campaign of resisting Western influence had been manifested in the slogan since the Meiji period, *Wakon-Yosai*, meaning "Japanese spirit with Western skill," which called for preserving the essences of native culture as the core when learning Western techniques.

52   For a detailed discussion of the controversies caused by the design competition for the Imperial Museum of Tokyo, see Hajime Yatsuka, *Shiso toshite no Nihon jindai kenchiku*, 374–384.

53   *Shinden* literally means "palace." It was used to represent an important traditional style in Japanese architecture, commonly used in the construction of the residence of the court and noble class during the Heian Period (794–1194).

54   Ryuichi Hamaguchi, *Hyumanizumu no kenchiku* (*Architecture of Humanism*) (Tokyo: Yukeisha, 1947).

55   Tomo-o Iwata, "Toward the Discovery of Tradition and People," *Shinkenchiku* (July 1956): 13–15. Tomo-o Iwata was Kawazoe's pseudonym for this article.

56   Ibid.

57   There are still debates regarding Jomon's and Yayoi's exact period of duration. Some historians hold that they actually paralleled each other in history. Arata Isozaki, *Japan-ness in Architecture* (Cambridge, MA: MIT Press, 2006), 33–46.

58   In Paris, Okamoto was close to members of the College of Sociology, including Emmanuel Levinas, Georges Bataille, and Roger Caillois. Okamoto returned to Japan in 1940, and was fascinated by the beauty of Jomon earthenware. The intellectual proximity with the College of Sociology had influenced his understanding of Jomon as a populist style and Yayoi as an elitist one. This point of view was expressed in his book *The Rediscovery of Japan: Records of Art of*

the Land (Tokyo: Shinchosha, 1958). For details of Okamoto and the role he played in the Jomon/Yayoi debate, see Isozaki, ibid, (see note 57).

59 According to Isozaki, Okamoto's argument against Yayoi and preference of Jomon came with a political implication. In the 1950s, Yayoi style was often associated with American modernism, and further linked to the American occupation of Japan. The influence of Yayoi in the notion of Japan-ness was manifest in Junzo Yoshimura's Japanese house *Shofu-so* (House of pine breezes) exhibited at MoMA in 1954. In contrast, the beauty of Jomon in line with Okamoto's notion of European modernism nurtured a native dynamism opposing the gaze from outside. Isozaki, ibid, 39 (see note 57).

60 Tange argued in his essay: "The shoin of the Katsura Palace belongs fundamentally to the aristocratic Yayoi tradition as it developed from the shinden-zukuri to the shoin-zukuri style. Accordingly, the building is dominated by the principles of aesthetic balance and continuous sequence of patterns in space. And yet there is something which prevents it from becoming a mere formal exercise and gives its space a lively movement and a free harmony. This something is the naive vitality and ever-renewed potentiality of the Jomon tradition of the common people. The Jomon element is strong in the rock formation and the teahouse of the garden. There, however, the aesthetic canons of the Yayoi tradition act as a sobering force which prevents the dynamic flow, the not-quite formed forms, the dissonances, from becoming chaotic. At Katsura, then, the dialectic of tradition and creation is realized. It was in the period when Katsura Palace was built that the two traditions, Jomon and Yayoi, first actually collided. When they did, the cultural formalism of the upper class and the vital energy of the lower class met. From their dynamic union emerged the creativeness seen in Katsura – a dialectic resolution of tradition and antitradition." Kenzo Tange, *Katsura: Tradition and Creation in Japanese Architecture* (New Haven, CT: Yale University Press, 1960), 35. An analysis of Tange and Kawazoe's debate on Jomon/Yayoi can also be found in Jonathan M. Reynolds, "Ise Shrine and a Modernist Construction of Japanese Tradition," *Art Bulletin* 83 (June 2001): 316–341.

61 *Béton brut*, or "raw concrete," was a French term used by Le Corbusier to describe his choice of material. It led to Brutalism in architecture in the 1950s, featuring the work of the English architects Alison and Peter Smithson and, later, the other architects including Louis Kahn and Paul Rudolph. The term gained currency when the British architectural critic Reyner Banham used it in the title of his 1966 book, *The New Brutalism*, to identify the emerging style. Reyner Banham, *The New Brutalism: Ethic or Aesthetic?* (London: Architectural Press, 1966).

62 "Age of Metabolism," in "Metabolism 2001," special issue, *Kikan Obayashi* 48 (2001): 96.

63 Noboru Kawazoe, "Metabolism 1960–2001: The Experiment of the 21st Century," in "Metabolism 2001," special issue, *Kikan Obayashi* 48 (2001): 3.

64 Noboru Kawazoe, "Thirty Years of Metabolism," *Thesis, Wissenschaftliche Zeitschrift der Bauhaus-Universität Weimar* 44 (1998): 147.

65 Kenzo Tange, *Katsura: Nihon kenchiku ni okeru dento to sozo* (*Katsura: Tradition and Creation in Japanese Architecture*) (Tokyo: Zōkeisha, 1960). Kenzo Tange, Noboru Kawazoe, and Yoshio Watanabe, *Ise: Nihon kenchiku no genkei* (*Ise: Prototype of Japanese Architecture*) (Tokyo: Asahi Shinbunsha, 1962).

66 Kisho Kurokawa, *Metabolism in Architecture* (Boulder, CO: Westview Press, 1977).

67 Arata Isozaki, "Theory of Process Planning (1963)," in *Arata Isozaki 1959–1978* (*GA Architect* 6), 30. The concept of process planning was further elaborated in a later essay. Arata Isozaki, "On Process Planning," *Kōkan he* (*Towards Space*) (Tokyo: Bijutsu Shuppansha, 1971), 76–97.

68 Arata Isozaki, "Invisible City," in *Architecture Culture, 1943–1968: a Documentary Anthology*, ed. Joan Ockman (New York: Rizzoli, 1993), 403–404.

69 Ibid, 404.

70 The work of Aika Takayama, Tange's senior colleague at the University of Tokyo, was also included in the Saibu exhibition.

71 David Stewart, *The Making of a Japanese Modern Architecture* (Tokyo: Kodansha International, 1987), 235.

72 Yatsuka and Yoshimatsu, 36 (see note 8). Otani was another associate in Tange's laboratory. His design of the Kyoto International Convention Center in 1966 won him an international reputation. Otani's early involvement in visionary city planning included the plan for Kikumachi in 1961, which resembled Metabolist projects. He proposed concepts of "composition,

organization, structure." But in contrast to Tange and the Metabolists' mega-form, Otani stressed that architecture should be part of the city and the urban context should be respected. For Otani's urban theory and design works, see Yatsuka and Yoshimatsu, 242–244 (see note 8).

73 Kenzo Tange, "Michelangelo shō: Le Corbusier ron he no jisetsu toshite" (Ode to Michelangelo: As an Introduction to the Study of Le Corbusier), *Geidai Kenchiku* (Dec. 1939): 36–47.

74 Tange's autobiography was published in English in *Japan Architect*, Apr. 1985–June 1986. The series is entitled "Recollections: Architect Kenzo Tange" and is an augmented translation of the thirty installments of "Watakushi no Rirekisho" (A History of My Life), originally appearing in *Nihon Keizai Shimbun* (Japanese Economic News).

75 The Imperial University of Tokyo was renamed the University of Tokyo after the Second World War.

76 Aika Takayama established the Urban Engineering Department at the University of Tokyo in 1964, of which Tange became a professor and Chair of the Urban Design program.

77 *Manchukoku* was the name of the puppet state established in Manchuria and eastern Inner Mangolia by Imperial Japan in 1932, with Puyi, the last Qing emperor, as the nominal regent and emperor. The government was abolished in 1945 after the defeat of Japan at the end of the Second World War. A detailed history of Japan's ambitious attempts to control Manchuria and to transform it into the new frontier of a total empire is included in Louis Young's *Japan's Total Empire: Manchuria and the Culture of Wartime Imperialism* (Berkeley: University of California Press, 1999).

78 Kenzo Tange, "Recollections: Architect Kenzo Tange, n.2" *Japan Architect* (May 1985):10.

79 The South Manchuria Railway Company (*Mantetsu*) was founded in 1906 after the Russo-Japanese War to operate the railroad and to develop settlements and industries along its route in Manchuria. Its first president was Shimpei Goto, the former governor of Taiwan and later the Mayor of Tokyo. Mantetsu expanded dramatically after its inauguration and, by 1930, had become the largest and most profitable corporation of Japan. Its research wing provided sponsorship to a large number of progressive intellectuals and became the central piece of Japan's colonial program. For details of the role of the South Manchuria Railway Company in the development of Japanese-occupied Manchuria, see Louis Young's *Japan's Total Empire: Manchuria and the Culture of Wartime Imperialism* (Berkeley: University of California Press, 1999).

80 Kenzo Tange, "Recollections: Architect Kenzo Tange, n.2" *Japan Architect* (May 1985): 7.

81 Ibid., 10.

82 Ibid.

83 The Greater East Asia Co-Prosperity Sphere (*Dai-to-a Kyoeiken*) was a concept created and promulgated during the Showa era by the government and military of the Empire of Japan which represented the desire to create a self-sufficient "bloc of Asian nations led by the Japanese and free of Western powers." The Sphere was initiated by Prime Minister Fumimaro Konoe, in an attempt to create a Great East Asia, comprised of Japan, Manchukuo, China, and parts of Southeast Asia, that would, according to imperial propaganda, establish a new international order seeking "co-prosperity" for Asian countries, free from Western colonialism and domination. However, this was one of a number of slogans and concepts used in the justification of Japanese aggression in East Asia in the 1930s through to the end of the Second World War.

84 Shigetaka Shiga, *Nihon Fukei-ron* (*Theory of the Japanese landscape*) (Tokyo: Iwanami Shoten, 1937). Shiga was an editor of the magazine *Nihonjin* (*Japanese*) during the Meiji era, and an advocate of Japanese tradition and opponent of Westernization. For details of Shiga's argument about Mt. Fuji and his influence on Tange's planning concept, see Hajime Yatsuka, "The 1960 Tokyo Bay Project of Kenzo Tange," in Arie Graafland and Deborah Hauptmann, eds, *Cities in Transition* (Rotterdam: 010 Publishers, 2001), 178–91.

85 The nationalist ideology continued to grow in Japan as the country engaged in a few wars in the first half of the twentieth century, including the Sino-Japanese War in 1894–1905, the Russo-Japanese War in 1904–05, and the First World War in 1914–18, before launching into the Second Sino-Japanese War and later the Pacific War.

86 Kenzo Tange, "Recollections: Architect Kenzo Tange, n.2" *Japan Architect* (May 1985): 12.

87 Reynolds, ibid, (see note 47).

88 Chuta Ito, "Ise Daijingu" (Ise Grand Shrine), in *Ito Chuta chosakushu: Nihon kenchiku no kenkyu* (*Chuta Ito's Research: Research of Japanese Architecture*) (*Tokyo: Hara Shobo*, 1982), 227.

First published as an article in *Tokyo mainichi shinbun* (*Tokyo Daily News*). Chuta Ito (1867–1954) was regarded as the first architectural historian in Japan. Although best known for his research on Buddhist architecture, he also published articles on Shinto architecture, including Ise. Through his prolific writing and teaching at the Imperial University in Tokyo, Ito had a profound influence on people's understanding of pre-modern Japanese architecture. Jonathan M. Reynolds criticized Ito's essay on Ise for its nationalist rhetoric and having "blurred a religio-political discourse with an architectural discourse." There were also authors, including Isozaki, who argued that shrine architecture was in fact not the original prototype of Japanese architecture. It was, rather, an "invented tradition," as Shinto did not appear until the seventh century. It was created in order to counter Buddhism that had been imported from China a few centuries before. Arata Isozaki, "Ise: no modoki" (Ise: The Artificial Origin), in *Ise Jingu* (*Ise Shrine*), ed. Arata Isozaki (Tokyo: Ishinami shoden, 1995). Architecturally, the appreciation of Ise was foreshadowed by Taut's writing after he visited Japan in 1933. He compared Ise to the Acropolis and wrote: "(the Parthenon) is the greatest and most aesthetically sublime building in stone as the Ise shrine is in wood." Bruno Taut, *Houses and People of Japan* (Tokyo: Sanseido, 1937), 139.

89   Mantetsu inaugurated the "Asia Express," the high-speed train from Dalian to Shinkyo in 1934. Reaching a top speed of 134 km/h (83mph), the "Asia Express" was arguably the fastest train in the world in the 1930s, and was the precursor of the *Shinkansen* Express Train System emerging in the 1960s in Japan. Hajime Yatsuka, "The 1960 Tokyo Bay Project of Kenzo Tange," in Arie Graafland and Deborah Hauptmann, eds, *Cities in Transition* (Rotterdam: 010 Publishers, 2001), 178–191.

90   Jacqueline Eve Kestenbaum, "Modernism and Tradition in Japanese Architectural Ideology, 1931–1955" (Ph.D. dissertation, Columbia University, 1996), 203.

91   Tange talked about the issue of "new tradition" when he interviewed Antonin Raymond for a Japanese radio program broadcast on April 27, 28, and 29, 1960. A partial English version of this interview was published in *Architectural Design*, Feb. 1961, pp.56–57. In the interview, Raymond responded to Tange's question about tradition with skepticism, insisting that "I find true Japanese tradition in exact agreement with the principles of good design as formulated by the founders of modern architecture early in this century." Raymond also criticized the works of "some of the young Japanese architects" for being "too sophisticated" and against the "true Japanese tradition." In his autobiography, Raymond cited Tange's Hiroshima Peace Center as one of the structures that imitated his own Reader's Digest Building built in Tokyo in 1951, and claimed that those young architects had been "attracted by the exterior only." Antonin Raymond, *An Autobiography* (Tokyo: Charles E. Tuttle, 1973), 213, 249–250.

92   Oscar Newman, ed., *New Frontiers in Architecture: CIAM'59 in Otterlo* (New York: Universe Books, 1961).

93   Watanabe's photos of Ise were taken in 1953, when the main sanctuary of its Inner Shrine performed its first ritual reconstruction after the Second World War. Watanabe's work was the first ever authorized photograph of Ise Shrine. A selection of these photos appeared in the book *Architectural Beauty in Japan*, published by the Society for International Cultural Relations in 1955, and other publications, including *Shikenchiku* and Arthur Drexler's *The Architecture of Japan* (New York: Museum of Modern Art, 1955). These photos stirred strong interest among architects to study Ise as a site of important Japanese tradition. Jonathan M. Reynolds, "Ise Shrine and a Modernist Construction of Japanese Tradition," in *Art Bulletin* 83 (June 2001): 316–341. Kenzo Tange and Noboru Kawazoe, *Ise: Prototype of Japanese Architecture* (Cambridge, MA: MIT Press, 1965).

94   Tange and Kawazoe, ibid., 16 (see note 93).

95   Ibid., 206.

96   According to *shikinen zokan*, each building in Ise's Inner Shrine and Outer Shrine complexes has an identical double, one of which is in use while the other is disassembled, then rebuilt. This ritualistic and performative rebuilding is said to have started in 685 CE. The period of rebuilding was a little in flux in the past. In earlier times, it was nineteen years; and due to turmoil in the Middle Ages, there occurred a complete interruption of more than one hundred years. Later it was officially set at twenty years. It is believed that the period of around twenty years is dictated by the lifespan of building. Some also say it may be the time needed for passing down the necessary carpentry techniques. The last rebuilding happened in 1993, the sixty-first on record. Arata Isozaki, *Japan-ness in Architecture* (Cambridge, MA: MIT Press, 2006), 131, 323.

97   Chuta Ito, 227 (see note 88).

98   Yatsuka and Yoshimatsu, 40 (see note 8).

99   Yatsuka and Yoshimatsu observe that the countries that had lost in the Second World War, such as Japan and Italy, nourished left-wing nationalist movements, which demanded reevaluation of tradition. Ibid, 36 (see note 8).

100 *Kenchiku Zasshi* (Architectural Journal), no. 690 (Sep. 1942). It is translated and quoted in Arata Isozaki, *Japan-ness in Architecture* (Cambridge, MA: MIT Press, 2006), 106.

101 Kenzo Tange, "Kensetsu o meguru sho mondai" (Some Questions Related to Construction), *Kenchiku Zasshi* (Jan. 1948).

102 Ibid.

103 Kenzo Tange, *Chiiki keikaku no riron* (*Theory of Regional Planning*) (Tokyo: Bureau of Resources Investigation, 1950); Kenzo Tange, "Geidai daitoshi no chiiki kōzō to kenchiku keitai" (The Regional Structure and Architectural Form of Contemporary Large Cities) (Ph.D. dissertation, University of Tokyo, 1959).

104 Fumihiko Maki, *Investigations in Collective Form* (St. Louis, MO: Washington University Press, 1964); Reyner Banham, *Megastructure: Urban Future of the Recent Past* (New York: Harper & Row, 1976).

105 Kenzo Tange, "Technology and Humanity," *Japan Architect* (Oct. 1960), 11–12.

106 Ibid.

107 The full name of the US–Japan Security Treaty was the "Treaty of Mutual Cooperation and Security between the United States of America and Japan." It was first ratified in 1952, when the American occupation of Japan ended, and was due for a renewal in 1960. This treaty allowed the American military to continue to use important bases in Japan for the defense of the Far East and to intervene in Japan to put down internal disturbances should the Japanese government request such assistance. While the Japanese government and a majority of the public supported the ratification of the new treaty, a sizable portion of the public did not, because they felt that the treaty compromised Japan's independence.

108 *Zengakuren* is an abbreviation of *Zen Nihon Gakusei Jichikai Sorengo* (National Federation of Students Self-Government Associations). It was first organized in 1948. Around 1960, it split into various factions that then coalesced as the "new left movement," in opposition to the Japan Communist Party. Arata Isozaki, *Japan-ness in Architecture* (Cambridge, MA: MIT Press, 2006), 323.

109 For details of the 1960 upheaval, see George R. Packard, *Protest in Tokyo: The Security Treaty Crisis of 1960* (Princeton, NJ: Princeton University Press, 1966) and David E. Apter and Nagayo Sawa, *Against the State: Politics and Social Protest in Japan* (Cambridge, MA: Harvard University Press, 1984).

Chapter 2

Metabolist utopias

Metabolists' urban designs, which often proposed sea and sky as the site for human habitats of the future, appear wholly impracticable at first glance. However, they were not simply illusive fantasies that architectural historians tended to portray. Just like modernist precursors Bruno Taut and Le Corbusier who believed architecture was the foundation for social change, Tange and his disciples were inspired by the prospect that a revolution of architecture and a radical reconstruction of the city, more than anything else, could lead to a new order for modern society.[1] Their proposals followed a long tradition of utopian planning, but their unique interpretation of modern technology added fresh ideas to this tradition.

Japanese society in the postwar decades had the necessary ingredients to stimulate utopian projects, that is, a combination of drastic change and the impotence of dealing with such change within the existing system, a situation that had been seen in other countries during periods of significant transition such as Italy in the early Renaissance and England and France at the beginning of the Industrial Revolution. In Japan, social and technical changes, heightened by the recent experience of war, engendered a decisive break with the past and a sense of emerging order, which visionary architects and planners wished to capture. The various intellectual and political movements in the postwar period were indications of such social conditions, culminating in the Anti-Security Treaty mass demonstrations in 1960. The same conditions also gave birth to the Metabolist movement. Political constraints and limited resources, especially those related to land, often frustrated these ambitious architects and forced them to express their ideas in theoretical projects.

Metabolists' ideal cities were thus directed toward the particular urban crises of Japan and addressed its social transformation in the postwar period. The architects were not only dismayed by critical challenges facing large cities, but also frustrated by political conflicts and the impotence of authorities to cope with the situation. Intensified urban ills and social dilemmas, often

concentrated in Tokyo, spurred the architects to seek radical alternatives. Problems associated with the rapid growth of large cities were among the initial factors that stimulated the architects' utopian speculations. Since the end of the Second World War, urban populations in Japan had grown at an unprecedented pace, yet the development of urban infrastructure lagged far behind, causing a chaotic urban scene. As the cities expanded into the surrounding countryside with reckless speed, they lost the coherent structure of a healthy organism. The Metabolists looked at these monstrous and untidy cities as cancers in the society. In their point of view, the confusing urban structure of Tokyo, with its labyrinth-like street system, was a remnant of Japan's archaic feudal system, hindering the continuing development of the modern industrial society. In *Metabolism: The Proposals for New Urbanism*, Kikutake claimed:

> We do not suggest a proposal for the future city. The state of con-
> fusion and paralysis in metropolitan areas and the lack of systematic
> planning is forcing us to make these proposals. . . . The huge city of
> Tokyo is badly sick. She has lost the proper control of the city because

2.1
**Arata Isozaki, City in the Air,
1961. Model view**

of her mammoth-like scale. She is even trying to conceal her illness
and to justify present conditions by relying on the adaptability of her
inhabitants.[2]

Metabolist architects dreamed of new cities which, once built, would provide the
environment for the true order they saw as inherent in an advanced industrial
society. However, because of the general paralysis in implementing large-scale
plans in Tokyo and the critical decay of the city's infrastructure, they determined
that they should leave existing cities as they were, while starting to build new
ones. What they sought was not an improvement of the city, however comprehensive, but a revolution in the way it was built and operated.

In an article published in 1991, the renowned architectural historian
Teiji Ito recalled something Arata Isozaki had said thirty years before. The
ambitious young architect told Ito:

Tokyo is hopeless. I am no longer going to consider architecture that
is below 30-meters in height. . . . I am leaving everything below

30 meters to others. If they think they can unravel the mess in this city, let them try. I will think about the architecture and the city in the air above 30 meters. An empty lot of about 10 square meters is all I need on the ground. I will erect a column there, and that column will be both a structural column and a channel for vertical circulation.[3]

Thus came Isozaki's famous project, "City in the Air." By 1963, the building code in Tokyo prescribed that no structure could be built taller than 31 meters. This height limit was set after the 1923 Great Kanto Earthquake that destroyed the majority of the city, causing a loss second only to the severe bombing at the end of the Second World War. Although miserable scenes after the earthquake must have remained in the memory of Tokyo's citizens and planners for many years, few effective measures had been taken to fundamentally improve the physical layout of the city. The city was still dominated by a medieval urban texture with numerous zigzag alleys and high-density low-rise buildings, many of which were built of wood. One of the complicated issues that paralyzed Tokyo's city planners in the postwar reconstruction was land ownership. Japan was notorious for its dispersed land ownership; urban land was held by numerous small property owners, making any large-scale intervention difficult. Land reformation carried out by the US Occupation Force right after the war further aggravated this situation, because the reform focused on economic egalitarianism in Japanese society and tended to divide up land parcels further.

Isozaki determined that he would not accept the constraints of building height and zoning as premises in design, so he made his city soar into the air. He also wanted his new city to have nothing to do with the existing urban areas, which for him were "hopeless." However, instead of erasing the old city as Le Corbusier proposed to do in his famous 1925 Voisin Plan for Paris, Isozaki decided to leave old Tokyo as it was.[4] What he proposed was to erect several cores, each occupying only around "10 square meters" on the ground to house vertical circulation and other basic equipment. When the cores rose above the 31-meter level, that is, the skyline of old Tokyo, cantilevered members began to grow horizontally out from the cores in various directions. These cantilevers extended useable spaces for housing and offices, forming self-contained human habitats in the air. The whole image was like a few gigantic trees growing up from a dense forest of shrubs. Although not intended as a blueprint for implementation, the concept was so powerful that Tange integrated it into his later design for the Shizuoka Press and Broadcasting Center, on a much more modest scale, after Tokyo's height restriction was officially removed in 1963.

Isozaki's uncompromising attitude was shared by all the Metabolists. Stimulated by both the energy and the chaos of a rapidly changing society, these architects called for a new pattern that would eventually revolutionize the existing urban structure. Within the movement, individual architects proposed different solutions to the problems facing postwar Japanese cities: Kikutake was fascinated by the idea of "marine city," Kurokawa advocated the concept of "urban connector," Otaka and Maki studied the possibilities of "artificial land"

ata Isozaki,
y in the Air,
61. Plan

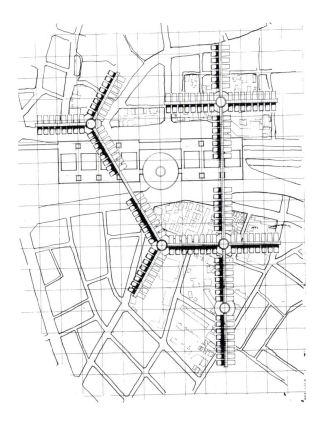

and "group form," and Tange tried to tie these concepts together and incorporate them in a linear city form. None of the schemes, however, was based on the existing urban framework. The architects determined that their society needed a new type of city: not only a new urban form, but also a new way of organization and operation. Critical of the status quo, they were fearful that any link to the existing city would allow urban confusions and social conflicts, as well as unpleasant memories of wartime, to persist.

Paradoxically, the Metabolists also argued that the radical reconstruction of the city, intended to cure Japan's urban ills of the time, was not a turn away from tradition. Instead, they argued, it would restore the dignity of Japanese tradition as well as solve the social crises and cultural dilemmas the nation was facing. In fact, formal similarities between the City in the Air and the traditional bracket set typical in Japanese wood structures have been recognized.[5] Particularly, the complex bracket sets of the South Gate at Todai-ji Temple in Nara, with stepping cantilevered members sitting on the top of gigantic columns and supporting the beams and the roof, were often referred to as the most likely inspiration for Isozaki's articulated megastructure.[6]

The futuristic urban projects were the Metabolists' instruments to promote their political ideals and social ambitions. On the one hand, like many progressive intellectuals of their time, these architects called for the social values characteristic of the modern era, such as democracy, egalitarianism, liberation from land, and freedom of movement. On the other hand, their schemes often conceptualized urban organization featuring hierarchy, centralized administration, and regimentation that had been themes of classic utopian schemes. A similar paradox also existed in their projects attempting to marry the virtues of the Eastern tradition with the power of modern technology. These contradictions of their urban ideals stemmed from the various influences the architects received, both architecturally and ideologically. They tried to combine these inspirations with Japan's particular urban and social context in plotting a future society. The Metabolist urban projects represented different solutions of issues of modern cities, and some even included criticisms of others' utopian planning concepts. They demonstrated diverse design ideas and social ideologies within this group of architects. Such diversity was manifest in the architects' different attitudes toward technology, a debate between concepts of megastructure and group form, and a dystopian notion of "city as ruin." This variety of design and social ideas made the Metabolist movement a unique phenomenon in the study of utopian urbanism.

Communal society

Admittedly, the Metabolists' central concern was the physical form of the city. Apart from Kawazoe, they barely elaborated coherently on the constitutions and social conditions they expected in these ideal cities, as Robert Owen, Charles Fourier, and even Frank Lloyd Wright had done.[7] The Metabolists' extraordinary urban forms nevertheless conveyed strong political messages. When one examines these various schemes and combines them with the manifesto and other sporadic writings by these architects, it is not difficult to see an integrated, though somewhat obscure, picture of their ideal societies.

The foremost characteristic shared by the Metabolists' proposals stemmed from a vision of modern communal living. Metabolist cities often consisted of a number of self-contained collective communities, with populations ranging from 2,000 (Agricultural City) to 500,000 (Ocean City). The land would be publicly owned, and the city would be governed by a central administration. The Metabolists wanted to dissolve the large cities and replace them with urban clusters, which would form a regional network or a linear urban system. The difference between city and country would no longer exist, as they would be united into new urban clusters. The architect would be the mastermind of this new type of city: not only should he be in charge of the design of the major structures and the prototypes of individual units, he would also be responsible for the education of citizens. Individuals, however, should have the freedom to choose their own style of living within the public framework. The city would be abundant economically and democratic politically. People would lead peaceful and romantic lives just like in a pastoral town, while enjoying the conveniences of up-to-date technologies. In short, the Metabolists' ideal cities were characterized by the fusion of several classical contradictions: city and country, centralization and democracy, order and freedom, tradition and modernity. These ideas derived from different sources in intellectual history, demonstrating continuity with classical utopian thought. They were also, in a particular way, related to the modern Japanese society.

The land and the major structures, or "artificial lands" as the Metabolists referred to them, of the city would be publicly owned and managed. They formed the permanent elements of the city. In contrast, private houses and office spaces were conceived of as modules. They were not occupying the land or artificial land, but rather simply attached to them. By putting land into public ownership, the Metabolists rejected other models of ideal society such as democratic individuality exemplified by Frank Lloyd Wright's Broadacre City or cooperative socialism as seen in Ebenezer Howard's Garden City.[8] For the Metabolists, public land ownership would prevent any speculation and guarantee true equality within the society.

Metabolists organized their projects such that each community was based on a gigantic spatial structure, housing a fixed population. For instance, the Tower-shaped Community in Kikutake's Ocean City would provide 1,250 housing units for 5,000 people in total, and his Mova-blocks could accommodate a population ranging from 10,000 to 30,000; Kurokawa's Agricultural City would be built on a 100 by 100-meter concrete slab and support the living of 2,000 people, and Tange's community on Boston Bay envisioned two A-shaped blocks accommodating a total population of 25,000. Most Metabolists insisted on strict population control in their ideal cities. When the population grew and exceeded the prescribed limit, a new urban unit would be generated in a similar way, as in cell division. The city would maintain a consistent population and could therefore avoid the chaos associated with overcrowding.

A model for the Metabolists' idea of collective community appears to be modernist mass urban housing projects. Since the early twentieth century, architects, planners, and public agents had been enthusiastically developing large-scale public housing to accommodate ever-growing populations in industrial cities. This trend started in Europe, where the prevalence of Socialist ideologies paralleled the development of modernism in architecture. It resulted in the *Siedlungen* (settlements) in Germany and the *Gemeindebauten* (municipal projects) in Austria. Both were new communities sponsored by municipalities to provide housing for low-income families. The best-known examples include a series of public housing projects for workers in Frankfurt am Main, under the direction of Ernst May, and the Karl Marx Hof in Vienna, planned by Karl Ehn during the Socialist Democratic regime.[9] These projects, both built in the late 1920s, were joint endeavors of a Socialist municipal government, a powerful city planner, and ambitious modern architects. They aimed to improve the living conditions of the proletariat with the help of modern architecture and modern building technologies like standardization. When this trend spread to the United States after the Second World War, it was often realized as high-rise buildings in large cities, but the previous social agenda was missing in this transmission. Mies van der Rohe's glass-curtain-wall high-rise apartments at Lake Shore Drive in Chicago, built around 1950, became the archetype of mass urban housing in

2.3
Karl Ehn, Karl Marx Hof, Vienna, 1930

America. This pattern was followed by the Marina City, again in Chicago, designed by Bertrand Goldberg in 1959. The latter, which stacked luxurious apartments on the top of multi-level parking garages in cylindrical twin-towers, inspired Tower-shaped City by Kikutake, who included a photo of Marina City's model in his essay in *Metabolism: The Proposals for New Urbanism*. Otaka, the elder Metabolist, was in fact involved in several public housing projects beginning in the 1950s.[10] When he worked for Kunio Maekawa in 1958, he designed the Harumi Apartment Building, located in a reclaimed area in Tokyo Bay, which was developed by the Japanese Housing Corporation as part of a systematic effort to solve Tokyo's housing crisis.

A more substantial influence on the Metabolist concept of collective living, however, came from Le Corbusier's Unité d'Habitation. Commissioned by the municipal government of Marseille, the complex comprised 337 apartments arranged over seventeen stories suspended on large *pilotis*. It not only housed around 1,600 inhabitants, but also incorporated commercial services for daily needs, such as shopping, laundry, catering, medical offices, and education facilities, as well as hotel rooms on two communal levels. The flat roof could also be used as a public terrace, offering recreational spaces including a swimming pool, a 300-meter track, and a children's play area. In contrast to these communal services, the apartments were strictly private. Despite generous exposure to nature through their large windows, the flats could only be accessed through somber interior "streets." Conceived of as a self-contained mini-city situated in a park-like setting, Unité d'Habitation was described by Le Corbusier as a "vertical garden city" – and he expected it to serve as a prototype of a neighborhood unit for the massive redevelopment of industrial cities. The concept of

·trand
▮dberg, Marina
y, Chicago,
▮4

creating a sense of intensely private life within a large community was inspired by the architect's experience of medieval monasteries. When Le Corbusier first visited the Monastery of Ema near Florence, the surreal setting had deeply touched him through "the harmony which results from the interplay of individual and collective life, when each reacts favorably upon the other."[11] The monastic integration of individuality and collectivism shaped a fundamental dualism that Le Corbusier later continued to pursue in his ideal cities. The Monastery of Ema, however, was not the only source of inspiration for the architect's concept of communal living. The nineteenth-century French social philosopher Charles Fourier played an equally important role in this process.[12] In one of his best-known writings, *Phalanstère*, Fourier described the physical form of his utopia, which was based on a collective residential quarter for 1,800 inhabitants. Le Corbusier's concept of *unité* thus fused two traditions of utopia – monasticism and Fourierism – to reinterpret the ideal city in modern society.

When Tange, a lifetime follower of Le Corbusier, attended the eighth CIAM meeting in Hoddesdon, England, in 1951, he managed to travel to Marseille to visit the recently completed *Unité d'Habitation*. The building impressed the young architect so much that he later recalled:

The two-month tour of Europe that followed left me profoundly moved by classical architecture and by the works of Le Corbusier. . . . I was tremendously excited by seeing the great works of Greek, Roman, and Gothic, and Renaissance architecture and the paintings and sculpture in the museums. Furthermore, I was impressed even more strongly than ever with Le Corbusier's greatness when I visited the Marseilles *Unité*, which was about ninety percent complete at that time and which had an impact in no way inferior to that of the architectural classics.[13]

2.5
**Le Corbusier,
Unité d'Habitation
Marseille, 1952**

Through Tange, the idea of a collective community was disseminated among the Metabolists. They pushed the two contrasting elements of collectivity and individuality to extremes, presenting them as megastructures and cells in their futuristic schemes. While the communal component was enlarged to include the infrastructure, public facilities and civic spaces of the city, the individual component was reduced to the minimal living space. These homogeneous cells implied a city life not unlike the medieval monastery, centered on the highest ideal of egalitarianism.

Influences of Socialism and Soviet city planning

There was another school of thought in the modern age that sought to build an egalitarian world through new forms of associated living: Marxist Socialism. Karl Marx and Friedrich Engels had provided arguably the most ambitious social vision in modern time, connected to a political conviction that capitalism, with its individualistic bourgeois culture, would soon be replaced by an era of collective life. Their numerous writings elaborated on the institution of communism, including a series of ideas that Kristan Kumar defined as utopian: extreme material abundance, an absence of alienation and exploitation, the interrelation of all men and women and the natural world, and absolute equality.[14]

The 1950s saw a strong revival of Marxism in Japanese intellectual circles, which paralleled the leftist political movements active in this period, climaxing in the Anti-Security Treaty demonstrations of 1960. In this political climate, Marx's critique of capitalism and his vision of a communist society influenced many progressive architects, including the Metabolists. They became interested in Soviet ideas of urban planning, especially the new forms of communal living which emerged in the 1920s and 1930s. It was thus no surprise that Metabolist projects often advocated the utopian ideals of putting land under public administration, eliminating the boundaries between city and country, and asserting absolute equality within the society. Through their ideal plans, Metabolist architects tried to reconcile the collective and the individual, not only to create a new urban form, but also to establish a new social order.

Dismissing the possibility of directly translating his vision into practice, Marx claimed: "I do not write recipes for the cookshops of the future."[15] The absence of any clear model in his writing regarding built forms in the new socialist society left plenty of room for invention. While they were united in the conviction that the existing city was inappropriate for the new communist man, Soviet city planners of the 1920s divided into two camps over the fundamental issue of urban form. Urbanists, led by the economist Leonid Sabsovich, advocated the construction of urban "agglomerations," while Disurbanists, represented by Nikolai A. Miliutin, recommended the establishment of linear cities.[16] Both the Urbanist and the Disurbanist ideas influenced the Metabolists' concepts of the future city.

The Urbanist schemes were characterized by cities of large-scale collective living. In an ambitious text entitled *The USSR in Ten Years* (1930),

Sabsovich advocated the construction of municipal housing complexes, where everything would be collectivized immediately.[17] He envisioned that current cities and villages would be replaced within ten years by a series of new towns, each consisting of 25 to 50 huge collective blocks. Each block would house 1,400 to 2,000 people and provide well-developed communal facilities. Moisey Ginzburg, another vanguard planner during this period, called such collectivized cities "social condensers," well adapted to instilling people with the communitarian attitudes required by the new world. Other Urbanists went even further in their proposals. In a plan for Kuznetsk, Aleksandr Vesnin and Victor Vesnin suggested that traditional family homes should be replaced by a series of dormitory buildings with extensive communal installations dispersed across the countryside. According to their scheme, 35,000 people were to be housed in several grouped neighborhood units. Each unit consisted of four identical three-story blocks, with 1,100 people in each block. Corresponding to such ideal urban forms were radical ideas about society. For instance, marriage and property would be obliterated, with individual rooms for men and women, irrespective of marital status. Everyone in the super block was a potential "bachelor," "bachelorette," "husband," or "wife."

Although Joseph Stalin abruptly halted Urbanist debates by demanding the dissolution of all informal art groups in 1932, Soviet urbanistic ideas emerging in the interwar period had influenced not only Western architects like Le Corbusier, but also Japanese visionaries. To progressive intellectuals across the world, the Soviet Union appeared a new civilization in the making, one that contained the promise of liberation for all. Like America, it aimed to challenge Western Europe's economic status as well as its leadership in the technology sphere. Unlike America, however, it proposed to do so without the inhumanity of capitalist exploitation. It thus offered an alternative model of economic and social development that promised to avoid consigning sizeable portions of the population to a life of poverty and squalor. In Krishan Kumar's words, it was a "utopian theory made reality."[18] The new urbanism emerging from this socialist society also showed the promise of providing a physical environment with equality and freedom for all. Therefore, when Japanese intellectuals and engineers gathered in occupied Manchuria in the late 1920s for the ambitious experiment of building a new state, they looked to the neighboring Soviet Union for a potential model. The revolutionary urban concepts, along with the explosive development of Soviet productivity during this period, had impressed them so much that they decided to carry out their own "Five-Year Plans" in Manchuria.[19] They also attempted to build new cities in Changchun and Datong, based on the principles of collective living, although their sources of inspiration were a little more eclectic.[20]

The socialist planning continued to influence Japanese architects and planners in the postwar years. Uzo Nishiyama (1911–1994), a Marxist scholar and professor of architecture at the Kyoto University, became a leading figure in combining architecture with a commitment to social reform. Although he had never traveled abroad until after the war, Nishiyama read widely in Russian and

German, and was familiar with recent developments in international planning as well as socialist movements. He spent many years studying Japan's housing problems, proposing standards of domestic design in order to improve the life quality of workers and farmers. His involvement in city planning indicated his strong socialist consciousness. Nishiyama called for the construction of large-scale public housing complexes to accommodate the overgrowth of cities while preserving arable land. Because of Japan's mountainous geography and limited resources of land, he proposed the creation of towns on mountain slopes in order to preserve the plain for agriculture and guarantee food supply for the growing population. In his 1946 scheme called "Mountain Slope City," residential blocks were modeled after the social housings in Europe and the Soviet Union. According to Nishiyama, some twenty new cities of 50,000 inhabitants each could be built annually to accommodate population growth in Japan. In urging a more comprehensive approach to urban issues, Nishiyama's social consciousness set a tone for postwar city planning in Japan.[21]

The Metabolists, who were influenced by the avant-garde planners of the Soviet Union as well as domestic Marxist scholars like Nishiyama, regarded themselves as social architects, believing in the capacity of planning as an effective force for social change. Like the Soviet Urbanists, they aspired to overcome the physical isolation of individuals and families by reorganizing social structures into communities. Because of Japan's growing urban density, Metabolists advanced industrial technologies for the construction of highly concentrated urban units, in which all activities would be integrated in a tightly knit pattern.

Noriaki Kurokawa, a pupil of Nishiyama at the Kyoto University, coined the concept of the "urban connector," possibly inspired by Sabsovich and Ginzburg's idea of "social condenser." The urban connector referred to a super-scale structure, or what people later termed "megastructure," which served as the medium between urban scale and human scale, and between the collective and the individual. It would gather individual forces into collective power, integrating the environment as a whole. Kawazoe argued for the application of megastructural planning in the modern age:

> The Gigantic City will be an apparatus designed to connect, on the one hand, machinery, energy, and speed on a vast scale with, on the other hand, human beings who have been reduced to individuals. . . . To express it more accurately, there will be a huge engineering structure to control nature and the city – that is, what is called the major structure, the city structural unit, or the urban connector. This will be constructed as the "perch" or "nest" of the individual human beings who move about and grow and develop. Within this structure all necessary city utilities will be provided, and each individual will be able to attach thereon his own dwelling.[22]

By separating the construction of urban connectors from individual dwellings, Kurokawa and Kawazoe expected this new planning method would bring order to

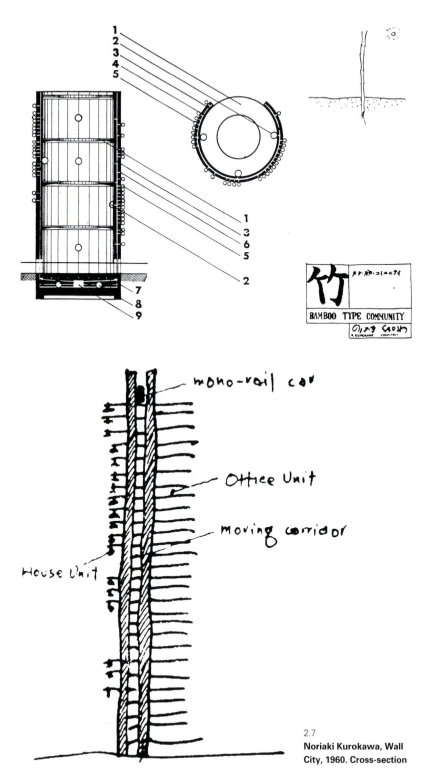

2.6
Noriaki Kurokawa
Bamboo Type
Community, 196

BAMBOO TYPE COMMUNITY

mono-rail car

Office Unit

moving corridor

House Unit

2.7
Noriaki Kurokawa, Wall
City, 1960. Cross-section

riaki Kurokawa,
tamorphosis,
55. Plan

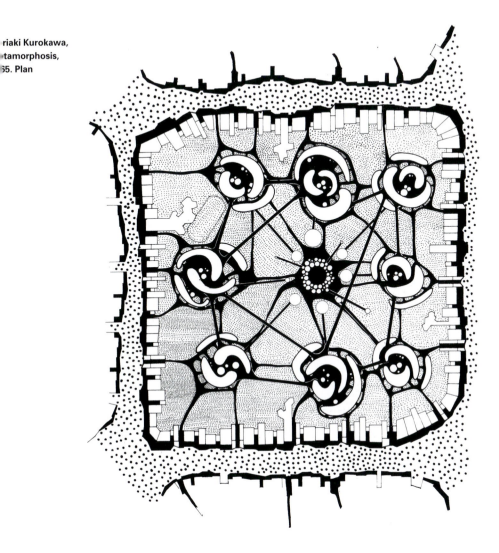

the scattered and jumbled big cities like Tokyo, as urban connectors would reorganize their enormous populations more effectively.

Kurokawa proposed two types of megastructure as urban connectors. One was called "Bamboo Type Community" and the other, "Wall City." Their vertical main structures took the shapes, respectively, of a multi-segment core and a giant free-curved wall. These megastructures would integrate urban infrastructure and a massive number of living units into a three-dimensional system, while dissolving the traditional social organization based on the family. Kurokawa claimed:

> Family life is disintegrating. Gone are the days when a living unit was a space only for one family unit. A living unit is now based on one generation and will eventually change into a per person unit. . . . The

entire city will turn itself into a gigantic compact architectural construction, where the fixed living space of a city will be inseparable from the working space.[23]

In his megastructures, urban life would be "condensed" to an unprecedented extent, thanks to the new prospect of "atomic energy." Living spaces and working spaces could be located on either side of the gigantic "wall," which enclosed transportation and other infrastructural systems. Thus, the distance between home and office would be as short as the "thickness" of the "wall." Kurokawa declared that the "wall," as an urban connector, would "stabilize the vitality of an intense way of life and bring hope for tomorrow."[24]

Isozaki also believed super-scale urban structures could fundamentally transform the way the city was operated. Both his City in the Air and Joint-core System were characterized by megastructures intended for generating new civic life. His megastructural proposals recalled the images of El Lissitzky's radical project of Cloud Prop (1923–25). Aiming to animate the banal city of Moscow, this Russian avant-garde artist and Urbanist proposed a series of identical horizontal skyscrapers to be suspended over the major traffic intersections in the city like "clouds," supported only by a few vertical cores. These "clouds," featuring massive cantilevered volumes "floating" over the old city center, preceded Isozaki's urban clusters in the air. Lissitzky anticipated that his megastructure would be capable of automatically transforming the space of the existing metropolis, ultimately changing its structure and fundamental relationships. He argued in his book *Russland* of 1929:

Up to now, in these buildings one cannot notice anything of the new conception of the open street; of the conception of the city as an

2.9
El Lissitzky, Cloud Prop, 1923–25. Montage

aggregate of new relationships; a notion even in the case of the old city, allows new mass and space relationships to come into being. The new social attitude to the building task has thrown up some radical propositions; building types have arisen which attack the old city in such a way as to have a changing impact on its entity.[25]

The didactic impulse to violate spatially the rectilinear grid of a classical city or to open up the tortuous street of an old medieval town had been a consistent theme in Lissitzky's works. In order to open up the space of an existing metropolis, he proposed to "minimize the foundations that link to the earth."[26] This statement again coincided with Isozaki's declaration that he needed just "ten square meters" on the ground for his City in the Air. Like Lissitzky, Isozaki and his peers in the Metabolist group believed the modern city required a new structure that should be divorced from the old urban fabric. The giant objects in their schemes represented great collective power. They were expected to "dynamicize" any given, pre-existing architectural or civic context, and to overthrow old urban patterns for a new spatial and social order.

Integration of city and country
The influence of Soviet planning also came from the other side of that cultural dialogue: the Disurbanists. Disurbanist theory played a decisive role in shaping the Japanese architects' concepts of regional and national planning. Article Nine of Marx and Engels's 1848 *Communist Manifesto* demanded "Combination of agriculture with manufacturing industries; gradual abolition of the distinction between town and country, by a more equable distribution of the population over the country."[27] In response to this articulation of the forthcoming communist society, the Soviet Disurbanist Movement arose in the 1920s. The Disurbanist ideal of city design was characterized by a diluted mix of both linear city and garden city theories, extending the power of planning to the regional scale. In *Literature and Revolution* (1923), Leon Trotsky called for the replacement of old cities with new "city-villages" and for the restoration of land to its natural conditions by employing new technologies.[28] The rapid urbanization and Soviet building boom of the 1920s provided opportunities to experiment with such ideas. A series of plans was put forward to create new socialist towns, with populations of up to 100,000, to be dotted across the country. Commenting on one of these schemes, Lissitzky said:

> Today we are familiar with two opposite poles: the large city as a concentration of industry and the village surrounded by agrarian production. In this particular urban system, both are possible. The parabolic sectors may either be planned so as to enclose the means of industrial production or laid out as open land for agricultural cultivation.[29]

The Disurbanists viewed large cities as products of capitalism which should hold no place in socialist society. Instead, they suggested redistributing the inhabitants of large cities such as Moscow into a continuous megalopolis, in which residents working in industry or agriculture would share communal facilities and live in prefabricated, portable residential units.

The Disurbanists were particularly enthused by the linear city, a concept initiated by the Spanish engineer Soria y Mata in 1882. It was regarded as an urban form that could establish a closer relationship between industry, agriculture, and domestic life, thus eliminating the boundary between city and country. In the Soviet Union, many of the difficulties Soria y Mata's linear project had encountered due to land ownership were overcome by the nationalization of land under Socialism. The idea of linear cities was widely adopted by Russian architects and town planners during the first Five-Year Plan from 1928 to 1933.[30] With full administrative support, Miliutin developed a comprehensive linear city proposal to promote collectivization and industrialization. He outlined his linear city in *Sotsgorod: The Problem of Building Socialist Cities* published in 1930.[31] His ideal city consisted of six parallel zones arranged in a prescribed order: railway zone, industrial zone, green zone, dwelling zone, park zone, and agricultural zone. Vehicular and pedestrian roads linked these zones perpendicularly. The city as a whole could accommodate 100,000 to 200,000 people. Ginzburg and Mikhail O. Barsh also developed a radical linear city project around 1930 and suggested the path to its realization. They envisioned that Moscow would gradually be evacuated and transformed into a leisure park, while its industrial and administrative functions would be rearranged along a series of linear routes. The result would be a comprehensive network covering the entire country, consisting of small towns, industrial estates, and highways flanked on both sides by factory-produced homes.

When introduced to Japan, socialist ideals of integrating city and country and decentralizing population across the nation through linear cities were justified by the country's geographical conditions. As noted earlier, Nishiyama proposed building community clusters on mountain slopes while reserving plains

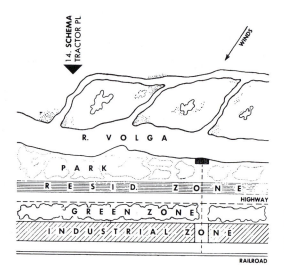

2.10
N. A. Miliutin,
Linear City
proposal in
Sotsgorod, 1930

for agricultural production. Reorganizing urban areas in this manner, however, required a transformation to public land ownership. It also meant that many large cities would need to be relocated in order to establish a closer relationship between city and country. Kurokawa adapted his professor's idea in the Agricultural City project, intended to serve as a model of a "village-city." As Hajime Yatsuka notes, this scheme in some way resembled the Bavirov Brothers' student project in the Soviet Union, which had also called for drastic disurbanization.[32] In Kurokawa's scheme, the parallel activities of human society were now to be stratified into a vertical pattern, consisting of a work level, a social level, and a private level. This meant that agricultural production would occupy the ground, with communal activities one story higher in the main structure, and private life further up in so-called "mushroom houses." Kurokawa expected Agricultural Cities would dot the whole country, serving as prototypes of an urban form which could bring to the countryside an urbanized organization and modern lifestyles while releasing Japan's large cities from overcrowding. The architect developed variations of this scheme, demonstrating a capacity to adapt to different topographies by stretching out the platform to become a more flexible structure.

With its gridiron pattern, Kurokawa's Agricultural City resembles Frank Lloyd Wright's 1934 Broadacre City in several aspects. These two projects are

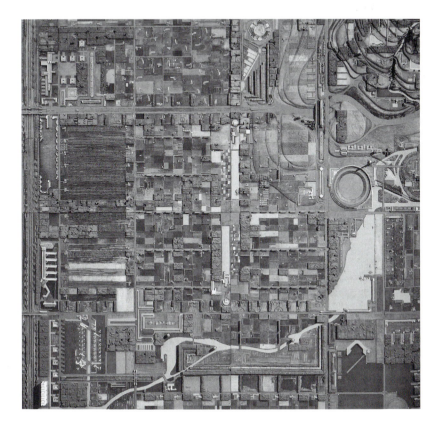

1
ank L. Wright,
oadacre City,
33–34.
construction
the original
odel, 1990

2.12
Noriaki Kurokaw
Agricultural City
1961. Model view

comparable in that both propose alternatives to large cities, emphasize land and agriculture as the city's economic base, and tend to combine the benefits of city and country.[33] However, there are some fundamental distinctions between Kurokawa's and Wright's projects. Whereas land in Broadacre was to be distributed equally to individuals, Kurokawa's plan was to put all land under public ownership so that an egalitarian and harmonious society would come into being, with the land to be used in the most efficient way. Wright's plan was based on faith in Emersonian individuality and Jeffersonian democracy, whereas Kurokawa was attracted by the prospect of a communal society influenced by Marxism. Inspired by modern techniques of transportation, Wright envisioned that automobiles and highways would supply the backbone of the future city. Kurokawa, however, seemed less interested in the impact that modern technology would make on his ideal city. His plan did not even show any roadway connecting the agricultural city with the world outside. It was like a medieval town, self-contained, harmonious with nature, but isolated from human society at large.

Other Metabolist projects appeared more in tune with modern society and, accordingly, pursued different approaches to the integration of city and country. Their proposals, emphasizing the role of modern technology, moved beyond the scale of a city to the domain of regional planning, often involving a linear urban form. Tange's 1960 Plan for Tokyo represented the most sophisticated linear plan to date in attempting to decentralize one of the world's megacities. The modern technologies of automobile and expressway would become decisive factors in this fundamental restructuring of the country's urban system. An enormous linear spine, loaded with a state-of-the-art highway system and the city's central administrative and business areas, extended over the bay to link Tokyo and Chiba. Tange envisioned that this spine would penetrate Tokyo's existing urban areas before moving further west to connect with Mt. Fuji and then the large cities in western Japan. This pattern would establish a continuous urban cluster, later known as a "megalopolis."[34]

The long and narrow belt of Japan's archipelagos seems to justify the idea of a linear urban network. Most of Japan's large cities, including Tokyo, Yokohama, Nagoya, Osaka, Kobe, Kyoto, and Hiroshima, are situated in the

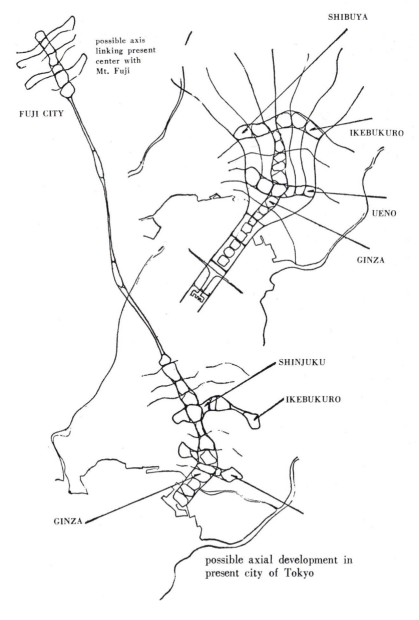

3
nzo Tange, the
ear extension of
e Tokyo Bay
:y, 1960. Sketch

possible axial development in
present city of Tokyo

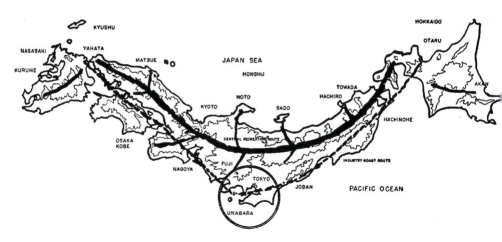

2.14
**Kiyonori Kikutak
Ocean City
Unabara, 1960.
Vision of Japan
a linear urban
network**

southern seaboard on the Pacific coast, while the northern coast along the Japan Sea, is chiefly occupied by mountains. This geographical character inspired Metabolist architects to formulate comprehensive ideas about linking the whole country via a linear network. In *Metabolism: The Proposals for New Urbanism*, Kikutake proposed that a series of Ocean Cities would be built in the inner bays along the Pacific coast.[35] They would be located near big cities like Otaru, Hashinohe, Chiba, Yokohama, and North Kyushu. Gradually, these existing industrial cities would move toward the sea. As the Ocean Cities grew, an "industrial highway" would be built connecting all the cities along the Pacific coast, like a strand of "newly crystallized gems."[36] In the meantime, another major highway would be built running through the "backbone of the Japanese archipelago" (the northern inland belt), and function as a "recreational highway."[37] Thus, the whole country would be connected by two parallel highways running east to west and serving different purposes.

Tange's and the Metabolists' approach to regional planning indicated their technocratic ambition, that is, to control the development of the whole nation by means of modern technology, management, and planning. This notion had also found its root in Soviet Russia. As Yatsuka pointed out, Russian Constructivism of the 1920s was not only an avant-garde movement of architecture and arts, but embodied the seed of an economic theory that believed in the capacity of technocrats to program the economic and social development of an entire country.[38] This notion, passed on by the Soviet Disurbanists, was manifest in Metabolists' works. Metabolists' projects were dominated by a utopian desire to overcome the distinction between city and country, and explored the scale of utopia by expanding the domain of planning to the whole country with extensive linear cities.

Urban life in the future society

In one of the earliest writings to introduce Metabolism to the Western world, Günter Nitschke contended: "For a European the most striking aspect of the Metabolist dream schemes is firstly the scale of the operations proposed, from an architectural point of view, and secondly the obviously different concept of human happiness inherently present from a social point of view."[39] There is no doubt that the scale of planning interventions proposed by the Metabolists was enormous, often involving regional and national restructuring. Their ideal plans, taking the form of either linear clusters or marine cities, represented fundamental undertakings in social organization. However, questions arise regarding the social micromechanism within such peculiar urban settings: how did these visionary architects conceptualize individual life in this system? How did they integrate modern values of freedom and democracy, which they strongly advocated, into their mega-projects? What kind of role would the architect play in the future society?

The Metabolists envisaged that their future cities would not only construct the physical environment that people desired, but ensure a harmonious combination of freedom and order, efficiency and leisure. Human happiness would be based on a new system of land ownership, with land to be put under public control in order to ground a communal setting. Whereas most planners, Frank Lloyd Wright in particular, thought people would lose their freedom living in a collective society where the individual did not own any land, the Metabolists believed that a lack of ownership would liberate them from the constraints of land and provide people true freedom. Historically, urban and rural inhabitants had limited mobility because of private land ownership. This was especially apparent in the feudal society that Japan had experienced for more than fifteen hundred years until the second half of the nineteenth century.[40] In a society characterized by strict social hierarchy, peasants, artisans, and lower-level samurais were tied to the land. Modern society, with its new technologies and new patterns of production, provides new possibilities to free people from their attachment to land. It demands new physical layouts and social constitutions compatible with such new mobility. Talking about the emerging urban pattern, Alison Smithson claimed: "This new sort of society needs a new sort of environment. An open society needs an open city. Freedom to move – good communication, motorways and urban motorways, and somewhere to go – both inside and outside the city"[41] Following the Team 10 theorists, the Metabolists also emphasized the mobility of modern society that potentially weakened the link between man and land. Kawazoe argued: "The ceaseless metabolic changes in the city, the restless movements of population, have caused people to abandon their attachment to definite plots of land."[42] For the socialist utopians, a modern communal society based on public land ownership was a natural outcome of the age of mass production. It would lead to rational planning of economic and social development, as well as a more appropriate use of resources to ensure maximum efficiency and productivity. According to these principles, the Metabolists argued that the communal city, while ensuring the abundance of life, would liberate people from the constraints of land and allow them to enjoy the mobility and freedom.

The Metabolists also envisioned this new flexible and mobile city, freed from private land ownership, as a classless, egalitarian, and harmonious society. When Kikutake discussed the Tower-shaped Community, he described the rite of celebrating a new family's joining the community:

> In order to celebrate the new-birth of a family, the new unit will be going up with slow rotation around the tower to the higher part in the sky. Both the inhabitants in the same tower and those living in neighboring towers will cheer and send their sincere and warm welcome to the new life of a fresh couple when their living unit is lifted to the top.[43]

According to his dynamic, everyone would have at least a chance to stay at the highest point of the tower-city. As new members are added to the tower, the other "houses" would move down gradually. Finally the old-style houses would be replaced by new ones whose design has been improved. Through this highly symbolic process Kikutake wanted to convey his faith in egalitarianism: with no hierarchy and no exploitation, everyone would enjoy the same opportunities.

The Metabolists believed that, as standardization made production more efficient, and as people were freed from the constraints of land, they would enjoy more leisure time. For instance, Kurokawa anticipated that workloads would be significantly decreased in the future society, allowing people three to four days for recreation.[44] Therefore, they called for people to take up constructive pastimes rather than simply spending their time on consumption. Kawazoe praised the trend of the so-called "Sunday carpenter," and suggested that in such voluntary activities people would "experience an enjoyment of their own freedom and expression."[45] Engaging in such spare-time constructive activities, he believed, was important to gain "entry into the new society."[46] Kurokawa was thinking the same. A series of renderings of the Kasumigaura project based on his Helix City concept depicted some attractive scenes in which amateur fishermen enjoyed leisure fishing. With a spectacular megastructural city erected on the sea in the background and futuristic flying machines in the air, the picture immediately conveyed strong senses of both Romanticism and Futurism.

Many Metabolist schemes were characterized by differentiating various scales of construction, which they believed would provide the flexibility for a modern society. With future buildings composed of prefabricated parts, the architect's job would mainly involve choosing from various components and joints and installing them into a house according to people's needs and tastes. Kawazoe wrote:

> The dwelling of the future will be reduced to "parts" and attached on to the "city structural unit," but these factory-produced parts will be capable of endless combinations and change by means of standard-ized systems and joints. People will be able to select suitable shapes, colors, and qualities according to their liking, and to put them together in entirely free sizes on the necessary scales.[47]

15
Noriaki Kurokawa,
Kasumigaura
Project, 1965.
Rendering

16
Noriaki Kurokawa,
Kasumigaura
Project, 1965.
Rendering

17
Noriaki Kurokawa,
Kasumigaura
Project, 1965. Plan

Therefore, he claimed: "The idea that only an architect can make a house must be discarded."[48] The "Sunday carpenters" should be able to assemble buildings by themselves. To teach people how to build, architectural schools would be established like Japanese "schools of flower arrangements or tea ceremony;" some master architects would become the heads of these schools, with schools to be named accordingly, such as "School of Le Corbusier" or "School of Tange."[49] In so doing, Kawazoe contended that the city would become more diverse, as would the society.

The idea of "Sunday carpenter" sounds like the Metabolists were expecting architects to play a less important role in the future, as they would no longer be responsible for designing buildings. In fact the opposite was true: architects occupied an unparalleled position in the Metabolists' utopian cities. In the city that Kawazoe depicted, a few selected architects would design the prototypes of dwelling units, test all kinds of combinations, and train people to build their own houses.[50] After the city was built up, they would continue to invent more variations so that the city could keep renewing itself with new designs of cells. The most significant person in such organization is a city architect charged with planning the city's main structure. The main structure controls the development of the city and its relation to nature and provides all necessary public utilities, so individual buildings could rest on it. By creating the skeleton of the entire city and setting up the mechanism of its development, the master planner was the virtual leader of the society. He played a crucial role both architecturally and socially in the city because, for the Metabolists, the transformation of the physical environment determined the organizational structure of the society.

The Modernist movement that swept the European continent in the interwar period had substantially expanded architects' role in society. They were often given the power to lead the transformation of an entire city, the prominent examples being Ernst May in Frankfurt, Martin Wagner in Berlin, and Karl Ehn in Vienna. However, utopian architect-urbanists like Le Corbusier and Frank Lloyd Wright were even more ambitious, seeking to create a new order for the world at large. They believed that an individual and his imagination could change history. They attempted to turn their social values into workable plans, and thus direct social change with their prophetic leadership. With the powerful concepts like Radiant City and Broadacre City, they tried to initiate an architectural revolution as an assertion of human rationality over impersonal forces.

The Modernist utopian faith in architects' omnipotence significantly influenced the Metabolists, and Tange in particular, who regarded themselves as "social architects."[51] They believed architects alone held the talent to combine the imaginative sensibility of artists with logical clarity of engineers, leaving them the sole guides to the development of modern society. In his address to the World Design Conference in 1960, Tange claimed: "Architects and designers are the only people who stand in the middle ground between technology and humanity, and it is therefore essential that with the advance of science they manifest more and more creativity."[52] Like Le Corbusier and Wright, Tange and the Metabolists believed that acceptance of responsibility for the future of cities presupposed total planning, which was inconceivable without a master planner with impartial wisdom and supreme power.

This desire for a powerful master planner actually contradicted the Metabolists' vision of designing democratic societies. Peter Smithson was particularly critical of Tange's Tokyo Bay Plan for its political implications, writing "whatever may be explained, it is, above all, centralized, absolutist, authoritarian."[53] He continued:

> I am, of course, sure that this was not the intention of its authors – far from it – but somehow it has crept in at all levels – into its basic thinking, into its organization, and residually, into its imagery – for only the natural sensitivity of its designers has taken the hard edge off its ruthlessness."[54]

Unlike traditional autocratic societies, however, there was no distinction between hereditary ruling classes and ruled classes in the Metabolist cities. Rather, a group of professionals would take command in leading the society, charged with imagining, for the common good, a complete system that should be just, coherent, efficient and sustainable. Architects and engineers were evidently candidates for this post.

Such a technocratic idea influenced several Metabolists' ideal city projects. While the younger architects' concepts were not fully developed in terms of social institutions, Tange's Plan for Tokyo clearly indicated the notion of city as a "machine," the ultra-rational entity with systematic organization governed by the elites of the industrial world. He placed the most important components of his ideal city, including administration, business, and communication, on its central spine. Like Le Corbusier's skyscrapers in the center of *Ville contemporaine*, Tange's central spine provided spaces for the masterminds of the entire society – architects, engineers and industrialists.

From the Metabolists' point of view, people would paradoxically achieve freedom through comprehensive planning. Public ownership would liberate people from the constraints of land, establishing the foundation of a just and egalitarian society. People would enjoy more leisure time, and devote themselves to constructive activities. To maintain its order and continuous development, however, the city should be put under the leadership of architects and professionals who represented the progressive force of the modern era. In short, the Metabolist urban schemes attempted to reconcile a series of contradictions of social values: collective and individual, order and freedom, city and country, autocracy and democracy. They manifested the multiple influences of both international intellectual movements and domestic social conditions. This unique synthesis put Metabolism in line with great traditions of utopianism, and allowed Tange and the Metabolists to develop a series of urban design concepts, rooted in the notion of city as an organic process which constituted Metabolism's most significant contribution to contemporary urbanism.

City as process

Classical utopias were often presented as completed works, their structures forming a perfect whole that gave no hint of further development or change. The same applied to traditional ideal city projects. Although the visionary architects provided plans for total transformation and often acquired a wealth of brilliant details, they gave no indication of social evolution. It was in this sense that Robert Fishman claimed: "The ideal city has no history; indeed, it is an escape from history."[55]

Metabolists, however, declared that their proposals were explicitly created to accommodate change. This notion constituted the foundation of their city designs, and was evident in the name of the group: Metabolism.[56] In contrast to the general conceptions that viewed the city as a passive object, the Metabolists considered it a living and mutable entity, with an inherent aptitude for change. From their point of view, the primary characteristic of the contemporary city lay precisely in its capacity for ceaseless transformations, like any organism in nature. The idea of city as process thus distinguished Metabolists' planning methodology from the conventional approach of master planning, which tended to envision a final, stable state of the city and provide the best layout with reasonable zoning. Metabolists suggested that there should be no physical destination for a city, as it continued to grow and renew itself; in fact, the transformation of cities had been accelerated in the modern age. Under these circumstances, any civic blueprint would become irrelevant. Otaka and Maki argued:

> In city planning the concept of "master planning" has been often criticized for the following shortcomings: First, the whole plan cannot be comprehended until it is completed. Second, when completed, it may well become socially obsolete or at least obsolescent. Then, at the worst, the plan is never completed. A master plan is basically a static concept, whereas the concept of master form we are proposing here is dynamic. Master form is an entity that is elastic and enduring through any change in a society.[57]

Instead of a master plan, the Metabolists proposed "a system which can be followed consistently from the present into the distant future."[58] This system requires due consideration to future growth. In other words, traditional master planning, authoritatively decisive in respect to both quantity and quality, should be replaced by system planning, which sees any given cluster as self-developing and self-regenerating and would be a complete form in each stage of its growth.

The notion of city as process informed the majority of Metabolists' urban schemes. Kikutake, who was first trained as a medical student before turning to architecture, claimed that his Marine City could accommodate any future external growth and internal regenerations.[59] On the one hand, the towers, serving as the main structure of the city, could continue to grow as population increased. The model of Marine City intentionally showed a cluster of tower-shaped communities in different stages of growth: some have fully matured, and some just emerged from the base. On the other hand, individual living cells attached to the towers would conduct a process of self-renewal: new cells could be added, old ones might "die," and, when the design became out-of-date, they would be replaced. Such replaceability was represented in Kiyoshi Awazu's graphic work entitled "Hand and Eye." The city as a whole would have its own life too. When a tower was no longer suitable for living, it would move to the center of the ocean to be sunk.[60] Kurokawa's Helix City, also to be erected on the sea, embodied the same idea. Inspired by the recent biological discovery of the structure of deoxyribonucleic acid (DNA), the architect proposed a double helix structure for the city and anticipated that it would perform the organic process of duplicating itself like DNA.[61]

18
Kiyonori Kikutake,
Marine City, 1963.
Model view

2.19
**Kiyoshi Awazu,
Hand and Eye,
1963. Print**

In his Tokyo Bay Plan, Tange presented the concept of city as process in a different way: the linear city. He compared a linear city to a vertebrate with a central spine as its main structure, extending as the creature grew while maintaining an organic whole.[62] Tange envisioned that Tokyo linear city would extend gradually from the existing center of Tokyo across the bay, reaching Chiba on the opposite shore in twenty years. After that, it would grow further into the region, and into other parts of the country.

By stressing change and transformation in the city, Metabolists introduced a fourth dimension into city planning, in which the dynamic elements of time played a crucial part. Their schemes anticipated change and sought to structure it. They thus transcended ideal city proposals of the past by demanding incompleteness, open-endedness, and fluidity. These characteristics would provide a vitality that was missing in the existing cities.

The biological metaphor that Metabolist urban schemes invoked was not without precedent. In the early twentieth century, Scottish urban theorist Patrick Geddes had articulated a city/organism analogy in his *Cities in Evolution* (1915).[63] Trained as a biologist, Geddes was an ardent advocate of the theory of evolution, which fundamentally influenced his urban thinking. Using biological concepts, he compared the city to an organic entity, studying its temporal pattern as well as a sophisticated relationship between city and region. Ernest Burgess, a member of the Chicago School of Sociologists, had also written an article entitled "The Growth of the City" in 1925, in which he described the growth

20
Noriaki Kurokawa,
Helix City, 1961.
Diagram

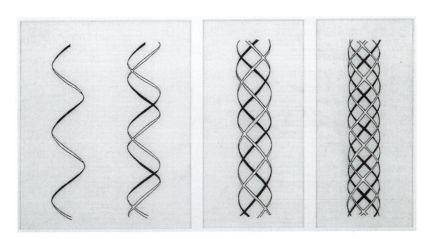

21
Noriaki Kurokawa,
Helix City, 1961.
Sketch

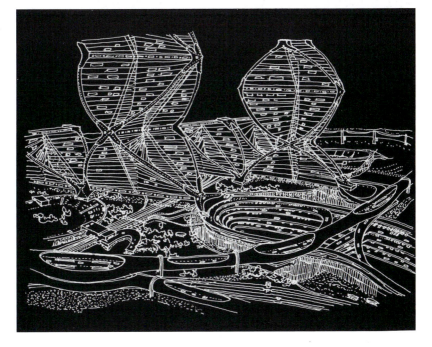

patterns of the city as "metabolism."[64] Instead of dealing with urban "expansion as physical growth," he called for a new approach which treated growth as a social process. Burgess applied this approach in the study of urban population patterns in Chicago and suggested that many questions could be answered by "thinking of urban growth as a resultant of organization and disorganization analogous to the anabolic and katabolic processes of metabolism in the body."[65]

Kawazoe declared, however, that what distinguished Metabolists' ideas from their Western predecessors lay in the notion of reproduction. He argued that the Marxist understanding of metabolism centered on the exchange

2.22
**Noriaki Kurokawa,
Helix City, 1961.
Model**

of matter between man and nature as represented by production. By contrast, reproduction, with its emphasis on renewal as well as propagation, was based on "information, tradition and culture, as symbolized by the genes."[66] As opposed to the Western "organic-body" urban analogy, Metabolists insisted that their theory could not be reduced to a purely biological model. Rather, their idea of city as process demanded a historical and cultural accountability that was particularly distinctive to Japan.

Undoubtedly, Tokyo's dramatic urban transformation in the postwar years stirred the strongest sense of a city as an ever-changing organic entity. On the one hand, Tokyo, burned into ash during the war, revived at a speed never before witnessed in the world. In merely one and a half decades, its population soared from less than three million to nearly ten million. Large rural areas in the periphery were quickly turned into new urban districts. The city became larger and more prosperous than ever before. On the other hand, the economic prosperity since 1955 resulted in significant changes in urban life, such as the popularization of automobiles, TVs and other electronics. Frequent replacement of merchandise and accelerated speed of movement led to a new urban culture centered on consumption. Kawazoe noted:

Movements within the city of Tokyo are rapid and drastic. Buildings that were here yesterday are gone today, and the morrow will surely bring more. There is probably no other city in the world where the rate of change is so startling. Within this movement exists the excitement, the joy, and the sadness of the city. And from this movement will doubtless spring the buds of a new culture.[67]

The Metabolists, observing these dramatic changes with their own eyes, could not help but view the city as an organism, in a constant process of change and evolution, and project this image to its future development.

Such observations of rapid change in the contemporary world were met by particular sensibilities grounded in Japan's cultural tradition. This intersection with tradition indicated a different dimension embodied in the Metabolist concept of the city as process. In an article published in *Architectural Design* in 1964, Günter Nitschke noted that Eastern philosophy, originating from China and most prominently presented in the book of *I Ching* (*Book of Transformation*), saw the world in the constant mutation of all things.[68] This complex notion of change has deeply influenced Japanese life since ancient times, and has been reflected in various aspects, including language (Kanji), religion (Zen and Shintoism), and architecture (Teahouse). In particular, the unique practice of periodic reconstruction of Ise Shrine every twenty years presents the dialectic relationship between eternity and ephemerality in a striking way. This symbolic rebuilding, celebrating the fundamental idea of transformation and regeneration in Shintoism, became an essential inspiration for Metabolism. As mentioned previously, the first ritual reconstruction of Ise after the Second World War sent a strong political message: Japan had regained its political and cultural autonomy. Architects looked to this tradition for new inspirations of design. Metabolists, in particular, were enthusiastic in interpreting this tradition of transformation and regeneration with their urban schemes. Tange and Kawazoe reflected on this idea in their 1965 monograph *Ise: Prototype of Japanese Architecture*.[69] They wrote:

> The vigorous conceptual ability of the ancient Japanese who fashioned the form of Ise was sustained by the energies released during the nation-building process. The form of Ise partakes of the primordial essence of the Japanese people. To probe this form and the way it came into being is to go to the very foundations of Japanese culture."[70]

They thus called for incorporating this unique tradition into a new design methodology and developed a system of replaceability on the urban scale underpinning the idea of the city as organism.

"Metabolic cycle"

Believing urban development is an organic process, Metabolists hoped to establish a system that would accommodate growth and regeneration in the modern city. Such a system needs to distinguish between urban elements with long-term and short-term lifespans, or, as Metabolists referred to them, different "metabolic cycles." Large-scale urban infrastructure and projects altering natural topography, such as dams, harbors, and highways, have long-term life cycles; small-scale constructions like houses, shops, and street furniture have shorter life cycles. Modern consumer society has made this distinction more obvious than ever before. Responding to the different metabolic cycles in built environments, the Metabolist urban projects applied different forms to elements of long-term and short-term cycles, often presenting them with the combination of a megastructure and numerous individual cells. For instance, Kikutake's Tower-shaped City was characterized by the contrast between a central tower structure and individual housing units attached to it; Otaka and Maki's enormous artificial ground, spanning over railroad tracks at Shinjuku, served as a "permanent" platform upon which the commercial, business, and entertainment clusters could grow; Kurokawa's Helix City also featured numerous cell-like units attached to the gigantic double-helix structure.

The gap between so-called "permanent" and "transient" elements was getting wider in contemporary society because of the development of building technologies, particularly technologies of prefabrication and standardization. Megastructures would be constructed on site; and cells would be prefabricated and then installed on the megastructure, and they could be moved or replaced whenever needed. By differentiating their structural and functional mechanisms, megastructure and cells would maintain a highly flexible relationship distinctive from conventional constructions.

Japanese building traditions provided other perspectives to draw on. Japan's wooden architecture had long been an important influence on modern architecture, and its formal simplicity and structural clarity impressed many modernist masters including Bruno Taut, Frank Lloyd Wright, and Walter Gropius. After visiting Japan in 1954, Gropius even encouraged young architects to "forget Rome and come to Japan!"[71] No prior attempt, however, had been made to apply the design principles of traditional wooden architecture on the scale of a city. Kikutake was particularly interested in the replaceability of components in wooden construction, a potential consequence of his participation in several restoration projects of historic structures. He studied the relationship between the major structure and small wooden members, as well as the joints that connected the two, and observed that a "wooden structure possesses a superb structural system: the possibility of dismantling and reassembling it. In other words, a recycling system had quite ingeniously been developed."[72] Of particular inspiration was a unique module system that coordinated the standardized building components, made them interchangeable, and related the parts to the whole. This system was used in both institutional and residential buildings. From the traditional building techniques Kikutake developed the concept of a "system of replaceability," applying it to various scales of design from a house to a city.[73] To him, the relationship between a megastrucutral city and its housing units was no different from the relationship between the wooden framework of a

3
yonori Kikutake,
ee-shaped
mmunity, 1968.
ndering

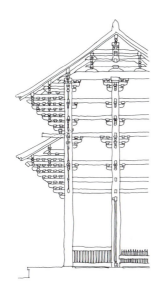

24
e Great South
ate of Todaiji
mple in Nara,
th century.
rtial section

Buddhist temple building and its smaller components like bracket sets or slide windows. The larger and smaller elements maintained relative independence and had different metabolic cycles.

The ideas of metabolic cycle and system of replaceability characterized a number of Metabolist urban projects. Although such structural concepts were not completely worked out in Metabolists' designs due to the technological limitations of the time, they influenced their formal inclinations. In fact, Kikutake's Tree-shaped Community scheme (1968) and Isozaki's City in the Air project, both featuring a series of cantilevered blocks extruding from a central core, were often referred to as much-enlarged versions of the bracket sets as seen in traditional Chinese and Japanese architecture.[74]

The combination of megastructure and cell, a dramatic representation of the Metabolists' concepts of metabolic cycle and replaceability, emerged as the distinctive trademark of the group. Although it has never been realized as an entire city, Metabolist architects managed to apply this concept symbolically in specific building projects, prominently Tange's Shizuoka Press and Broadcasting Center and Kurokawa's Nakagin Capsule Tower. These two buildings, standing alongside an inner-city highway and less than one mile away from each other in Tokyo, were intended as prototypes of the architects' concepts of urban form. Both structures feature one or multiple central cores and inhabitable capsules plugged on to the cores with cantilevers. Although the capsules were conceived of as industrial products and mimicked shipping containers in appearance, the buildings were erected with conventional reinforced concrete construction, making the removal or replacement of capsules difficult if not impossible. It is not surprising that such ideas did not influence mass developments as the architects anticipated, and the realized buildings remain isolated monuments in Tokyo's bustling and ever-changing business district. Their seemingly incomplete silhouettes nevertheless showcase the idealistic concept of the megastructural city and the aesthetics of the "city as process."

Artificial land

The combination of megastructure and cell reflected the Metabolists' thinking about the relationship between the collective and the individual. These architects were obviously aware of the conflict between their reliance on mass production and standardization in modern society, and the social values of freedom and democracy that equally concerned them. They insisted that modern production patterns left enough room for individual opinions and tastes, and they by no means wanted to build a homogeneous society. Aiming to create a new social structure with maximum personal freedom, the Metabolists based their schemes on the concept of "artificial land." Kurokawa's Agricultural City, which envisioned a whole community built on an enormous concrete slab elevated over natural ground, offered an explicit example of artificial land. Other architects interpreted this concept with different vocabularies, such as "multi-level ground" in Tange's Boston Bay project and "vertical ground" in Kikutake's Tower-shaped Community and Kurokawa's Wall City.

Through the concept of artificial land, Metabolists tried to define a new relationship between nature and human beings. Starting with the idea that land does not belong to any individual, the foremost objective of artificial sites was to liberate the land as public property and cause it to revert to its natural state. The artificial land concept also allowed architects to create new forms of dwelling, often based on construction of *pilotis* or artificial islands on the sea. More importantly, it would provide a generic framework upon which human creativity could be brought to play in a variety of individual constructions. Artificial land and housing units constituted the basic components in a Metabolist city. While the former would be built with public investment and designed by a city architect, the latter would result from individual activities and reflect the diverse needs and tastes. Houses would be built from prefabricated components, but Metabolists argued that prefabricated parts could be installed in many different combinations, so people could express their individuality.[75]

Artificial land first emerged in Le Corbusier's urban visions, particularly a series of sketches for Rio de Janeiro, São Paulo, and Montevideo he drew when he traveled in South America in 1929. This concept was then articulated in his 1931 plan for Algiers, known as "Plan Obus," which served as a direct model for a number of Metabolist projects.[76] Plan Obus featured a massive multi-level structure providing artificial lands for 180,000 dwelling units and an interior elevated super highway. On these multi-level platforms, inhabitants could build two-story houses in various designs to meet their own needs. Among the architectural styles of the houses shown in this sketch, Le Corbusier included both his recently completed Immeubles Villas and a Moorish house, indicating the idea that everyone could build to his own taste.

Inspired by Le Corbusier's plan for Algiers, Tange appropriated the idea of artificial land in his Boston Bay project of 1959 and again for his Plan for Tokyo in 1960. The Boston project, also known as the "Plan for a Community of 25,000 Residents," was characterized by multi-level concrete platforms supported by two gigantic triangulated space frames. In addition to various public facilities (including school, church, and pedestrian walk), artificial grounds provided "ample room for unrestrained choices on the part of the residents."[77]

25
Corbusier, Plan
r Algiers, 1931.
ketch

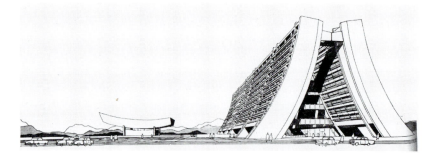

2.26
**Kenzo Tange,
World Health
Organization
Headquarters
building, 1959.
Unrealized
competition ent▶**

2.27
**Kenzo Tange,
competition ent▶
for World Health
Organization
Headquarters
building, 1959.
Model interior**

The housing units were to be assembled with factory-built components, the combination of these cells and their placements would be "arbitrary," and their details and decorations were also left to the "discretion of the residents." Therefore, Tange claimed that this project had the "significance of enabling the residents to identify themselves with their location within the over-all system."[78]

The A-shaped frame in the Boston Bay project was an improvement from Le Corbusier's artificial land, enhancing the natural lighting of the houses and bringing some variation to the civic spaces within the megastructure. Its triangular interior accommodated the infrastructure and public facilities of the community, including a motorway, a monorail, parking, elevators and a school.

The A-shaped megastructure first appeared in Tange's competition entry to the World Health Organization (WHO) headquarters building in Geneva earlier in the same year. In this scheme, the space between two leaning blocks was designed as intermediate between "the scale of highways and the scale of individual human," and a communal space for ambassadors and visitors from all over the world. It "symbolized the social vitality of the WHO."[79] Tange's scheme was dismissed by the jury as unbuildable; nevertheless, its symbolic formation of communal space, together with the spontaneous constructions of individual space characteristic of the Boston project, was integrated into the design of residential mega-blocks in Tange's Plan for Tokyo the following year. All these designs confirmed the architect's belief that the basic structure should be the property of the public and collectively developed, while individual dwellings would be built within the major structure and specified to individual needs and personal tastes.

Otaka's urban design projects were also dominated by the notion of separating private and public developments and making this separation formally recognizable. He applied the concept of artificial land to both residential and commercial projects. In his collaborations with Maki on the Shinjuku project, public facilities were housed underneath the artificial ground centered on the railway station. Above the "ground" was a variety of commercial developments. These private establishments were presented in dramatic architectural forms, including masculine office towers with boldly jutting elements, flower petal-like amusement structures, and massive shopping centers. These elements were grouped on the artificial ground in a random manner, indicating the outcome of market-driven construction activities. Otaka dealt with the same relationship of collective form and individuality when designing a collective housing project in Sakaide. Again, he employed artificial land, elevating it six to nine meters above the ground. The ground level was reserved for shops and parking, with private housing installed on the concrete platform according to the needs of individual families.

The Metabolists' urban concepts, emphasizing individual creativity and freedom of movement, coincided with the ideas of the Situationist International, a political and artistic movement of the 1950s and 1960s in Europe. Active in the 1950s and 1960s, Situationists rejected rigid urban planning and called for the creation of fluid urban "situations" in which people could create their own spontaneous forms of life and "do their own things."[80] They anticipated profound and provocative social change in their urban projects, and tried to create an environment suitable for post-industrial man. The urbanist in this group Constant Nieuwenhuys expressed this goal in his theoretical project called the New Babylon. Depicting everyday spaces that both reflected and induced the desires of "Homo ludens," the New Babylon envisaged a nomadic metropolis in a state of perpetual transformation. The urban form was characterized by giant frameworks upon which individuals would be free to build their own shelters. The Situationists' libertarian utopia not only inspired other avant-garde architectural movements in Europe, including Archigram and SuperStudio, but also gained

2.28
**Masato Otaka,
Sakaide Housing
Project, 1962**

2.29
**Constant
Nieuwenhuys,
New Babylon,
1956–74. Montag**

prominence in the 1968 May student upheaval in Paris, setting a tone for the postmodern intellectual culture.

There is no doubt that Metabolists, like Situationists, viewed freedom and individuality as fundamental human values; however Metabolists were equally concerned, if not more so, about the guidance of rationality in shaping modern society. Metabolists believed that just as the artificial land was to be the foundation of all individual constructions, planning should provide the foundation of freedom and individual creativity. Their schemes tried to strike a balance between a rational system of planning and spontaneous creation, using artificial land to promote individual freedom while putting it under effective control. The task was obviously difficult due to inherent contradictions between these two agendas that underpinned the idea of artificial land. These competing impulses witness one of the inherent contradictions in the idea of artificial land. As Peter Smithson observed, "from the time of Le Corbusier's Algiers project onwards, the romance of the idea of 'each man building his own house' on man-made platforms stands unsupported by a demonstration of how it is to be done."[81] In Metabolist cities, the paradox between a need for centralized authority and a striving for individuality persisted despite Metabolists' earnest planning. This irresolvable conflict, to some extent, explains the fact that almost none of their urban schemes were realized.

Marine civilization

Metabolists tended to envision that cities of the future would be built on the sea. They created a number of marine city schemes, prominent among them Kikutake's Marine City and Ocean City, Kurokawa's Helix City, Otaka's Tokyo Marine City Plan, and Tange's Community of 25,000 in Boston Bay and Tokyo Bay Plan. Although science fictions in the 1950s and 1960s often depicted cities built over or underneath the ocean, Metabolists have gone further than any other visionary architects in that period in exploring the physical environment of marine civilization through their urban projects.[82]

Metabolists' concepts of marine cities need to be read in light of the particular urban and social crises in postwar Japan arising from limited land and rapid population growth. As Japan failed to expand its territory through the conquests of war, new sites had to be found to accommodate future growth. Since 1958, a number of schemes have been developed for the reclamation of Tokyo Bay. Not only were Metabolist architects enthusiastic about this idea, many political leaders, industrialists, and planners were also convinced that expansion of Tokyo into the bay was the best answer to the land crisis. This idea was positively received because creating new land in the sea was in fact less costly than redeveloping the inner city, and doing so could evade the complicated land ownership issues often associated with large development projects. In one of his schemes for a marine city, featuring cylindrical residential towers built upon artificial concrete islands and an industrial base underneath the water surface, Kikutake called for a new urban form that would provide "land for man to live, sea for machines to function."[83]

However, building cities over the sea involved more than a search for land. Kenneth Frampton accurately comments on Japan's special relationship with the sea and its influence on Metabolism: "[When] the Metabolists looked to the sea as the locus of a new civilization, they looked to the one element which had always been deeply linked to the spiritual and material survival of Japan."[84] For the Japanese, the ocean was an element lived with and paid tribute to, and it has always been a critical factor in the development of its culture. A large number of traditional Japanese woodcuts depicting the ocean and lives of fishermen testify to the importance of the ocean to Japanese society, such as Katsushika Hokusai's famous The Great Wave off Kanagawa. This profound relationship between ocean and human life was fully expressed in Kurokawa's Helix City. In this scheme, the quest for a new type of marine civilization was duly rendered with illustrations of utopian urban scenes, depicting peaceful life of pre-modern fishermen in a dream-like setting with helix megastructures and futuristic flying machines.

The concept of city united with sea was pushed forward in Tange's Tokyo Bay Plan, which treated the ocean as a new topography. Tange made no fundamental difference between land and sea, with interlocking loops of highway extending continuously from the existing center of Tokyo into the bay and then reaching the Chiba Prefecture on the opposite shore. Residential blocks would also be erected directly on the sea, even without artificial islands as their base. This peculiar relationship demonstrated the architect's ambition of transforming the ocean into urban territory, and constituted a vivid Japanese character in modern city design.

That Metabolists regarded the sea as the seed of a new civilization and claimed their projects as universal models for the future echoed another great tradition. If one recalls classic literature, from Plato's *Atlantis* to Thomas More's *Utopia*, the sea has always been a favorite location for utopian authors' ideal cities. Both Atlantis and Utopia were described as islands. In order to make a "good place," a utopia had to be completely isolated from the world outside. The Metabolists shared a similar notion. They were convinced that a brand new civilization would only emerge once people were brave enough to reject the chaos, danger, and misery of "continent civilization" in its entirety and turn to the sea. Kikutake declared: "The civilization of continents was an accumulation of bloody struggles of human relations established on limited land, so it was a history of endless wars."[85] Referring to the Cold War, he continued: "Eventually, the civilization of continents has brought about the present opposition between two big continents which is terrifying the everyday life of the people in the world."[86] As opposed to it,

2.30
Katsushika Hokusai, The Great Wave off Kanagawa, 1832. Color woodcut

the sea is awaiting a new discovery which will promise true happiness for human beings. It is just a matter of time that the civilization of continents hands over its part to the prospective civilization of the sea commenced by Marine City, just like the coal era handed over its part to the oil era.[87]

To Kikutake, launching a marine city required a revolution of existing society to establish a new society that is free of war and other social evils. This would be the future of human civilization.

Building a new "marine civilization" therefore not simply sought to increase land surface or to flee from the land. It aimed to reshape the relationship between man and his environment, as well as between men themselves. Kawazoe argued: "Just as life originally came from the ocean, so will the metabolism of the city be given the opportunity to develop in a smoother manner by being floating on the ocean."[88] Marine civilization would provide opportunities to restore land to its natural state, to take advantage of the natural resources of the ocean, and to build compact and sustainable towns. Most importantly, it could transform the fundamental organization of human society. As Kikutake said, "the Marine City will be a unit of human community, not the individual life."[89] He suggested that in solving the problem of land scarcity by moving the city to the sea, a new marine civilization would eliminate traditional contradictions caused by land. People would now be able to unite into a new communal society.

Kikutake claimed that the Industrial Revolution had brought "a most important opportunity to liquidate the continued causation between man and continent."[90] Technology, he believed, was gradually making it possible to build a new human habitat on the sea. His most comprehensive proposal – Ocean City Unabara – was intended as an industrial city floating on the sea accommodating 500,000 inhabitants. In Kikutake's mind, Unabara would become the center of a linear series of urban clusters as the result of a nationwide urban reconstruction. Located along the Pacific coast, these urban clusters would concentrate the country's production centers.

During the 1960s and 1970s, Kikutake continued to develop his idea of a marine city, incorporating in it his concern for the environment. Fifteen years after the original concept was proposed, he finally had a chance to realize a miniature marine city called "Aquapolis." Built as a floating pavilion for the Okinawa Marine Exposition, Aquapolis's 100 meter by 100 meter platform provided a self-contained environment, connected to land only by a floating bridge. Visitors were able to "experience the stability, safety and pleasure of the environment in this marine city."[91] Aquapolis was made of prefabricated parts and equipped with desalination and power-generating plants. Devices for purification and garbage-treatment were also provided to avoid contaminating the sea. Although Aquapolis demonstrated the potential of available technologies to build a self-supported environment over the sea, it has by no means proved that such artificial islands could sustain the social organization that the Metabolists envisioned.

2.31
Kiyonori Kikuta[
Aquapolis,
Okinawa Marin[
Exposition, 197[

Megastructure versus group form

Although their urban projects shared similar values regarding the city and society, Metabolists were far from a homogeneous group. United in the notion of a harmonious collective society and the desire for a new spatial order that would accommodate growth and constant change, these architects developed distinct approaches to urban design. Based on fundamentally different conceptions of the relationship between the part and the whole in the composition of a city, two competing ideas emerged within the Metabolist movement: megastructure and group form.

Kikutake, Kurokawa, Tange, and Isozaki were fascinated by the idea of megastructure. They conceived of the city as one gigantic building, proposing hierarchical organization centered on three-dimensional super-scale structures that predetermined the configuration of individual elements. Kikutake's Marine City, Kurokawa's Agricultural City and Helix City, Isozaki's City in the Air and Joint-Core System, and Tange's Tokyo Bay Plan, all fell in the megastructure category. Fumihiko Maki, however, counteracted megastructure with the concept of group form, which, instead of moving from a major structure to individual units, suggested that order should arise from grouping smaller elements together. He argued that group form created a flexible urban system more responsive to the fluctuating conditions of contemporary society. Later other Metabolists also integrated the idea of group form into their design works, such as the 1968 Housing Competition of Peru, a collaboration among Maki, Kikutake and Kurokawa, and Tange's plan for Mekka in 1974.

Maki's concept of the group form was first formulated in "Towards Group Form," the essay co-authored with Otaka and included in *Metabolism: The*

Proposals for New Urbanism. He elaborated on this concept in *Investigations in Collective Form*, published in 1964.[92] This booklet introduced three prototypes of collective urban forms: "compositional form," referring to the conventional method of composition based on a two-dimensional plane; "megastructure;" and the "group form." This book is remarkable for a few reasons, first and foremost of which is its status as the first written work to define the concept of megastructure. Maki described a megastructure as an open structure made possible by present-day technology and a man-made landscape upon which a city would thrive and continue to progress through its different metabolic cycles. Although he recognized its great promise in several public realms – including environmental engineering, multi-functional complex, and infrastructure – Maki was quick to point out the "certain static nature" inherent in the megastructural approach.[93] To him, the problem of megastructure lay in the fact that it formed a rigid system concentrating all functions in one place. He argued:

> The ideal is not a system, in which the physical structure of the city is at the mercy of unpredictable change. The ideal is a kind of master form which can move into ever new states of equilibrium and yet maintain visual consistency and a sense of containing order in the long run.[94]

The "master form" he advocated is group form, a structuralist approach of adding dynamic individual elements to create a cluster. Through this process a group shares its character with its components. Instead of providing a powerful physical structure, group form offers a master key or a visual grammar, through which one can cope with an expanded scale of operations and rapid transformation. In contrast to top-down planning, group form encourages cumulative growth that results in a non-hierarchical collective form.

Maki confirmed that his understanding of the distinction between "form" and "system" was inspired by Kahn's concepts of "form" and "design," which the master had presented at the World Design Conference in 1960: "There is need to distinguish 'form' from 'design.' Form implies what a building, be it a church, school, or house, would like to be, whereas the design is the circumstantial act evolving from this basic form, depending on site condition, budget limitation or client's idea, etc."[95] Maki added his interpretation: "As soon as a form is invented, it becomes the property of society. . . . A design, on the other

32
umihiko Maki,
lagram of three
ollective forms:
ompositional
rm, mega-form,
nd group form,
964

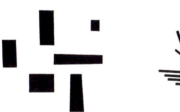

2.33
Japanese linear village Iga, presented in Maki's *Investigations in Collective Form*

hand, belongs to its designer."[96] He thus argued that, while a design is an individual creation, a form is a collective act. Form should provide an internal order that serves to coordinate the design of multiple elements.

Order is inherent in each of the elements composing the group. Maki called such order "a system of generative elements in space," meaning that individual elements, rather than a major structure, were the key to the "form."[97] He cited European medieval cities, Greek island towns, North African villages, and sixteenth-century Dutch towns as examples of this approach to town planning. In particular, Maki looked into the relationship between Japanese vernacular villages and the houses in the villages, for it embodied the essential spirit of the group form. In Maki's words:

> Many Japanese villages in the past developed along major country roads. Houses are generally U-shaped, and juxtaposed one against another perpendicularly to the road. The front part of the house is two stories high and forms a tight continuous village façade together with other units. Behind it is an enclosed yard, which is used for domestic work, drying crops, making straw, etc. A barn is located at the other end of the house, and faced an open country field. . . . Here the house unit is a generator of the village form, and vice versa. A unit can be added without changing the basic structure of the village. The depth and frontage of the unit, or the size of the court or barn may

differ from unit to unit. But there prevails an understanding of basic structural principles in making the village.[98]

This text articulates a reciprocal relationship, both in form and in operation, between the individuals (houses) and the whole (village) in a group form. Individual units are defined by a prototype, which determines the character of the ensemble at large. As this link is built, the individual elements can differ from each other in details, but the group's characteristics as a whole would remain consistent. Such a relationship also allows the village to grow and renew itself without affecting its comprehensive image, because the system maintains a dynamic equilibrium. Maki stressed that group form was not arbitrary; rather, it evolved from the social structure embedded in vernacular establishments like Japanese villages, Italian hill-towns, or Dutch canal towns. He wrote: "I saw in those collective forms an expression of regional culture."[99] The vernacular settlements Maki visited during his Graham Foundation-sponsored travels in the late 1950s impressed him with their formal cohesion and non-hierarchical multi-directional social structure supporting their particular aesthetic order. The principles of group form derived exactly from this regional culture and natural order.

Maki's urban theory, drawing inspiration from vernacular settlements, was not an isolated attempt to transform such natural order into contemporary urbanism. The 1960s witnessed departures from orthodox modernist principles of urbanism and explorations of new concepts of urban form. Architect-theorists, prominent among them Aldo van Eyck and Bernard Rudofsky, enthusiastically studied the primitive and the vernacular, drawing lessons from patterns arising from spontaneous gatherings of similar or diverse parts. Van Eyck, one of the leaders of Team 10, was inspired by primitive dwelling forms in central Africa, in which he detected a reciprocal relationship between part and whole, small and large, and house and city. He thus developed the theory of "configurative discipline," suggesting that such a reciprocal relationship reinforced the identities of each other. His Amsterdam Orphanage, completed in 1960, exemplified an approach to urbanism based on generative elements. In 1964, the same year Maki published *Investigations in Collective Form*, Rudofsky's exhibition Architecture without Architects was staged at the Museum of Modern Art in New York, along with a publication of the same title.[100] The exhibition brought to light the beauty of architecture not designed by professionals, but rather as the result of spontaneous construction of individuals sharing a common heritage, culture, and everyday life. The exhibition was enormously influential and inspired architects and designers by drawing their attention to the original creativity embodied in vernacular buildings and settlements.

Also in the early 1960s, a University of Tokyo research team led by Teiji Ito and Arata Isozaki conducted an extensive survey of Japan's traditional towns. The results of their survey were published as "Nihon no Toshi Kukan" (Japanese Urban Space) in the magazine *Kenchiku bunka* (*Architectural Culture*) in December 1963, and included a number of case studies of vernacular villages and traditional urban spaces.[101] Typological analyses spoke to their organizational structure, compositional elements, sequential experience, and, more importantly, cosmetic metaphor and symbolism of urban space. The authors argued that Japanese cities did not have plazas in the Western sense, and no Western-style tradition of picturesque urban scenery was to be found; rather, temporal or visual enclosures were set up for communal events like street markets, rituals, and festivals. The publication came with an introduction by Isozaki entitled "The Invisible City." His essay had a distinctively Metabolist tone to it: "The city has no permanent form. It is constantly in a state of flux to meet new urban conditions and requirements. The main concern of Japanese planners has been the creation of the symbolic urban space."[102]

What distinguished Maki's study from other investigations regarding traditional urban spaces was his attentiveness to the sociological implication of vernacular group forms. Jennifer Taylor observes that Maki was concerned with establishing a flexible order that would encourage fluctuation of both spatial and social organization; such an order arose from hermeneutical relationships established between part and whole, participant and place, at all scales.[103] It was in sociological terms that Maki commented on the fundamental distinction between mega-form and group form:

> The element in mega-form does not exist without a skeleton. The skeleton guides growth and the element depends on it. The element of group-form is often the essence of collectivity, a unifying force, functionally, socially, and spatially. It is worth noting that generally group form evolves from the people of a society, rather than from their powerful leadership. It is the village, the dwelling group, and the bazaar which are group forms in the sense we are using this term, and not the palace complex, which is compositional in character.[104]

Maki's notion of urban form, which embraces both social and physical organizations, draws the conclusion that group form emanates from the people themselves, and this form represents a more democratic and flexible system than mega-form, which embraces centralized power.

Maki's academic and professional experiences in the United States might have influenced the formation of urban concepts that distinguish him from the other Metabolists. During his extended stay in America, from 1955 to 1965, the country witnessed the rise of community movements against modernist urban renewal projects, and the cities where Maki stayed – Boston, New York, and St. Louis – were centers of this new movement.[105] During those years, Maki was exposed to the work of the urban theorists Jane Jacobs, Kevin Lynch, and Aldo van Eyck. These influential authors and educators criticized the Modernist approach to city building from different perspectives, but all stressed that urban vitality stemmed first and foremost from the everyday life of people who occupied and experienced the city and influenced the development of the city.[106] Reflecting general community concerns in America at the time of Maki's university appointments, the humanistic disposition of these theorists must have contributed to his awareness of a social dimension in urban design, and led him to a more democratic approach to collective form.

To Maki, order is not necessarily evident and more often hidden. In a studio project involving urban design students at Harvard, Maki investigated the possibility of reorganizing Boston's urban infrastructure. The study was published in 1965 as *Movement Systems in the City*.[107] As Taylor notes, Maki's study of Boston represented a remarkable contrast to the Boston Bay project drawn up by Tange and students at Massachusetts Institute of Technology in 1959. While Tange's project presented a strong visual order characterized by gigantic A-frame megastructures, Maki's proposal was strategic in intention without necessarily suggesting a concrete composition. The overall idea proposed loose organization based on communication networks rather than on control of physical form. It was in this sense that Taylor contended that the project was "decidedly Japanese."[108]

The debate between megastructure and group form also raised an essential issue about the relationship between order and chaos. In Maki's view, the order of a city could reside in the seemingly chaotic scenes; it was the task of planners to reveal the order by providing a conceivable organization or, in Kevin Lynch's terminology, the imaginability of the city. In the Boston study, Maki pointed out that the word "chaos" should not refer to "the lack of structure, but to the difficulty of perceiving it, and the problem is not one of restructuring but of making understanding easier." He continued: "A person moving through a city must be given visual clues and explanations of where he is and where he is going, of what these places are, and how they are related to each other."[109] Group form was thus intended for a cohesiveness based on a sensory order rather than a material one. Such order resided in each individual unit in a city, which came together to form an assemblage with the same structure and created collective unity.

Maki also tried to emphasize the temporal dimension of group form, using it as a critique of the static modernist concept of "master planning." He claimed that group form "can move into ever-new states of equilibrium and yet maintain visual consistency and a sense of continuing order in the long run," because its image "derives from a dynamic equilibrium of generative elements, not a composition of stylized and finished object."[110] Although the basic typology and ordering system should remain consistent, the form of individual components might vary through time in response to changing contexts. Group form should remain sustainable as an open-ended process and continue to energize the evolution of the city. This notion, known as "sequential group form," derived from "ways of thought that embraced the incomplete, the unpredictable and the transient, and suggested ways by which the current urban condition, with its demands and complexities, might well be addressed."[111]

The Hillside Terrace project in Japan, arguably the most engaging urban project in Maki's career, provides a remarkable manifestation of his idea of group form, involving spatial, social, and temporal dimensions of the concept. Privately commissioned by the Asakura family, the project is in fact a series

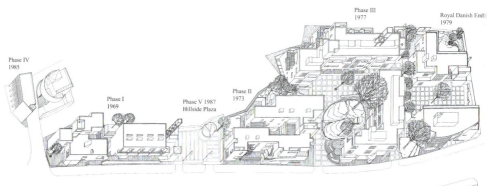

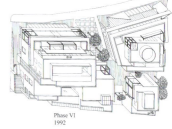

2.34
**Fumihiko Maki,
Hillside Terrace,
Tokyo, 1967–92.
Axonometric**

2.35
**Fumihiko Maki,
Hillside Terrace,
1967–92.
Courtyard of an
early phase**

Fumihiko Maki,
Hillside Terrace,
1967–92. Street
facade of a later
phase

Fumihiko Maki,
Hillside Terrace,
1967–92. Aerial
photo

consisting primarily of mixed residential, commercial, and cultural uses, but also including the Royal Danish Embassy.[112] These buildings line both sides of Kyu-Yamate Avenue, forming a continuous townscape of approximately 250 meters in the Daikanyama district in Tokyo. Since the design of the first increment in 1967, the project continued to grow for thirty years, progressing through seven stages. Each stage of the development grew out of the pattern set by previous designs but distinguished itself by reflecting the revision of planning regulations, development of technology, changing consciousness of the architect, and the shifting character of the urban context, as Daikanyama evolved from a quiet residential area to a bustling commercial district. For instance, while the early buildings were built of concrete, clad with cement and ceramic tile, and often appeared visually heavy and spatially enclosed, later developments saw an increasing use of steel structure, metal panel, and glass, and were lighter and more transparent in appearance. Daikanyama's public spaces also became more open and inviting.

Despite the environmental changes over thirty years, the general ambiance of the complex remains remarkably consistent. Buildings maintain an overall accord in their figure/ground composition – the relationship between building and street and the way public spaces are introduced into the building massing – and in the modernist simplicity of their general architectural style. There is a mutual harmony between the buildings, as well as what Maki called a "morphological dialogue" between the buildings and the street. The layout of buildings affords visual references to one another, but without the rigidity of axis and hierarchy. They maintain a close scale through the subdivision of buildings into smaller groupings. A ten-meter height limit along Kyu-Yamate Avenue is obeyed. Although this height restriction had in fact been removed from the local zoning regulation when later phases were designed, Maki continued to set his buildings beneath the line to maintain a consistent street profile. Overall, the project is dominated by a conceptual openness, which allows multiple penetrations into the assemblage. A variety of courts and corridors compose a cinematic sequence of public spaces along the slightly sloping road, effectively serving as nodes in the complex and linking the buildings to the city.

Hillside Terrace thus constitutes a "group form at its most dynamic, growing and evolving organically over time."[113] It demonstrates that both consistency and diversity can be accomplished through the orchestration of various forms and spaces, each of which remains independent while at the same time suggestive of a governing structure. An open system with a certain degree of ambiguity makes the project responsive to uncertainty and celebrates the aesthetic of transformation as group form continues to evolve, always ready to accommodate new additions and changes, but complete in form in each stage. In Maki's point of view, such a cumulative townscape based on group form has become the essential character of Tokyo and suggests a new urbanity for the modern city.

Utopia and dystopia: Issue of technology

Maki's theory of group form and his design works became, in essence, a critique of the Metabolists' megastructuralist approach to planning. This should not be a surprise since from the beginning the Metabolists were a coalition loosely formed for a special event. Rejecting the postwar status quo of Japan's urban developments, these architects were aware of social reform and anticipated that a higher standard of social order would emerge from a new urban form. They were engaged in integrating social and technological aspects of contemporary civilization into a comprehensive system of architecture. Their urban concepts, however, were divided over the prospect of technological progress and the role that such large-scale urban interventions would play in the evolving social system. Although they believed it necessary to provide a structure for urban growth using technology, some of them were doubtful – even fearful – of the impact of a technocratic approach on the human environment. The incompatibility of their attitude toward technological means and their goals for social progress resulted in a persistent ambivalence in their urban concepts.

Ambivalence was already immanent in the short essay written by Isozaki in 1962 entitled "The City Demolisher, Inc.," taking the form of a dialogue between "Arata" and "Shin."[114] As Yatsuka notes, the essay contrasted a passion for city-design and a quasi-Dadaistic desire for city demolishing so strongly that this contradiction could only be left unresolved.[115] This contradiction remained true for Isozaki's works throughout the 1960s. Though never a formal member of the Metabolist group, Isozaki shared the Metabolists' sphere of theoretical influence as well as an enthusiasm for megastructural form and futurist technology. As Tange's student and lieutenant, Isozaki developed a concept of urbanism that emphasized cybernetics, an influence that also characterized Tange's city design methodology.[116] However, in contrast to the Metabolists, who were mainly concerned with a biological process as metaphor for environmental and sociological transformation, Isozaki was skeptical of anticipating a social revolution that could be mediated by technological proposals. He was in sympathy with Metabolists' basic ideas when he wrote: "The city is a process, and there is no concept more certain than this;" but he argued against their optimistic view that the development of nature and society was a harmonious and continuous process.[117] For Metabolists, urban growth and transformation were more or less predictable and thus could be planned, structured, and controlled. Isozaki instead contended that sudden catastrophic ruptures could occur in the development of an urban society as well as in nature. He later recalled:

> I was in agreement with most of what they (the Metabolist group) said but could not see eye to eye on one cardinal point: drawing a direct analogy between organic metabolism and architectural composition. For rather than being systemic, change is dramatic and destructive, lying outside the bonds of human control. It is the result of complicated accumulations of overlapping, unforeseeable coincidences. Method and logic originate on the basis of a toleration of the natural course of change.[118]

The dramatic and destructive changes he suggested included wars and atomic bombing, which still lived vividly in the memory of most Japanese. Such tragic happenings completely interrupted the process of urban development. For Isozaki,

Metabolists' urban models failed to take such instances into consideration. Isozaki's view of urban transformation in the form of metamorphosis resonated with Tange. The latter argued: "The understanding of city as solely a process is to admit the natural development of the city which is a retrogressive opinion." Tange thus stressed that architects and urbanists' needed to grasp "the point when big metamorphosis takes place" in the uninterrupted process of metabolism.[119]

2.38
Arata Isozaki, Incubation Process, 1962. Montage

Isozaki's conception of the urban process as metamorphosis led him to the idea of "ruins," referring to the state of a city after a catastrophe. He presented his notion of ruins in a photomontage entitled Incubation Process at the exhibition of "City and Life of the Future" in 1962. It featured his 1960 Joint-Core System project, originally designed as an alternative scheme for the redevelopment of the Shinjuku Station area. Images of this futuristic city were superimposed on a picture of classical ruins. Fragments of giant Doric orders were recycled and became the base of a cluster of megastructures anchored by a strip of urban freeway. Accompanying the montage was text that reads:

> Incubated cities are destined to self-destruct
> Ruins are the style of our future cities
> Future cities are themselves ruins
> Our contemporary cities, for this reason, are destined to live only a
>   fleeting moment
> Give up their energy and return to inert material
> All of our proposals and efforts will be buried
> And once again the incubation mechanism is reconstituted
> That will be the future.[120]

In "Incubation Process," the ambivalence of Isozaki's notion of urbanism was evident. On the one hand, the rebirth of a city from classical ruins demonstrated the fundamental Metabolist conception of the ability of human society to revive and renew itself. Even if the city was entirely destroyed, new life would emerge from the ruins. On the other hand, the montage indicated Isozaki's reluctance to accept the Metabolists' somewhat naïve faith in the benevolence of technology

9
ata Isozaki, Oita
fectural
rary, 1966

and optimism in the future of cities. Isozaki contended that metamorphosis would be both destructive and constructive and, as a result, human society repeatedly cycled between city and ruins: "In the incubation process, ruins are the future state of our city, and the future city itself will be ruins."[121]

Incubation Process thus allowed Isozaki to distinguish himself from the Metabolists' technological orientation, rejecting the idea that "a social revolution could be achieved by means of new technology."[122] Ruins symbolized death and counteracted the literal-minded manipulation of utopian strategies. Revealing an ironic and somewhat pessimistic attitude toward the notion of "progress," Isozaki's concept of ruins was less characteristically Metabolist in its presentation and feeling, but it was distinctively prophetic. The montage to a certain extent presaged the downfall of the technological universe and the rise of a postmodern ideology barely a decade later. David Stewart observed:

> The vision of a contemporary city rising amid classical ruins of a markedly primitive type and bespeaking an already known capacity for future growth – but also for decline – is supremely an image of its time. It is tinged with the vitalistic sensibility of Metabolistic origins but, with hindsight, can also be explained as a precursor of a certain "postmodern" thinking, defined in the narrowest sense as a preoccupation with neoclassical resurgence. . . . With the new device of ruins, a flavor of vague ambivalence and subtle artificiality has been introduced, adding a formal and historical dimension to societal and demographic references that until now furnished Metabolism's main focus.[123]

The idea of transformation between city and ruins also provides hints of Isozaki's later architectural works. For the Oita Prefectural Library project completed in 1966, he designed horizontal volumes resembling giant beams abruptly cut to show the section, implying a state of ruins as the result of metamorphosis. This symbolic approach indicated early thinking of the postmodernist movement of architecture, in which Isozaki was a pioneer.

For the metaphor of ruin Isozaki was indebted to Louis Kahn, who might have transmitted his enthusiasm for the subject during his short Japanese sojourn in 1960. Inspired by the ancient monuments in Italy, Greece, and Egypt that he viewed during his four-month tenure as architect-in-residence at the American Academy in Rome in 1950, Kahn consistently incorporated images of ruins in his architecture to give the buildings a timeless character.[124] Sporadic destruction of cities, however, had long been a part of life in Japanese society due to the vagaries of fire, typhoon, earthquake, and war across the archipelago. This resulted in the acceptance of the precariousness of life and the ephemerality of all things. Isozaki reflected:

> Throughout my youth, until I began to study architecture, I was constantly confronted with the destruction and elimination of the physical objects that surrounded me. Japanese cities went up in flames. Forms that had been there an instant earlier vanished in the next. . . . The ruins that formed my childhood environment were produced by acts of sudden destruction, unlike those of Greece and Egypt, which had long been in a ruinous state. Wandering among

2.40
Arata Isozaki, "Destruction of the Future City," 1968. Montage

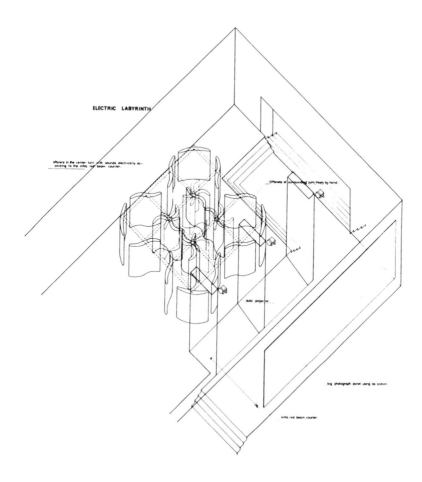

ELECTRIC LABYRINTH

2.41
**Arata Isozaki,
Electric Labyrint▮
installation for th
Triennale in Mila
1968. Axonomet▮**

them instilled in me an awareness of the phenomenon of obliteration, rather than a sense of the transience of things.[125]

Isozaki's experience of war as a teenager might have contributed to his awareness of the obliteration and rebirth of cities. The city of Oita, Isozaki's hometown in the island of Kyushu, is only about a hundred miles away from Nagasaki and Hiroshima, the two cities hit by atomic blasts at the end of the Second World War. These devastated cities and the trauma of their people had induced the young architect to conceive of the city as ruins. Isozaki later recalled:

> The experience of Hiroshima had to be accepted as the indelible origin of the reconstruction process. I belonged to the generation that had experienced once and for all the bankruptcy of Japan as an export commodity, the destruction of its cities, the transformation of the social structure, and above all, the end of history at Hiroshima. Stained upon my eyes was the scene of destruction and extinction that came *first*, before the beginning of everything else. Yet the reality of

construction and growth proceeded apace. Though the architect and urbanist are dedicated to progress, it is nonetheless impossible to escape altogether a recurring premonition of total collapse.[126]

Hiroshima offered a key to the "destructive" posture assumed henceforth by Isozaki in his work. He presented this theme in another photomontage entitled "Destruction of the Future City," created as part of an installation for the 1968 Triennale in Milan. The installation, known as "Electric Labyrinth," featured an electric labyrinth consisting of sixteen revolving curved Plexiglas panels, covered with representations of hellfire from Japanese medieval paintings and supernatural figures from eighteenth-century Japanese prints. The photomontage was projected on a large screen in the background. Collaged over a large panoramic depiction of devastated and charred Hiroshima were pairs of megastructures depicted as ruins. These once gigantic futuristic buildings, now merely burnt down to their frames, were silhouetted against the horizon. Stewart has written that in this work, the motif of future urban ruin moves even further from the theme of "Incubation Process." Instead of expecting the birth of a future city upon the ruins of past and present cities, "it has been turned against itself – and us – the locus of the ultimate man-made destruction treated now as a mere vignette over which to impose the decay of a futuristic utopia." He wondered: "Or is it, alternatively, a prophecy of the willed self-destruction of all such utopian visions?"[127] In the end, this ironic concept of city as ruins turned Isozaki away from the Metabolists' utopian concepts of city and toward a rather dystopian one. Also noteworthy is the fact that "Electric Labyrinth" was completed in the aftermath of 1968. Coupled with synchronized effects of light and sound in a dark room with an infrared beam controlling the movement of panels, the whole installation was bathed in a mysterious, ominous atmosphere characteristic of many avant-garde works of the post-1968 era. It is telling yet ironic that even before the exhibition was opened at the Milan Triennale, the Triennale was itself occupied by student demonstrators.[128]

Notes

1 Both Bruno Taut and Le Corbusier influenced Japan's modern architecture. Taut stayed in Japan between 1933 and 1935, and wrote a few books on Japanese culture and architecture. Bruno Taut, *Houses and People of Japan* (Tokyo: Sanseido Co., 1958). Taut's utopian urban concept was presented in *Alpine Architektur* (Hagen: Folk-Verlag, 1919). Le Corbusier traveled to Japan after the Second World War to design the Museum of Western Arts in Tokyo. David B. Stewart, *The Making of Modern Japanese Architecture: 1868 to the Present* (Tokyo: Kodansha International, 1987), 206–210.

2 Kiyonori Kikutake, "Ocean City," in *Metabolism: The Proposals for New Urbanism* (Tokyo: Bijutsu shūpansha, 1960), 10–13.

3 Teiji Ito, "Moratorium and Invisibility," in David Stewart and Hajime Yatsuka, eds, *Arata Isozaki: Architecture 1960–1990* (Los Angeles: Museum of Contemporary Art), 90.

4 Le Corbusier's Voisin Plan was included in his *Urbanisme* (1924), translated as *The City of To-morrow and Its Planning* (New York: Dover, 1987). Among criticisms of this plan and Le Corbusier's concepts of contemporary city planning in general are Lewis Mumford's "Yesterday's City of Tomorrow" in *Urban Prospect* (New York: Harcourt, Brace & World, 1968) and Robert

Fishman's *Urban Utopias in the Twentieth Century: Ebenezer Howard, Frank Lloyd Wright, Le Corbusier* (Cambridge, MA: MIT Press, 1982).

5 Günter Nitschke, "The Metabolists of Japan," *Architectural Design* 34 (Oct. 1964): 522; and David Stewart, *The Making of a Japanese Modern Architecture* (Tokyo: Kodansha International, 1987), 219–221.

6 Todai-ji is a large Buddhist temple in Nara. Its South Gate was built in the eighth century, and is regarded as one of the oldest existing wood structures in the world.

7 There were some changes after the late 1960s. Some of the Metabolists became more involved in political discussions. For example, Kurokawa divided his company into two offices in 1969, a design firm focusing on architecture and urban design, and an institute of social research called Social Engineering Inc.

8 Wright and Howard's concepts of the ideal city are elaborated in their respective books. Frank Lloyd Wright, *The Living City* (New York: Horizon Press, 1958); Ebenezer Howard, *Garden Cities of To-morrow* (London: S. Sonnenschein & Co., 1902). For comparison of their ideologies, see Robert Fishman, *Urban Utopias in the Twentieth Century: Ebenezer Howard, Frank Lloyd Wright, and Le Corbusier* (Cambridge, MA: MIT Press, 1982).

9 Ernst May served as the city planner for Frankfurt am Main from 1925 through 1930. He was influenced by the British Garden City movement, but reformed it with Modernist architecture. Under his direction, the city built more than 15,000 housing units in five years, forming a series of residential communities. May tried to convey this model of public housing development to the Soviet Union in 1930, but this attempt was less successful. Karl Marx Hof in Vienna was built between 1927 and 1930 under the administration of Socialist Democrats in Vienna. Karl Ehn, a follower of Otto Wagner, was the planner. It held 1,382 apartments and was called the *Ringstrasse des Proletariats*. Designed for a population of about 5,000, the premises included many amenities, including laundromats, baths, kindergartens, a library, doctors' offices, and business offices. For details of these two projects, see William Curtis, *Modern Architecture since 1900* (New Jersey: Prentice Hall, 1996); and Kenneth Frampton, *Modern Architecture: A Critical History* (New York: Thames & Hudson, 1992).

10 Otaka's involvement in the design of public housing community continued into the 1980s and 1990s, when he participated in the planning of several new towns. One of them was the Tama New Town on the outskirts of Tokyo, also intended as self-contained urban clusters.

11 Le Corbusier, *L'unité d'Habitation de Marseille*, trans. by Geoffrey Sainsbury as *Marseilles Block* (London: Harvill Press, 1953), 45. A thorough investigation of the inspiration of monasticism to Le Corbusier's social ideals is included in Peter Serenyi, "Le Corbusier, Fourier and the Monastery of Ema," *Art Bulletin* 49 (Dec. 1967): 277–286.

12 Serenyi, 281 (see note 11). For a detailed description of Fourier's *Phalanstére*, see Victor Considerant, *Description du Phalanstére et considerations socials sur l'architectonique* (Paris: Librairie Sociétaire, 1848).

13 Kenzo Tange, "Recollections: Architect Kenzo Tange, Part 3," in *Japan Architect* (June 1985): 12.

14 Krishan Kumar argued that it was the socialist utopia, from Saint-Simon to Marx and Engels, that became the inspiration of the literary utopia when it revived at the end of the nineteenth century, including Edward Bellamy's *Looking Backward*, William Morris' *News from Nowhere*, Theodor Hertzka's *Freiland*, and H. G. Wells' *A Modern Utopia*. Socialism was established as the modern utopia, the only one that could seriously command the attention of writers of utopia. Krishan Kumar, *Utopianism* (Minneapolis: University of Minnesota Press, 1991), 61–62.

15 Quoted in Kumar, 61 (see note 14).

16 For a summary of ideas and urban schemes of the Soviet Urbanists and Disurbanists, see Ruth Eaton, *Ideal Cities: Utopianism and the (Un)Built Environment* (New York: Thames & Hudson, 2001), 195–196. For Miliutin's Disurbanist ideas, see N. A. Miliutin, *Sotsgorod: the Problem of Building Socialist Cities*, trans. by Arthur Sprague (Cambridge, MA: MIT Press, 1974).

17 Leonid Sabsovich, *SSSR cherez 10 let* (Moscow: Gosizdat RSFSR "Moskovskii rabochii," 1930).

18 Kumar, 80 (see note 14).

19 For a detailed description of Japan's ambitious attempts to build a total empire in Manchuria, see Louis Young's *Japan's Total Empire: Manchuria and the Culture of Wartime Imperialism* (Berkeley: University of California Press, 1999).

20 Sakakura's famous plan of South Lake Residential Quarter showed the influence of his mentor Le Corbusier's concept of Radiant City. However, Radiant City had been, in turn, inspired by the Soviet planning ideas.

21 For a detailed discussion of Nishiyama's planning visions, see Carola Hein, "Visionary Plans and Planners," in Nicolas Fiévé and Paul Waley, eds., *Japanese Capitals in Historical Perspective: Place, Power and Memory in Kyoto, Edo and Tokyo* (London: RoutledgeCurzon, 2003), 333–341.

22 Noboru Kawazoe, "City of the Future," in *Zodiac* 9 (1961): 110.

23 Kiyonori Kikutake et al., *Metabolism: The Proposals for New Urbanism* (Tokyo: Binjutsusha, 1960), 84.

24 Ibid.

25 El Lissitzky, "Alte Stadt – Neue Baukorper," in *Russland* (1929), reprinted in *Ullstein Bauwelt Fundamente* 14: 32–38.

26 Ibid.

27 Karl Marx and Friedrich Engels, *Communist Manifesto* (1848), ed. Fredric L. Bender (New York: W. W. Norton & Company, 1988), 75.

28 Leon Trotsky, *Literature and Revolution* (Ann Arbor: University of Michigan Press, 1960), 249.

29 Quoted in Kenneth Frampton, "Notes on Soviet Urbanism, 1917–32," in David Lewis, ed., *Urban Structure: Architects' Year Book*, v.12 (1968), 238–252.

30 For a detailed description of the development of linear cities in Soviet Union, see Frampton, ibid, (see note 29).

31 N. A. Miliutin, *Sotsgorod: The Problem of Building Socialist Cities,* trans. Arthur Sprague (Cambridge, MA: MIT Press, 1974).

32 Hajime Yatsuka and Hideki Yoshimatsu, *Metaborizumu: 1960 nendai no Nihon kenchiku avangaruto* (*Metabolism: Japanese Architectural Avant-garde of the 1960s*) (Tokyo: Inax Publishing Co., 1997), 17.

33 Frank L. Wright's Broadacre City was first published in *The New Frontier: Broadacre City* (Spring Green, WI: Taliesin Fellowship, 1940) after a series of exhibitions. Later it was integrated in another book, *The Living City* (New York: Horizon Press, 1958). For a discussion of this utopian plan, see David G. De Long, ed., *Frank Lloyd Wright and the Living City* (Weil am Rhein, Germany: Vitra Design Museum, 1998) and Robert Fishman, *Urban Utopias in the Twentieth Century: Ebenezer Howard, Frank Lloyd Wright, and Le Corbusier* (Cambridge, MA: MIT Press, 1982).

34 Jean Gottmann, *Megalopolis: The Urbanized Northeastern Seaboard of the United States* (New York: Twentieth Century Fund, 1961).

35 Kiyonori Kikutake et al., *Metabolism: The Proposals for New Urbanism* (Tokyo: Binjutsusha, 1960), 27.

36 Ibid.

37 Ibid.

38 Hajime Yatsuka, "The 1960 Tokyo Bay Project of Kenzo Tange," in Arie Graafland and Deborah Hauptmann, eds, *Cities in Transition* (Rotterdam: 010 Publishers, 2001), 178–180.

39 Günter Nitschke, "The Metabolists of Japan," *Architectural Design* (Oct. 1964): 524.

40 Japan entered the feudal era in roughly 350 AD when the Yamato regime was established. Peter Bleed et al., *Japanese History: 11 Experts Reflect on the Past* (Tokyo: Kodansha International, 1996), 23 and 168.

41 Alison Smithson, ed., *Team 10 Primer* (Cambridge, MA: MIT Press, 1968), 61.

42 Noboru Kawazoe, "City of the Future," in *Zodiac* 9 (1961): 110.

43 Kikutake et al., 18–19 (see note 35).

44 Kikutake et al., 84 (see note 35).

45 Noboru Kawazoe, "City of the Future," in *Zodiac* 9 (1961): 107.

46 Ibid.

47 Ibid.

48 Ibid.

49 Noboru Kawazoe, "City of the Future," in *Zodiac* 9 (1961): 110.

50 Ibid.

51 For the difference between the "social architects" in the 1960s and the postmodernists in the

1970s in Japan, see Hajime Yatsuka, "Architecture in the Urban Desert: A Critical Introduction to Japanese Architecture after Modernism," *Oppositions* 23 (Winter 1981): 2–35.

52 Kenzo Tange, "Technology and Humanity," *Japan Architect* (Oct. 1960), 11–12.

53 Peter Smithson, "Reflections on Kenzo Tange's Tokyo Bay Plan," *Architectural Design* (Oct. 1964): 479–480.

54 Ibid.

55 Robert Fishman, *Urban Utopias in the Twentieth Century: Ebenezer Howard, Frank Lloyd Wright, and Le Corbusier* (Cambridge, MA: MIT Press, 1982), 95.

56 Kawazoe later explained his understanding of the word: "The reason that we chose the word "metabolism" is that Engels said in *Dialectics of Nature*: 'The basic way of existence of life is metabolism.' However, this concept is actually not complete. The basic difference of an organism from other physical existence has another aspect, that is, propagation. But the Japanese word "Metabolizumu" actually also contains the meaning of propagation or generation development. This word represents 'vital force.'" Masato Otaka and Noboru Kawazoe, eds., *Metabolism and the Metabolists* (Tokyo: Bijutsu Shupansha, 2005), 16.

57 Kikutake et al., *Metabolism: The Proposals for New Urbanism* (Tokyo: Binjutsusha, 1960), 59.

58 Noboru Kawazoe, "The City of the Future," *Zodiac* 9 (1961): 100.

59 Kikutake's early training in medical school might have contributed to his idea of city as organism. See David Stewart, "Irony and its Fulfillment," in Arata Isozaki, *Arata Isozaki: Four Decades of Architecture* (New York: Universal Publications, 1998), 19.

60 Kikutake et al., 21–23 (see note 57).

61 The double helix structure of DNA was discovered by James Watson and Francis Crick at Cambridge University in 1953.

62 Kenzo Tange, *A Plan for Tokyo, 1960: Toward a Structural Reorganization.* (Tokyo: Shikenchikusha, 1961), 13. More discussion of Tange's analogy of the linear city to an organism is included in Chapter 3 of this volume.

63 Patrick Geddes, *Cities in Evolution: An Introduction to the Town Planning Movement and to the Study of Civics* (London: William & Norgate, 1915). Geddes was well known for introducing the concept of "region" to town planning. Moreover, he was arguably the first planner to recognize the importance of historic city centers, as demonstrated in his renewal work in Edinburgh. His urban theory combined all these concerns and addressed to the geographical, historical, and spiritual aspects of the city. For a detailed study of Geddes's urban theory, see Volker M. Welter, *Biopolis: Patrick Geddes and the City of Life* (Cambridge, MA: MIT Press, 2002).

64 Ernest Burgess, "The Growth of the City: An Introduction to a Research Project," in Robert Park et al., eds, *The City* (Chicago: University of Chicago Press, 1925), 47–62.

65 Ibid., 53.

66 Noboru Kawazoe, "Thirty Years of Metabolism," in *Thesis, Wissenschaftliche Zeitschrift der Bauhaus-Universität Weimar,* 44 (1998): 146–151; originally published in the Japanese journal *Approach* 116 (Tokyo, 1991).

67 Noboru Kawazoe, "A New Tokyo: In, On, or Above the Sea?" *This is Japan* 9 (1962), 65.

68 Günter Nitschke, "The Metabolists of Japan," *Architectural Design* (Oct. 1964): 509–524. Laotse, *I Ching*, trans. Richard Wilhelm (Princeton, NJ: Bollinggen, 1967).

69 Kenzo Tange and Noboru Kawazoe, *Ise: Prototype of Japanese Architecture* (Cambridge, MA: MIT Press, 1965).

70 Ibid, 18–19.

71 Carola Hein et al,, eds., *Rebuilding Urban Japan after 1945* (New York: Palgrave Macmillan, 2003), 200.

72 Kiyonori Kikutake, *Kiyonori Kikutake: From Tradition to Utopia* (Milan: L'Arca Edizioni, 1997), 10.

73 Kiyonori Kikutake, "On the Notion of Replaceability," in *World Architecture* 32 (1995): 26–27.

74 For details of Kikutake's "Tree-shaped Housing" project, see Kiyonori Kikutake, "Metabolism and Habitat," *World Architecture* 32 (1995): 38. The tree-shaped form was realized in one of the architect's later works, the Sofitel Hotel near Ueno Park in Tokyo.

75 Noboru Kawazoe, "The City of the Future," *Zodiac* 9 (1962): 110.

76 Plan Obus was the first of a series of plans that Le Corbusier made for Algiers. In the following years he produced several revised proposals, progressively reducing the scale of the intervention and concentrating on the architectural solutions for the business center. All the projects were

rejected. For a detailed discussion of Le Corbusier's plans for Algiers, see Mary Mcleod, "Le Corbusier and Algiers," *Oppositions* 19 (Winter/Spring 1980): 54–85.

77 Kenzo Tange, "Towards Urban Design," *Japan Architect* (Jan. 1971), 31.

78 Ibid.

79 Ibid.

80 The Situationist International movement was founded in 1957 as a merger between Asgar Jorn's International Movement for an Inagist Bauhaus and Guy-Ernest Debord's Lettrist International. Until its dissolution in 1972, Debord was the leading protagonist in this movement, which attracted around seventy members and helped precipitate the uprisings of May 1968 in France. For the urban ideas of the Situationist International, see Simon Sadler, *The Situationist City* (Cambridge, MA: MIT Press, 1998), Elizabeth Sussman, ed., *On the Passage of a few People through a rather Brief Moment in Time: the Situationist International, 1957–1972* (Cambridge: MIT Press, 1989), and Eaton (2001), 223–227 (see note 16).

81 Peter Smithson, "Reflections on Kenzo Tange's Tokyo Bay Plan," *Architectural Design* 34 (1964): 480.

82 A large number of science fiction novels depicting underwater living and ocean worlds appeared in the 1950s and 1960s, such as Kenneth Bulmer's *City under the Sea* (1957) and *Beyond the Silver Sky* (1961), Frederick Pohl and Jack Williamson's Undersea/Eden Trilogy: *Undersea Quest* (1954), *Undersea Fleet* (1956) and *Undersea City* (1958), Stanislaw Lem's *Solaris* (1962), and Gordon R. Dickson's *The Space Swimmers* (1963).

83 Kiyonori Kikutake, "Marine City," *Kokusai Kenchiku* 26 (Feb. 1959): 36–39.

84 Kenneth Frampton, "The Rise and Fall of Mega-architecture: Arata Isozaki and Crisis of Metabolism, 1952–66," in Kenneth Frampton and Yukio Futagawa, *Arata Isozaki* v.1 (Tokyo: A.D.A. Edita, 1991), 8–15.

85 Kikutake et al., 20–21 (see note 57).

86 Ibid.

87 Ibid.

88 Noboru Kawazoe, "The City of the Future," *Zodiac* 9 (1961): 111.

89 Kikutake et al., 20–21 (see note 57).

90 Kikutake et al., 22 (see note 57).

91 Kiyonori Kikutake, "Metabolism and Habitat," in *World Architecture* 32 (1995): 28–47.

92 Fumihiko Maki, *Investigations in Collective Form* (St. Louis, MO: Washington University, 1964).

93 Ibid, 8–13.

94 Ibid, 11.

95 Ibid, 20.

96 Ibid.

97 Ibid, 14.

98 Ibid, 18.

99 Fumihiko Maki, "Notes on Collective Form," in *Japan Architect* (Winter 1994): 248.

100 Bernard Rudofsky, *Architecture without Architects: An Introduction to Nonpedigreed Architecture* (New York: Museum of Modern Art, 1964).

101 Toshi dezain kenkyukai (Urban Design Research Group), "Nihon no Toshi Kukan " (Japanese Urban Space), *Kenchiku bunka* (Dec. 1963) whole issue. This study was republished as a monograph in 1968: Toshi dezain kenkyukai, *Nihon no Toshi Kukan* (*Japanese Urban Space*) (Tokyo: Shokokusha, 1968). The research team involved in this project included Teiji Ito, Arata Isozaki, Tsuchida Akira, Hayashi Yasuyoshi, Tomita Reiko, Omura Keiichi, Watanabe Jiro, Fukuzawa Kenji, Murai Kei, and Yamagishi Kiyoshi, among others. Arata Isozaki, *Japan-ness in Architecture* (Cambridge, MA: MIT Press, 2006), 325.

102 Toshi dezain kenkyukai, *Nihon no Toshi Kukan* (*Japanese Urban Space*) (Tokyo: Shokokusha, 1968), 46.

103 Jennifer Taylor, *The Architecture of Fumihiko Maki: Space, City, Order and Making* (Basel: Birkhäuser, 2003), 58.

104 Fumihiko Maki, *Investigations in Collective Form* (St. Louis, MO: Washington University, 1964), 19.

105 Jacobs featured Boston's West End and New York's Greenwich Village as examples of vibrant urban communities in her *The Death and Life of Great American Cities*, in which she attacked plans of urban renewal for these areas. St. Louis's Pruitt-Igoe social housing project, designed by Minoru

Yamasaki in 1955, was involved in another famous controversy. It was demolished in 1972. Jane Jacobs, *The Death and Life of Great American Cities* (New York: Random House, 1961).

106 Jacobs (see note 105); Kevin Lynch, *The Image of the City* (Cambridge, MA: Technology Press, 1960); Aldo van Eyck lectured extensively in the United Stated during this period.

107 Fumihiko Maki, *Movement Systems in the City* (Cambridge, MA: Graduate School of Design, Harvard University, 1965).

108 Taylor, 43 (see note 103).

109 Maki, *Movement Systems in the City* (Cambridge, MA: Graduate School of Design, Harvard University Press, 1965) 11.

110 Fumihiko Maki, "The Future of Urban Environment," in *Progressive Architecture* 45 (Oct. 1964): 178.

111 Taylor, 23 (see note 103).

112 The Hillside Terrace includes Hillside Stage I, 1967–69; Hillside Stage II, 1971–73; Hillside Stage III, 1975–77; Hillside Stage IV, 1985 (by Motokura Makoto, who previously worked in Maki's office); Hillside Stage V, 1987; and Hillside Stage VI, 1992. The Royal Danish Embassy which was built in 1979 on one of the parcels originally owned by the Asakura family, was also designed by Maki. In 1998, Maki designed Hillside West for a site only a short distance from Hillside Terrace. It continued the rhythm of development of the preceding series. For details, see Taylor, 132–138 (see note 103).

113 Taylor, 26 (see note 103).

114 Arata Isozaki, "The City Demolisher, Inc." In *Kūkan he* (*Towards Space*) (Tokyo: Bijutsu Shuppansha, 1971), 11–20.

115 Yatsuka Hajime, "Architecture in the Urban Desert: A Critical Introduction to Japanese Architecture after Modernism," in *Oppositions* 23 (Winter 1981): 2.

116 Isozaki first entered Tange's studio at the University of Tokyo as a fourth-year undergraduate in 1953. His collaboration with Tange lasted until 1963 when Isozaki founded his own firm of Arata Isozaki Atelier, with the ironic initials AIA – usually read as American Institute of Architects. David B. Stewart, *The Making of Modern Japanese Architecture: 1868 to the Present* (Tokyo: Kodansha International, 1987), 219.

117 Arata Isozaki, *Kukan he* (*Towards Space*) (Tokyo: Bijutsu Shuppansha, 1971), 39.

118 Arata Isozaki, *The Island Nation Aesthetic* (London: Academy Editions, 1996), 34.

119 Quoted in Noboru Kawazoe, "Metabolism 1960–2001: The Experiment of the 21st Century," in *Metabolism 2001, Kikan Obayashi* special issue 48 (2001): 2–19.

120 Arata Isozaki, *Incubation Process*, 1962, republished in Arata Isozaki, *Kukan he* (*Towards Space*) (Tokyo: Bijutsu Shuppansha, 1971), 40, and Arata Isozaki, *Japan-ness in Architecture* (Cambridge, MA: MIT Press, 2006), 87–88.

121 Ibid.

122 Isozaki claimed that his relationship with Metabolism was manifested in "Incubation Process": "this photograph was·frequently cited as a representative Metabolist work. But while I was certainly thinking in Metabolist terms in this montage, as I dealt with the flux of generation and the destruction of the city, I was never a member of the Metabolist group. Indeed, I always tried to make a clear distinction between myself and their technological orientation, their somewhat naïve pragmatism which allowed them to believe that a social revolution could be achieved by means of new technology." Arata Isozaki, *The Island Nation Aesthetic* (London: Academy Editions, 1996), 33.

123 Stewart, 219–221 (see note 116).

124 During his tenure at the American Academy in Rome, Kahn wrote to his colleague in Philadelphia: "the architecture of Italy will remain as the inspirational source of the works of the future." Eugene J. Johnson and Michael J. Lewis, *Drawn from the Source: The Travel Sketches of Louis I. Kahn* (Cambridge, MA: MIT Press, 1996), 72–73. Kahn talked about the idea of ruins at an interview in 1961: "I thought of the beauty of ruins. . . . of things which nothing lives behind. . . . and so I thought of wrapping ruins around buildings." Kahn's idea of ruin is discussed in Kent Larson, ed., *Louis I. Kahn: Unbuilt Masterwork* (New York: Monacelli Press, 2000), 38.

125 Arata Isozaki, *The Island Nation Aesthetic* (London: Academy Editions, 1996), 31.

126 Arata Isozaki, *Japan-ness in Architecture* (Cambridge, MA: MIT Press, 2006), 84.

127 Stewart, 222 (see note 116).

128 Ibid.

Chapter 3

The myth of Tokyo Bay

The Metabolist projects represented radical and systematic challenges to the established concepts of urbanism. Kenzo Tange's 1960 Plan for Tokyo, in particular, had the most profound influence on the practice of urban design in postwar Japan. This plan was not only the outcome of collaboration between Tange and some Metabolists, but also a concentrated expression of Tange's ideals regarding the modern city. Featuring an enormous linear series of interlocking loops expanding Tokyo across the Tokyo Bay, it culminated the decade-long megastructural movement that Reyner Banham documented in his 1976 *Megastructure*.[1] Another historian, Hajime Yatsuka, also lauded Tange's plan as "one of the most striking renditions of the crystallization of the ideas and philosophy of certain trends in urbanism during the twentieth century."[2]

Unlike most Metabolist schemes that suggested no specific location for their ideal cities, Tange's plan was based on an extensive analysis of Tokyo. It thus raises questions concerning the relationship of the architect's vision to the urban situations of this mega-city around 1960: What were the main problems that Tokyo was facing when Tange proposed his plan? What was the objective of this proposal, and what strategies did Tange employ to achieve his goals? To what extent did this plan distinguish itself from previous attempts? To understand Tange's proposal, one must first pay a visit to Tokyo in 1960.

Tokyo's urban crises

Japan's capital suffered from severe bombardment before the end of the Second World War. Many parts of the city had to be rebuilt from ground zero, but Tokyo was soon on its way to recovery. In particular, the start of the Korean War in 1950 sparked Japan's economic resurrection, and injected new energy for Tokyo's dramatic urbanization. The city expanded at an unprecedented pace, and its population exploded. Tokyo became once again a vital city.

Despite the massive reconstruction and rapid industrialization, Tokyo retained its pre-modern urban structure and predisposition inherited from its feudal era. The city continued to develop in a piecemeal fashion without any effective reorganization of urban layout. New buildings quickly filled in empty lots to meet the rapidly growing demand for housing, but the development of infrastructure lagged behind. Increased automobile usage led to huge traffic problems. Although a variety of solutions had been proffered, large-scale urban designs and planning measures suffered from a number of issues from the outset. These plans failed to cope with the complex problems arising from a city of such magnitude and in dramatic growth. The vast population movement, fast proliferation of automobiles, inadequacy of social services, shortage of land and widespread private land ownership, as well as initial inexperience of the authorities in charge all contributed to Tokyo's predicament.[3] Notorious for its chaotic urban scene and lack of efficient and coherent planning guidance, the city was scoffed as "the world's largest village."[4] To Japanese architects and industrialists, Tokyo was sick and incurable.

The dramatic growth of population during the postwar years made Tokyo bustling yet confusing. During the first five years after the war, the city's population swelled from 2.78 million to 5.38 million.[5] The population of the city center with its fifteen wards increased at an even higher rate, with some wards reaching seven times their original size. The rapid growth was the result of several factors: evacuees and soldiers returning from war, repatriated Japanese from lost colonies, and thousands upon thousands of desperate job seekers from impoverished prefectures and devastated cities. Tokyo's population continued to soar through the 1950s, reaching 6.96 million in 1955 and 8.31 million in 1960.[6] The population explosion raised serious problems for Tokyo, the first and foremost being the need to house the growing population. Air raids during the war burned 770,000 dwelling units to ashes.[7] Immediately after the war, illegal constructions quickly filled empty spaces to shelter the returning residents. Due to the economic condition in that particular period, it took several years for these makeshift constructions to be removed or replaced, making it difficult to plan and rebuild the city more coherently. Housing remained the most pressing issue through the 1950s, leaving a shortage of 420,000 dwelling units in 1960.[8]

Over-concentration of population and industries in the capital put huge pressure on its transportation system. The proliferation of private automobiles in the 1950s aggravated traffic congestion. The situation became so serious that newspaper columns even discussed the possibility of turning part of the Imperial Palace into a park and building a highway between the palace and the park to alleviate traffic in the city center.[9] Drastic ideas like this indicated people's anxiety about Tokyo's predicament. Contributing to the deterioration of traffic conditions was the fact that Tokyo's transportation system was based on a centripetal pattern. Official measures undertaken to broaden existing thoroughfares only resulted in greater concentration of urban functions at the center, inviting even more congestion.

Rapid growth of population and concentration of industries drove Tokyo's land prices to an astronomical level. Issues of land ownership complicated the situation further. Although most of Tokyo's original constructions had been obliterated in air raids, fragmental land ownership remained, as did the city's narrow street patterns inherited from the Edo period. Japan's first postwar constitution, adopted under the supervision of the Allied Forces, tended to protect existing land ownership rights and even scatter them further.[10] High land price as well as the complexity and fragmentation of land ownership made it difficult to assemble enough land for large-scale public developments in the inner city.

At the root of all these issues was the fact, agreed upon by architects and planners, that Tokyo lacked a powerful and coherent planning framework. There was little evidence of the coordinated land use or zoning restrictions that were present in most Western cities, and even less evidence of attention to aesthetics in urban design. This deficiency gave rise to many incongruities and resulted in a chaotic urban scene. To many, the city was a jumble of buildings with little relationship to each other whatsoever, and the streets were like a maze with no apparent plans for either beautification or meeting modern traffic needs. Erhard Hursch's report, in his 1965 book *Tokyo*, painted a vivid picture of the city's urban scene:

> Tokyo is a huge wilderness, a conglomerate mass of wooden cubes and concrete blocks, main arteries and narrow alleys, waterways and railbeds, of trees, cables and signs – a jungle crammed with people and filled with the roar of engines. . . . Whether you arrive by plane, ship or train, you do not enter upon the scene of a clear-cut urban structure; instead, you find yourself thrown immediately into a whirlpool. You are carried away by a violent current, bewildered by the profusion, submerged as by great drowning waves.[11]

Observing the confusion of Tokyo's urban development, Tange was struck by the urgency of implementing a powerful plan to give the city a coherent structure. He noted: "Tokyo has been formed as a result of totally planless spontaneous growth on the basis of self-assertion of the inhabitants. [There has been an] irritating lack of leadership on the part of governments in enforcing a rational plan for Tokyo."[12] But could Tokyo afford a modern plan?

Missed opportunities and mismatched plans

There had been opportunities for Tokyo in the twentieth century to transform its urban fabric. The city had been readied for comprehensive reconstruction at least twice, first after the Great Kanto Earthquake and then after the Second World War. The great earthquake of 1923 and the fire it caused destroyed over 63 percent of houses in Tokyo. Twenty years later, Tokyo was once again reduced to ashes by repeated air bombings, which wiped out 40 percent of buildings in the city.[13] Ambitious reconstruction plans were drawn up after both disasters, but they failed to make any significant impact on the city due to the costs involved, the urgency of rebuilding shelters, and the complexity of land ownership. The Imperial Capital Rehabilitation Plan for reconstructing Tokyo after the Kanto Earthquake was proposed by Mayor Shimpei Goto, and it was extolled as "the only genuine master plan in modern Japanese history."[14] The plan tried to take advantage of the destruction of the earthquake to reshape Tokyo into a modern city by Western standards, proposing a series of tree-lined boulevards and urban parks and improvement of municipal service. Carrying out Goto's plan in its entirety, however, required a financial outlay equivalent to three times the nation's annual budget. There were also oppositions from influential landowners, who feared losing their land holdings to public projects.[15] As a result, only a few elements of the scheme were actually implemented, and a majority of Tokyo was rebuilt much the way it was.

The reconstruction of Tokyo after the Second World War began under the American occupation. In addition to the goal of providing 300,000 prefabricated shelters, the 1945 War Rehabilitation Plan for Tokyo and the 1946 National Capital Region Development Plan, both prepared by the metropolitan government, addressed the issues of land readjustment, decentralization, and restriction of growth in the city's central districts.[16] These plans used the opportunity of wartime destruction to define greenbelts around the center city and extend green corridors deep into the core. It would thus restructure Tokyo and subdivide it into several specialized sub-cities using an extensive network of ring and radial parkways, greenbelts, and green corridors. One of the objectives was to keep the population in the center city within the limit of 3.5 millions. However, due to the incredible rate of population growth and limited financial capacity after the war, there was even less of a chance to introduce improved standards of urban design. While it is obvious that Tokyo was rebuilt very quickly and once again became a populous and vital city, it is equally clear that the reconstruction did not follow the carefully thought-out plans. By 1950, only 6.8 percent of the area damaged in the war and initially designated for comprehensive reconstruction was in fact rebuilt under the direction of the authorities. Private property owners rebuilt the rest, and the result was visual chaos in this rapidly growing mega-city.[17]

Since the mid-1950s, several factors emerged as new stimuli for Tokyo's urban regeneration. First of all, Japan entered a new phase of economic growth, paving the way for the Japanese economic miracle. Accompanying the nation's growing economic power was the privilege to host the Olympic Games of 1964, awarded to Tokyo in 1958. The Olympics demanded that Tokyo significantly improve the city's infrastructure and create new public facilities, which were both formidable challenges and great opportunities for city planners.

Economic growth was the unquestioned top priority of Japanese central government during the 1950s and 1960s. After the Korean War began in 1950, the Allied Forces used Japan as their military base as well as a source of supplies, boosting Japan's export-oriented economy. The record economic growth commenced in earnest in 1955 and continued into the 1970s with more than 10 percent annual growth of the Gross National Product (GNP).[18] It caused an unprecedented construction boom and accelerated metropolitan expansion. Tokyo was the engine of this economic miracle. People flocked to the capital

yo
ropolitan
ernment,
yo War
nage
abilitation
, 1946. Land
map

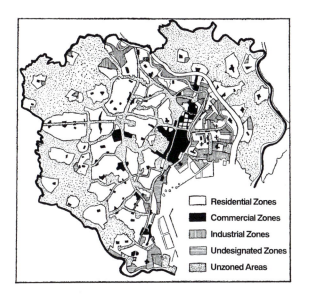

Residential Zones

Commercial Zones

Industrial Zones

Undesignated Zones

Unzoned Areas

from all over the country, leading to a new wave of population growth. The late 1950s saw the beginning of suburbanization in Japan, in which the outer circles of Tokyo absorbed most of the population increase. From 1955 to 1964, the total population of the Tokyo metropolitan region rose from 13.28 to 18.86 million.[19] Accompanying this population explosion was a significant trans-formation of the city's spatial structure. Instead of the concentration of business functions in a single core, a polycentric pattern came into being, with a number of mass traffic nodes emerging as new business and commercial centers, such as Shinjuku, Shibuya and Ikebukuro.

The 1964 Olympic Games, the first to be held in an Asian country, triggered another round of urban regeneration. The feverish preparation for the event brought significant improvements of infrastructure in the metropolis. Among many new Olympic venues and public facilities was the Tokyo Olympic Stadium designed by Tange. It was built on a site previously serving as the headquarters of the Allied Occupation Forces, thus assuming political symbolism. Several arteries were widened and straightened to become "Olympic thoroughfares." During the pre-Olympic frenzy, the city built its first elevated inner city highway, added several new subway lines, and extended existing ones.[20] All the Olympic projects, as much as the Tokyo Olympic Games itself, were intended to show the world Japan's complete recovery from the war and to demonstrate its mastery of new technologies in all fields. The most impressive accomplishment of the country was its cutting-edge transport technique: the Olympics were celebrated with the completion of the first section of the *Shinkansen* bullet train line between Tokyo and Osaka. This rail line has since been extended all the way to Fukuoka on Kyushu Island in the west and Hokkaido in the north, linking most major cities on the Japanese archipelago with a fast and convenient network. The result was the formation of Tokaido megalopolis, a linear agglomeration accommodating more than 40 percent of Japan's total population. The great constructive energy released during the economic miracle and the preparation for the Olympics offered fresh opportunities for planners to rethink Tokyo's urban future and, to a great extent, prompted the emergence of Tange's 1960 Plan for Tokyo.

Under such circumstances of extraordinary urban growth, it became more evident than ever before that exceptional methods were required to regulate Tokyo's pattern of expansion. The solution could only be found on a regional scale. Therefore, from the mid-1950s onward, a series of special steps leading to comprehensive city planning were taken. The national government took the initiative by creating the cabinet-level Capital Region Development Commission in 1956. One of the commission's major achievements was the publication of the National Capital Region Development Plan in 1958. This regional plan addressed all categories of land use and encompassed a huge territory with a radius of about 100 kilometers, centered on the expanded 23-ward nucleus. It was evident that this plan was in many respects influenced by

3.2
Kenzo Tange, Tokyo Olympic Stadium, 1964

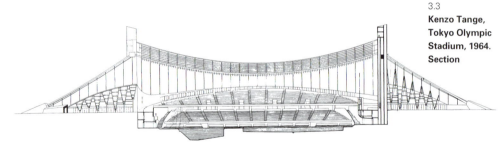

3.3
Kenzo Tange, Tokyo Olympic Stadium, 1964. Section

yo
ropolitan
ernment,
ional Capital
ion
elopment
, 1958

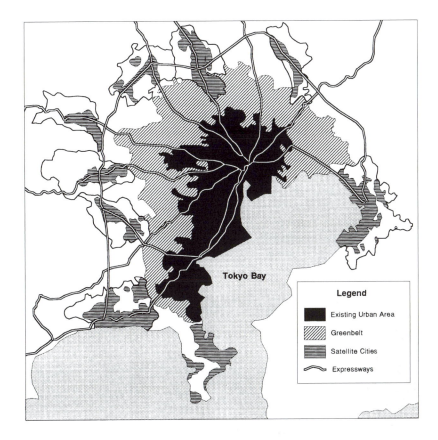

the British garden city movement and particularly Sir Patrick Abercrombie's 1944 Greater London Plan.[21] A main feature of the 1958 plan for Tokyo was a greenbelt zone 16 to 27 kilometers away from the city's center. New business and civic developments would be largely confined within the inner circle of this belt; housing and community projects would be directed to the more distant zones located between 27 and 72 kilometers from the center of Tokyo. These outer zones included a number of new satellite towns to absorb much of the region's population growth and industrial expansion. The plan also called for the construction of an extensive network of expressways to connect the newly urbanized areas and linking them to the center.

Tokyo Metropolitan Government officially carried out the Capital Region Development Plan, giving the city a new planning framework. Industry and urban sprawl, however, grew far more quickly than anticipated. As a result, many of the restrictions specified in the plan soon became outdated and were ignored. For instance, the Japan Housing Corporation, a semi-public agency established to ameliorate housing shortages in the urban areas, ended up using the greenbelt zone for many of its development sites. In 1965, a revised master plan erased the greenbelt altogether and offered this zone for suburban growth. In the meantime, the outer boundary of the capital region was substantially extended. Another significant revision of the 1958 plan was the abolition of the 31-meter building-height limit in the 23 wards of central Tokyo, taking effect in 1963.[22] The removal of the height limit reflected the intense demand for development space, and launched the city into an era of skyscraper construction.

The new frontier

What happened in Tokyo in the postwar years testified that urban planning had become a field sharply polarized between the ideal and the real. Although the government attempted to control Tokyo's expansion and plan reconstruction according to principles of modern urbanism, they failed to make any significant impact in the face of the city's exceptional pace of growth. At the same time, outside the policy-making circle, industrialists and architects actively sought alternatives for the city's future. Instead of directing urban growth to the newly urbanized metropolitan periphery, they set their eyes on a new frontier – the Tokyo Bay.

It was no surprise that industrialists became involved in city planning as Japan's postwar economy relied increasingly on its big corporations. Industrialists enjoyed a cozy relationship with the national and local governments, especially through the Ministry of International Trade and Industry (MITI). One of MITI's major missions was to coordinate the private sectors, promoting continuous development and making Japanese industries more competitive internationally.[23] A number of semi-public organizations, such as the Japan Housing Corporation, were established as the result of collaboration between government and industry, and they played an important role in the making of urban plans and public policies. During the 1950s, these agencies and corporations organized various seminars to encourage industrialists, economists, architects and other professionals to discuss Tokyo's economic and urban development. Tange was among the prestigious architects in close contact with government and industrial leaders, and participated in many of these seminars. Some of the diagrams he drew in the pre-1960 seminars indicated the idea of building an artificial island in Tokyo Bay, although the reclamation was modest in scale compared to his later proposals.

In April 1958, Hisaki Kano, president of the Japan Housing Corporation, published a visionary concept for Tokyo's urban development.[24] For the first time, the focus of a plan shifted to Tokyo Bay. Kano called for massive reclamations between Tokyo and Chiba, the prefecture on the opposite side of the bay, to create land accounting for one third of the total bay area. An industrial belt, several residential districts, an international airport, and a large park were proposed for these islands. The earth to fill in the bay would be taken from leveling the mountains in the Boso Peninsula.[25] Collaborating with the Industrial Planning Committee, Kano developed his idea into a more concrete Neo-Tokyo Plan in July 1959. According to this proposal, several artificial islands would be created for different uses, with the largest one in the middle of the bay serving as a city center. A double-loop expressway and a railroad would connect the new city districts with the existing ones.

Kano's proposal of filling up the bay was intriguing to both the public sector and the professional circles because he was a pragmatic business-man potentially capable of carrying out such a plan. His idea particularly inspired the visionary architects and urban designers, many of whom believed that the expansion of Tokyo into the bay was a reasonable, and probably the best, solution. Because of the scarcity of land and the startling price of real estate in the city, it was in fact less expensive to reclaim the sea, and, cost was not the only reason: creating land through reclamation would also avoid the extremely complicated land ownership issues that often plagued large development projects in Tokyo.

Metabolist architects embraced Kano's idea enthusiastically and pushed it further. They discovered that even though filling in the bay could create land, most constructions on the artificial islands would still require foundations laid directly on the solid rock underneath the sea. In areas close to the mouths of rivers, foundation piers would need to go down as deep as 50 meters to reach

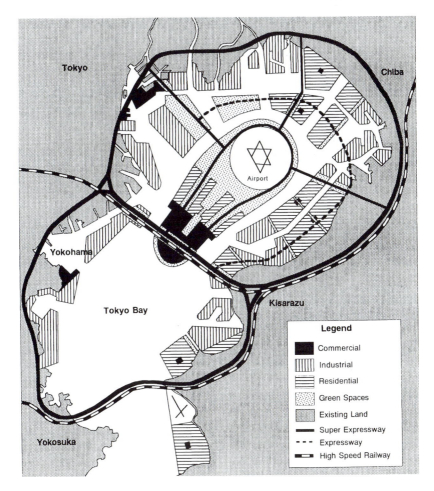

5
saki Kano and
e Industrial
anning
ommittee, Neo-
kyo Plan, 1959

the rock. It would therefore be easier and more economical to sink piers directly into the sea and erect buildings on them, instead of moving so much dirt. With this in mind, Masato Otaka published his Tokyo Marine City Plan in 1959, characterized by a horseshoe-shaped strip of reclamation along a transportation ring on Tokyo Bay.[26] A number of urban clusters consisting of high-rise housing blocks would be built on this linear city, based on the prototype of the Harumi Apartment Building recently completed by Otaka.

Otaka's concept might have influenced Tange's later plan for Tokyo in two aspects. In terms of building form, the Harumi project was supported by a system of massive A-shaped structures that allowed for the possibility of open floor plans. This idea found a stronger expression in Tange's 1959 MIT project, "Community of 25,000 on Boston Bay," which served in turn as the prototype of the residential structures in the architect's 1960 Plan for Tokyo. In terms of urban structure, Otaka's concept of a linear city foreshadowed Tange's "civic spine," an idea that dominated his 1960 plan.

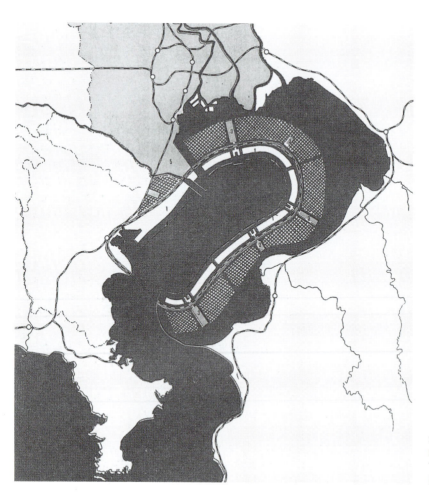

3.6
Masato Otaka,
Tokyo Marine Ci
Plan, 1959

nori Kikutake,
ting City of
yo, 1961

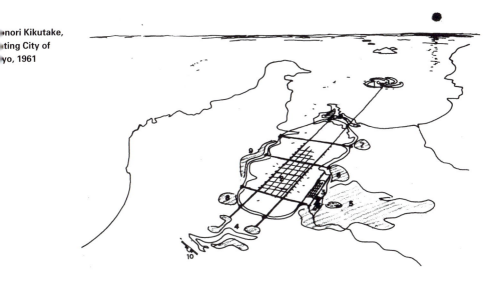

Otaka's younger peers in the Metabolist group were even more radical when developing Kano's Tokyo Bay concept. Instead of employing immoveable structures, Kikutake was the first to consider the possibility of a marine city floating on the sea. He contended that this approach would make the city adaptable to ever-changing demands of land and space usage. Based on his previous concept of Tower-shaped City, Kikutake proposed a Floating City of Tokyo in 1961, featuring an enormous rectangular floating island on Tokyo Bay carrying a gridiron layout of housings and factories. Individual installations would be linked together by a lattice road system, which also connected the island to the cities surrounding the bay. Should any change occur in the city, each urban block could be detached from the system and moved to other locations, or it could float out to the ocean and be sunk.[27]

1960 Plan for Tokyo

Inspired by Kano and the Metabolists' schemes, Tange's 1960 Plan for Tokyo was almost a natural progression toward a new Tokyo Bay city. However, it was only Tange who could integrate all these new ideas into a plausible proposal, combining the regional and local conditions of Tokyo with cutting-edge concepts of planning and striking a balance between two contrasting approaches: the pragmatism of industrialists and the idealism of utopian architects.

Tange had already been thinking about the future form of the city when he traveled to Otterlo for the eleventh and last CIAM meeting in September 1959. The conference asked each participant to "come with a project which he considered to express in the best way possible his conception of the task of the architect and urbanist, and his thoughts on how the architect and urbanist might rationalize and harmonize the connections between people and their surroundings."[28] In addition to his recently completed Kagawa Prefecture

Government Building, Tange brought with him two projects by Kikutake: the Sky House and the Tower-shaped City. These projects became the first Metabolist designs exhibited in an international event. Tange justified them on a pragmatic ground and claimed: "Tokyo is expanding but there is no more land, and we shall have to expand into the sea."[29] His inclination for the city's future could not be clearer.

In Otterlo, Tange met with people discontented with the established Modernist paradigm of planning. They actively sought new approaches to city design and, more specifically, to reorganizing the city as a human association with an emphasis on its sociological organization and symbolic meaning. Promoting this idea were Louis I. Kahn and Team 10 members including Alison and Peter Smithson, Aldo van Eyck, and Georges Candilis. These architects called for a new hierarchy of human association to replace the function-based division advocated in the Athens Charter. They agreed upon the pivotal role of a city's transportation system in shaping the city, and focused on issues like mobility, openness, and adaptability to growth and change as characteristics of the modern city. In practicing these ideas, they often employed a megastructural strategy. Their concepts of city design were demonstrated in projects like the Smithsons' London Road Study and Kahn's plan for central Philadelphia, both presented at the Otterlo meeting.

Another topic arousing ardent debate at the Otterlo meeting concerned regionalism in design. Supporting Peter Smithson's point of view, Tange repudiated Ernesto Rogers's notion of regionalism as backward-looking, and rejected the interpretation that his Kagawa Prefecture Government Building perpetuated Japanese tradition. He extended his argument to the issue of city planning and declared:

> We must reject "aestheticism" in town planning. Tradition and regional characters should be re-examined with critical eyes and minds. I shall repeat again that all I have said above begins with the positive denial of the attempt to make order out of existing reality. Vitalism is always destructive to existing reality, but is very constructive in the building of our future.[30]

Tange's resolution of breaking away from "existing reality" to pursue new paradigms of planning might have set the tone for the plan of Tokyo he introduced the very next year.

Tange's 1960 Plan for Tokyo was completed in his studio at the University of Tokyo, with the assistance of five young architects: Keji Kamija, Arata Isozaki, Sadao Watanabe, Noriaki Kurokawa, and Heiki Koh.[31] The plan was first disclosed on Japan's national television network NHK as a one-hour special TV program for the new year of 1961.[32] Two details about the plan, the date and the occasion of its debut, deserve some attention before the plan itself is examined. First, although the plan was titled "1960," it did not come out until January 1961. Second, the plan was first published through a popular media

nzo Tange
nding in front
a presentation
ard of the Plan
Tokyo 1960

rather than any architectural periodical. Actually, Tange's plan did not appear in *Shinkenchiku* (*New Architecture*) until March 1961, and the first foreign journal that covered this plan was *Architectural Forum* in the September 1961 issue.[33]

To explain the discrepancy in timing, Yatsuka reasoned that Tange might have called the scheme "Plan for Tokyo 1960" because of his original intention to publish the plan at the World Design Conference held in Tokyo in 1960.[34] It was delayed because Tange's staff were involved in the preparation of the conference, and also because of the political turbulence in May 1960. Kurokawa, one of Tange's key assistants, was engaged in the frequent meetings with other Metabolist members to prepare the program for the conference as well as the Metabolist manifesto. Another key designer, Isozaki, although not directly involved in the Metabolist group, was working on visionary projects including the City in the Air. The mass demonstrations against the revision of the US–Japan Security Treaty, which continued through the first half of 1960 and caused great upheaval soon after the close of the World Design Conference, was also responsible for the delay of Tange's work.[35] In this climate of political unrest, most progressive intellectuals and students went on the streets to demonstrate. Tange and his staff were no exception.

Tange later recalled that he had been mulling over the content of the Tokyo Bay Plan during his tenure as a visiting professor at MIT in fall 1959.[36] In addition to his original attempt to publish it in 1960, Tange may have put "1960" in the title of the plan to compete with the Metabolism's manifesto. Seeking a new paradigm of urbanism, the Metabolists' pamphlet drew immediate attention from the international community of architects. Some of the Metabolists were invited to the exhibition of Visionary Architecture organized by MoMA in the same year. Although Tange was recognized as mentor of these young architects, he was not directly involved in the founding of this group. The enthusiastic reception of Metabolism at the design conference might have stimulated Tange to publish his own visionary plan.

It is unlikely that Tange's plan was commissioned by the government or any organization; rather, it was the architect's voluntary effort. His decision to introduce this project through public media instead of professional periodicals, however, indicated that he did not conceive of this plan as a purely experimental scheme. Rather, he wanted his voice heard by the general public and, by so doing, to influence the authorities and official plans for the city. This conclusion is borne out by other evidence. Two and a half months before the project was completed, Tange previewed his idea in the popular news journal *Syukan Asahi* (*Asahi Weekly*).[37] The article he wrote, entitled "The Future City over the Sea: The Realization of a New Plan for Tokyo," presented a sketch of his vision of a "New Tokyo" through the reclamation of the bay. After the final plan was published, congressmen in the National Diet urged the Japanese Minister of Transportation to read Tange's report.[38] Tange's strategy of bringing the project to public attention was an indication of his wish to carry out this plan, however unrealistic it appeared to be. The plan itself also demonstrated the architect's commitment to a mission that would not only establish a new order for Tokyo's urban environment, but one that might demand a complete redefinition of its social system.

Mobility as nature of the pivotal city

As rendered on a large-scale model, Tange's plan envisioned a new Tokyo expanding across the bay to reach the opposite shore in Chiba. The most notable feature was a central spine carrying an elevated highway system, which consisted of a series of interlocking loops and spanned thirty kilometers over the sea. The spine started with a loop framing the existing city center of Tokyo, then it moved on to the sea. The third, fourth, and fifth loops, which would be entirely over water, would accommodate a new civic center and a port. The subsequent links would be occupied by office and public buildings until the spine landed on the shore again. The buildings on the spine took the form of habitable bridge trusses spanning gigantic service towers, which were arranged on a rectangular grid with 200-meter intervals. Beyond the fifth link,

3.9
Kenzo Tange, Pl
for Tokyo 1960.
Model

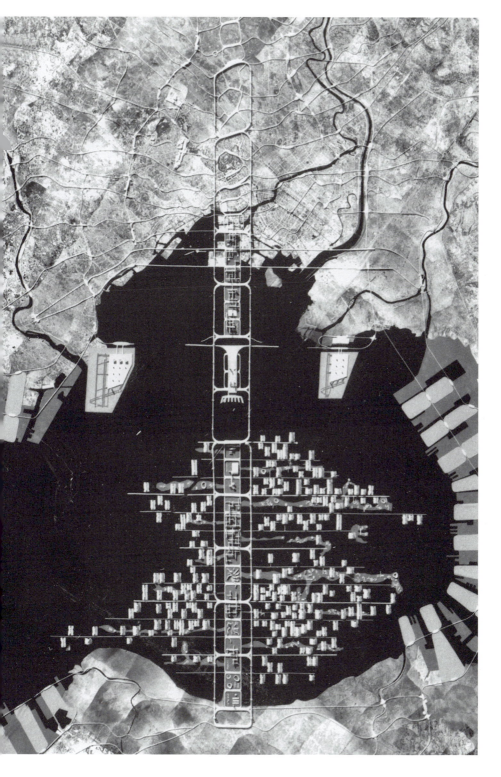

a number of secondary freeways departed from the central spine at right angles, connecting the main line to clusters of tent-like residential units that spread over the bay. These gigantic structures would serve as artificial grounds upon which residents could build their own houses.[39] The whole plan was conceived as an enormous megastructure with a hierarchical arrangement of circulations and programs.

Tange's spectacular plan stemmed from his interpretation of the characteristics of what he called the world's "pivotal cities," that is, cities with populations of ten million or more. In his view, such cities, including Tokyo, were in a state of confusion and paralysis because the physical structures of the cities had "grown too old to cope with the current rate of expansion," and the only way to save the cities was a radical transformation of their fundamental structures.[40] The vitality of a city in the postindustrial age was no longer based on the primary or secondary economic sectors, but its tertiary sector. As a result, the city should not be simply treated as a composition of separate functional zones, as orthodox Modernists suggested, but rather an open complex linked by a communication network. Tange argued that the transportation system was the physical foundation of a city's operation, and mobility was the factor that would bring a city vitality. The communication system was particularly important for the organization of a pivotal city like Tokyo. Tange articulated its significance with a metaphor: "It is the arterial system which preserves the life and human drive of the city, the nervous system which moves its brain. Mobility determines the structure of the city."[41]

Tange included a number of tables and graphics in his plan, illustrating recent trends of the demographic and economic conditions of Tokyo as well as Japan as a whole. The research had been conducted earlier and included in Tange's doctoral thesis entitled "The Regional Structure and Architectural Forms of Contemporary Large Cities," submitted to the University of Tokyo in 1959.[42] In the dissertation, Tange discussed the dramatic transformation that Tokyo was undergoing and the primary challenges it was facing. Many of the data involved comparisons between Tokyo and other mega-cities in the world. The investigation also manifested Tange's keen interest in regional planning. To him it was the inevitable next step when considering the development of contemporary cities on a larger scale and in a more comprehensive manner.

In Tange's opinion, re-planning Tokyo the mega-city was an urgent task mandated, first and foremost, by the rapid proliferation of individual automobiles. The automobile had changed the relationship between architecture and street, and the new relationship demanded a new system of transportation. He noted:

> In the past, people walked along streets until they came to their destination and then simply disappeared into the door. . . . With automobiles on the street, however, everything is different. In the first place, it is necessary to divide pedestrians from vehicles, to create highways and streets that are for the exclusive use of vehicles. Thanks

to the coming of the automobile, there is need for a new order in which a vehicle can move from a fast highway to a slower one and then come to a stop at the destination.[43]

Tange contended that the movement automobiles introduced into urban life had changed people's conception of space. This new sense of space, in turn, required a new spatial order in the city. Because the old transportation system could no longer meet the needs of a contemporary society, Tange called for replacing it with a new hierarchical system serving the automobile. Consciousness for greater mobility in a contemporary city underlay all parts of his plan for Tokyo.

The issue of mobility had been a theme of theoretical exploration among European Modernists since the early twentieth century. Le Corbusier's *Ville Radieuse* was a profoundly important step in introducing a new awareness of mobility into architecture and city design.[44] He not only recognized that the automobile would fundamentally transform the infrastructure of a contemporary city, but also implied that it would transcend the traditional role as means of transportation and become a communication symbol to unify the modern society. In his ideal plan of the Radiant City, Le Corbusier used *pilotis* as a basic structuring element of urban design to separate pedestrians from the automobiles. The ground would virtually be left open as an enormous green space for pedestrians, while automobile transportation was given unencumbered access in a separate system. The role of *pilotis* in urban design was partially realized in Le Corbusier's *Unité d'Habitation* in Marseilles, intended as a prototype of collective housing for large-scale urban reconstruction. There was no doubt that Le Corbusier's theory had influenced Tange. Tange introduced the *pilotis* system into his plan for Tokyo a few years later, and integrated it with the so-called "core system," that is, vertical shafts containing stairways, elevators, and other services.[45] The architect explained:

> *Pilotis* areas constitute spatial links between private and public areas. They are areas in which the flow of traffic meets with stable architectural space. Core systems, on the other hand, link urban arteries with the buildings. In this plan we propose to unify the core and the *pilotis* into a single system.[46]

With the "pilotis and core system," architects would not only be able to separate automobile transportation from pedestrians, but also give the city a more coherent structure because architecture and infrastructure would be virtually integrated into one system.

Tange claimed that the pilotis and core system could be used in the exploitation of new urban areas as well as in the redevelopment of existing districts. Therefore, he made his megastructure start right from Tokyo's city center and extend outward. The ultimate goal was to substitute the traditional two-dimensional planning method of zoning with this three-dimensional

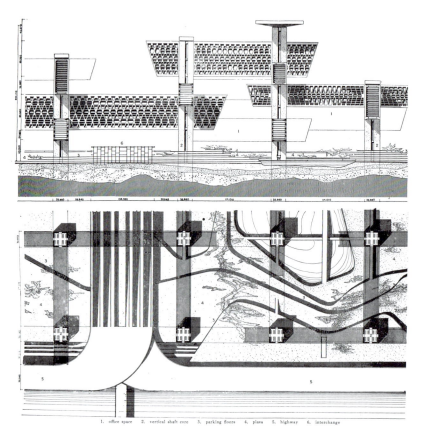

3.10
Kenzo Tange, P▮
for Tokyo 1960.
"Pilotis and cor▮
system

1. office space   2. vertical shaft core   3. parking floors   4. plaza   5. highway   6. interchange

generative system, through which a higher degree of mobility and social interaction could be developed. Tange claimed: "In this system, it would be possible, while taking into account the spaces that form the surroundings, to form well-planned continuous urban spaces that were not closed in nature. In effect, zonal planning methods used in urban planning to date would be replaced by organized spatial planning."[47]

Such an anti-zoning position and concerns with urban communication systems were shared by Tange's Western peers, particularly Kahn and the Smithsons. In a series of plans for Philadelphia dating from 1952, Kahn suggested that traffic patterns would become the generator of new city forms. His diagrams of urban circulation, defining different types of movement, became the departure point of his visionary plans. To him, transportation was not just a mechanical process, but also embodied the essence of a modern metropolis. His analogy between the flow of traffic and an urban canal system provided a novel analysis of the movement pattern in a large city:

> Expressways are like RIVERS. These RIVERS frame the area to be served. RIVERS have HARBORS. HARBORS are the municipal parking

towers; from the HARBORS branch a system of CANALS that serve the interior; the CANALS are the go streets; from the CANALS branch cul-de-sac DOCKS; the DOCKS serve as entrance halls to the building.[48]

This poetic analogy applied a symbolism to the banal transportation structures, and inspired Kahn to develop a new structure for the modern city. He used this approach in several plans for Philadelphia, most evidently the 1963 plan often known as "Viaduct Architecture."

Alison and Peter Smithson's 1958 competition entry for Hauptstadt Berlin was also based on studies of movement, both physically and in its social ramifications. Although it represented a less symbolic and more pragmatic approach, the plan went somewhat further than Kahn's plan for Philadelphia to envisage a drastic reordering of the city. There were separate systems for cars and pedestrians, each adopting distinct geometries and operating independently. Regarding mobility as an essential character of the modern time, the Smithsons called for celebrating it with an "aesthetic of change" in design to replace traditional Cartesian aesthetics.[49]

Pushing further Kahn and the Smithsons' ideas in his plan for Tokyo, Tange stressed mobility as a characteristic of postindustrial society, and rendered it concretely with a powerful form: the highway system, supported by large-spanned suspension structures, extended all the way from Tokyo across the bay to Chiba. By projecting the infrastructure of his new city directly on to the water, the highway system was presented with a startling clarity as the dominant element. The great size of this linear system, which stretched thirty kilometers

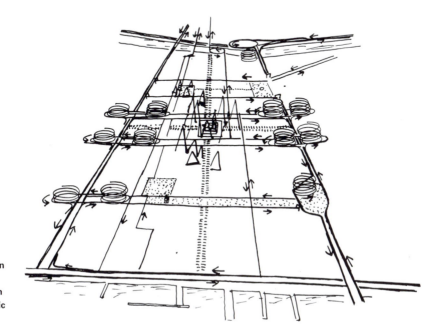

1
uis I. Kahn, Plan
Philadelphia,
51–54. Diagram
proposed traffic
ttern

3.12
Alison and Peter
Smithson,
competition entr
for Hauptstadt
Berlin, 1958. Plan

over the bay, the perspicuity of its loop and branch road network, and the formal inventiveness of the extraordinary buildings which were clipped on to the highway framework, all combined to make the plan an articulated statement of an urban form generated in the age of the automobile. Tange's symbolic attitude toward the issue of mobility was also evident in such a gesture: the striking form and structural hierarchy of the transportation system not only made it visually prominent in the plan, but also provided legibility of the social organization. To the architect, the articulated transportation pattern indicated a new spatial framework from which a new urban order would emerge. It would become the icon of the new city on Tokyo Bay and symbolize a contemporary society characterized by openness, mobility, and adaptability to continuous growth.

Linear civic axis as the symbol of open society
Tange declared that his plan for Tokyo had three objectives:

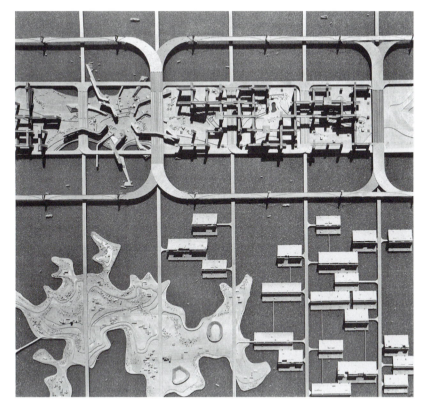

zo Tange, Plan
Tokyo 1960.
ial plan

1. To shift from a radial centripetal system to a system of linear development.
2. To find a means of bringing the city structure, the transportation system, and urban architecture into organic unity.
3. To find a new urban spatial order which would reflect the open organization and the spontaneous mobility of contemporary society.[50]

Apparently, the first and foremost goal of the plan was to transform the current radial centripetal structure, which Tange called a "closed system," into a linear structure, which represented an "open system" and would encourage the spontaneous mobility of contemporary society.[51] To his point of view, the current structure of Tokyo was a typical centripetal system organized around an urban core. Tange dismissed it as the form of a medieval city that was obsolete and dysfunctional for a city of Tokyo's magnitude. He wrote:

> In the age when cities developed around central squares or plazas and when people lived within limits prescribed by regional societies, the central square was the nucleus of communication, and the

cathedral, the castle, and the city hall were the spiritual supports, as well as the symbols, of city life. Horses and carriages moving along radial streets past rows of buildings must have formed a very harmonious ensemble. Now, however, mass communication has released the city from the bonds of a closed organization and is changing the structure of society itself. In the society with an open organization and in the pivotal city of this organization the mobility involved in free, individual communication is assuming a larger and larger scale. This movement, added to the fixed movement of regular commuters, has led to extreme confusion in the larger cities.[52]

Tange's argument clearly countered CAIM's concept of "urban core." The 1951 CIAM meeting called for rebuilding European cities with an identifiable core modeled after traditional civic centers such as Italian piazzas. Tange rejected this notion of civic center and instead advocated a linear form that he called the "civic axis." This civic axis, combined with the arterial movement that sustained urban life, would serve as the symbol of the open organization in a contemporary pivotal city, just as a cathedral sitting at the center of a centripetal organization was the symbol of the medieval city. In Tange's proposal, the future axis of Tokyo would take as its point of departure the present city center and gradually extend out over Tokyo Bay, thus transforming the "civic core" into a "civic axis."

Although Tange claimed the civic axis as a new concept, the linear form was hardly his creation. As early as 1882, Soria y Mata had introduced the first published linear plan, *Ciudad Lineal*.[53] Since then, the linear city concept had been developed with many variations by town planners in Europe and America. Among the best-known examples were Tony Garnier's *Cité Industrielle* in 1904, Edgar Chambless's Roadtown plan in 1910, and Le Corbusier's series of schemes for Algiers in the early 1930s. Tange's inspiration for the linear city might have also come from the world's other political camp – the Soviet Union. Russian Disurbanist planners had published a number of linear city projects during the Soviet Union's first Five-Year Plan from 1928 to 1933, such as N. A. Miliutin's *Sotsgorod*.[54] This theoretical project was developed with the Soviet government's support to accelerate the process of collectivization and improve industrial production. Such linear planning concepts in the Soviet Union had influenced Japan's modernist planners working for *Mantetsu* in Manchuria. For instance, Takayama and Uchida's 1939 plan for Datong followed the linear city principle and might have inspired Tange's plan to a certain extent.

After the Second World War, the linear city concept once again aroused widespread interest, for it appeared to possess the potential to control urban sprawl and direct urban decentralization in an orderly way.[55] Competing with the linear city was another paradigm of planning for organized urban decentralization: the Garden City, initiated by Ebenezer Howard at the end of the nineteenth century.[56] The Garden City concept had been influential since its inauguration, disseminated throughout the world through either governmental initiatives like the British New Town Movement or academic and

4
nzo Tange, Plan
Tokyo 1960.
ntral spine

professional movements like the Regional Planning Association of America. There were constant debates between advocator of the linear city model and the Garden City model, as people were usually in favor of one theory over the other. Two years before Tange's project, the Tokyo Metropolitan Government announced the National Capital Region Development Plan. Inspired by Sir Patrick Abercrombie's 1944 Greater London Plan and the subsequent New Town Movement, this plan envisioned a series of new towns on Tokyo's outer rings to absorb the region's population growth and provide new centers for economic expansion.

Tange's plan was apparently intended as a polemical counterthrust to the 1958 National Capital Region Development Plan. To him, the idea of creating satellite cities or sub-centers to decentralize population and industries

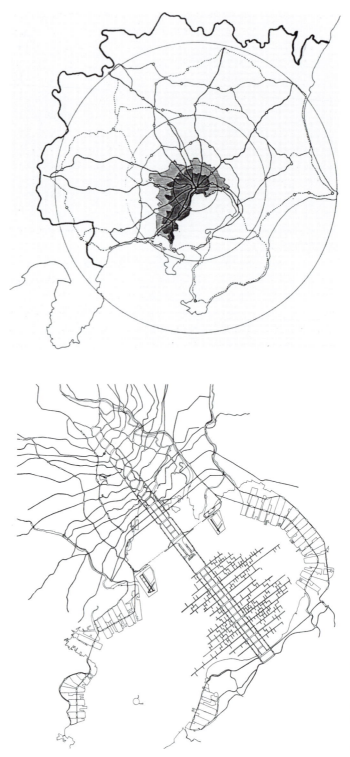

3.15
The Tokyo
Metropolitan
Government's
1958 National
Capital Region
Development Pl▮

3.16
Tange's linear pl▮
was a criticism o▮
the 1958 Nationa▮
Capital Region
Development Pla▮
which featured a▮
radiant pattern

from the city center would not solve Tokyo's fundamental problem. First of all, it was not certain that these satellite cities would succeed and people would be willing to move to a remote town; then, even if the satellite cities and sub-centers actually matured, the dispersion of population and urban functions would create even more transportation between the center city and the sub-centers. In the long run, this variable flow of traffic would add to the burden of the metropolitan center. Conversely, Tange advocated the linear city because it would allow the spontaneous mobility characteristic of the contemporary age on one hand, and maintain the proper relationship between different sections of the city on the other. Tange thus contended that the linear city was the optimum model of urban decentralization, and it embodied the very essence of social progress by promoting mobility. The significance of Tokyo's civic spine, powered by the new linear transportation system, would transcend the mere question of transportation to become the symbol of a postindustrial city.

What distinguished Tange's civic spine from earlier linear forms was a sophisticated cyclical system integrated into this transportation axis, which consisted of a double-loop composition in each link for different speeds of automobile traffic. The outer loops, which would carry high-speed through-traffic, were put on suspension bridges fifty meters above water. Its obvious prototype was the Bay Bridge in San Francisco, an indication of engineering Tange learned in America. Each loop was a three-kilometer span, and side of the loop would have one-way traffic, but cars could not travel straight-ahead. Instead, they had to move clockwise and counterclockwise alternately. In the middle section, where these two traffic flows overlap, cars on both sides of the loops would be moving in the same direction. The inner cycles organized the local traffic and provided access to buildings and communities. Each cyde spanned a kilometer. They were designed using the same principle as the outer loops and located on a lower level. The high-speed lanes and low-speed lanes would be connected by means of ramps. Despite the obvious inconvenience of such zigzag traffic patterns, its designers boasted that this cyclical system would avoid any intersection, and thus increase the capacity of the transportation system by ten to thirty times.[57] Tange also claimed that this cyclical unit would make gradual expansion of the civic axis possible: at each stage of development the system was complete, but it would always be possible to add another unit.

Although architects and critics admitted the ingenuity of such a highway system design, few were convinced by its practicability. In an essay written in 1964, Peter Smithson threw doubts on Tange's linear transportation system:

> The classic disadvantage of the linear town is that it concentrates all movement along the central spine – all movement must proceed via that spine even when it has no business there. In a linear road system this leads to a terrific number of lanes being necessary, each filled to capacity, with a probable redundancy of lane capacity in the feeders.

3.17
Kenzo Tange, Pla
for Tokyo 1960.
Model detail of th
suspension bridg

> As far as I can see, no reduction of the number of lanes is produced by the cyclical system, except in so far as one might get better usage of the lane capacity because the longer and shorter journeys need not use the same links in the system. But this separation would be possible to arrange in a more orthodox system.[58]

This observation plainly countered Tange's appeal and revealed the technical inefficiency of his linear system. To Smithson, Tange's plan represented a monumental urban form, responding symbolically to the call for mobility, however it failed to provide a plausible proposal to tackle the transportation problems of the mega-city.

There were also debates on the plan's metaphorical meaning. In order to convince people that linear development was inevitable as a city expanded, Tange, like the Metabolists, invoked a biological analogy. He compared the transformation of the city structure from a radial form to a linear form with the evolution and growth of living organisms:

> The amoeba and the asteroid have radial centripetal forms, but vertebrates have linear bone structures with parallel radiations. When the living functions of organisms differentiate and perform the composite function of life, the centripetal pattern evolves into a system of parallel lines grouped around an axis formed of a spine and arteries. The process whereby a vertebrate body hatches from an egg illustrates the possibility of gradual development on the part of a linear system.[59]

Most organisms initially take a radial form, but as they mature and are required to perform more complex functions, the radial pattern is no longer suitable so it evolves into a linear one. What was true for organisms was also true for cities, Tange asserted. Not coincidentally, the same belief was held by the Metabolists.

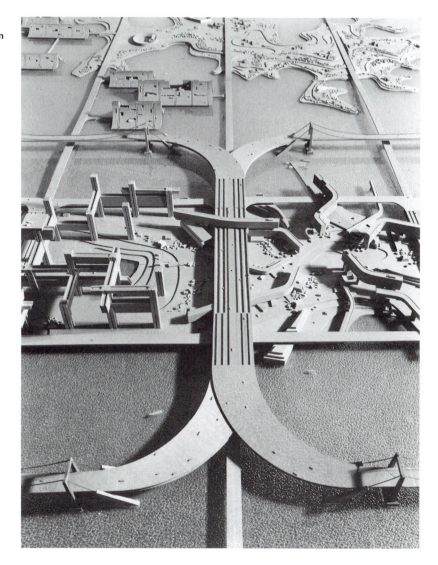

The team working on this plan under Tange's direction included Kurokawa and Isozaki, both of whom were sympathetic to the Metabolist theory and viewed the city as a vital process of continuous development.

Interestingly, when Christopher Alexander commented on Tange's plan in his essay "A City is not a Tree" published in 1965, he also introduced a biological analogy. He called city plans based on such kinds of organization "trees," and noted that the Tokyo Bay Plan was a "beautiful example" of the tree-like structure.[60] He harshly criticized the artificial cities created in the pattern of a tree for being monotonous and rigid, and having lost the necessary characteristics of human organization; and he believed they were doomed to fail. Alexander countered the "tree" model with a different urban pattern called "semi-lattice" characterized by intrinsic organic adjacencies, which resided in all natural cities and provided complexity, variety, and real openness.[61] In the end, both Smithson's technical critique and Alexander's biological analogy called into question the "openness" and "flexibility" which Tange repeatedly claimed for his linear plan. These criticisms indicated that Tange's monumental structure remained a model for urban growth and free movement that was unachievable practically.

As the most conspicuous feature of Tange's plan, the linear structure also represented the architect's political ideal of national organization. Yatsuka linked the Tokyo Bay Plan to Tange's earlier city design projects, more specifically, the 1942 competition entry of the Memorial for the Greater Asian Co-Prosperity Sphere, and pointed out Tange's longstanding ambition of regulating

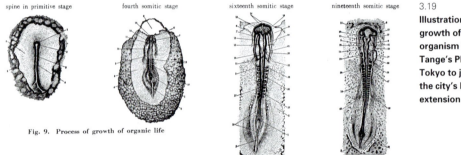

spine in primitive stage   fourth somitic stage   sixteenth somitic stage   nineteenth somitic stage

Fig. 9. Process of growth of organic life

3.19
Illustration of the growth of an organism in Tange's Plan for Tokyo to justify the city's linear extension

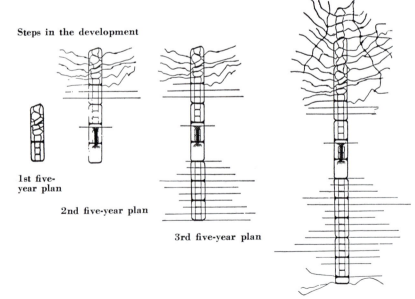

Steps in the development

1st five-year plan

2nd five-year plan

3rd five-year plan

4th five-year plan

3.20
Tange envisioned that the new city would be built in four phases

national development with systematic planning.[62] The 1942 scheme envisioned a linear transportation axis, which would serve as a national development spine linking Tokyo with Kyoto via the proposed memorial site. This concept of regional planning heralded the 1960 Plan for Tokyo, in which it was combined with Tange's futuristic enthusiasm about speed. The axis originally connecting Tokyo with Mt. Fuji in the 1942 plan was now turned in the opposite direction: toward the Tokyo Bay. Tange also drew a number of sketches for his Tokyo Bay project to study the extension of the axis to the inner land. The spine shown in one of these sketches was slightly bent to reach Shinjuku, the new urban center. Further west, it extended toward Mt. Fuji, reflecting the very idea that Tange had applied in his project some twenty years before. The same notion dominated both plans: the linear axis would not only give the city a new spatial framework, it should also become the economic and spiritual spine of the nation.

Metabolic cycles as presented in residential megastructures

The issue of how to cope with rapid growth and unpredictable changes in a contemporary city was a concern for both the Metabolists and Tange. In contrast to the conventional method of master planning which sought a final and stable state, Tange envisioned his Plan for Tokyo would make the city adaptable to both external growth and internal regeneration. External growth meant that the organization of the city was conceived as having a nature that could continue to grow and evolve in a systematic way. The internal regeneration was to allow components of the system, that is, architecture, to engage in a continuous process of self-renewal while the system as a whole maintained its quality. The key to establishing such a system was differentiating objects whose cycles of change were slow from those objects in cycles of more rapid change and evolution.

This attitude, seeing a city as an organic process that was constantly growing and changing, was articulated by Team 10 theorists Alison and Peter Smithson. They noted:

> Just as our mental process needs fixed points (fixed in the sense that they are changing over a relatively long period) to enable it to classify and value transient information and thus remain clear and sane, so the city needs 'fixes' – identifying points which have a long cycle of change by means of which things changing on a shorter cycle can be valued and identified. With a few fixed and clear things, the transient – housing, drug stores, advertising, sky signs, shops and at shortest cycle of all, of course, people and their extensions, clothes, cars and so on – are no longer a menace to sanity and sense of structure, but can uninhibitedly reflect short-term mood and need. If this distinction between the changing and the fixed were observed there would be less need for elaborate control over things for which no good case can be made for controlling, and legislative energy could be concentrated on the long-term structure.[63]

Applied to the planning of a city, this meant fixing only infrastructure along which development could take place and leaving the transient things to individual tastes. For instance, the transportation system should be more or less inviolable and protected as "fixed," while individual constructions would be conceived as "transient." This distinction between "fixed" and "transient" elements was first introduced by Le Corbusier in the 1931 plan for Algiers. In this plan the massive super structure served as the permanent framework of the city; within this enormous structure inhabitants could build their own houses that would reflect constantly changing urban life and diverse individual tastes. Inspired by Le Corbusier's utopian concept, Team 10 architects developed such notions into an "aesthetic of change" in architecture, and claimed that this aesthetic of change would generate, paradoxically, a sense of security, stability, and order.[64] Metabolists further elaborated the theme relating different cycles of change and combined it with a natural philosophy in their concept of "metabolic cycle."[65] They maintained that objects with different qualities were in different metabolic cycles: some were persistent while others were transient.

Obviously, Tange was also aware of the different metabolic cycles of various constructions, that is, the longer lifespan of large-scale construction like infrastructure as compared with the shorter lifespan of houses and articles of daily life. He contended that this gap continued to widen as a result of mass production and the emerging "throwaway" consumerist culture:

> Short-lived items are becoming more and more short-lived, and the cycle is shrinking at a corresponding rate. On the other hand, the accumulation of capital has made it possible to build in large-scale operations. Reformations of natural topography: dams, harbors, and highways are of a size and scope that involve long cycles of time, and these are the man-made works that tend to divide the overall system of the age. The two tendencies – toward shorter cycles and toward longer cycles – are both necessary to modern life and to humanity itself.[66]

While long-term large-scale structures curtailed individual freedom more and more, short-term elements became expressions of individual choice and contemporary susceptibility to novelty. In the Plan for Tokyo, the A-shaped dwelling structures demonstrated the effort to bring this contradiction in urbanism into a harmonious whole. The enormous concrete structures provided artificial grounds made possible by communal investment, upon which individual investments would take place in the form of private constructions that would reflect constant changes in taste. Tange expected the longer life cycles of infrastructure to be organically connected with the shorter life cycles of individual constructions and form a spatial system that would propel the city's evolution.

Tange's interpretation of metabolic cycles in city design, however, was not without controversy. Despite his shared concern with the distinction of "fixed" and "changing" elements in urban building, Peter Smithson disagreed with Tange in terms of his approach to the residential megastructure in the Tokyo Bay Plan. He wrote:

> The pyramidal housing units over-the-water are formally the finest things in the scheme, but unhappily as in a thousand student projects (from the time of Le Corbusier's Algiers project onwards), the romance of the idea of 'each man building his own house' on man-made platforms, stands unsupported by a demonstration of how it is to be done.[67]

Even within the circle of Metabolism, there were debates on the criteria for differentiating long-term structures and short-term elements. Fumihiko Maki noted that Tange's mega-form was based on the assumption that designers

6.21
Kenzo Tange, Plan
for Tokyo 1960.
Tent-shaped
residential blocks

3.22
**Kenzo Tange, Plan
for Tokyo 1960.
Tent-shaped
residential blocks,
plan and section**

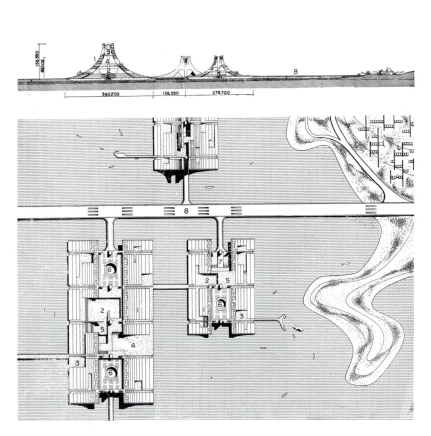

would be able to ascertain which functions to be dealt with had long cycles of change, and which shorter; however, he argued, this might not be the case. Maki wrote:

> Can the designer successfully base his concept on the idea that, to give an example, transportation methods will change less rapidly than the idea of a desirable residence or retail outlet? Sometimes, the impact and momentum of technology become so great that a change occurs in the basic skeleton of social and physical structure. It is difficult to predict to which part of a pond a stone will be thrown and which way the ripples will spread. If the megaform becomes rapidly obsolete, as well it might, especially in those schemes which do not allow for two kinds of change cycle, it will be a great weight about the neck of urban society.[68]

Here Maki implies that even though a megastructure allowed for changeable infill, the main structure itself could become obsolete and lead to the failure of the entire system. He thus dismissed the megastructural approach and instead turned to a method that "permits the greatest efficiency and flexibility with the smallest organizational structure," that is, the group form.[69] The debates between different understandings of metabolic cycle consequently betrayed Tange's symbolic approach to this issue as well as the utopian nature of his plan in general. Characterized by a rigid hierarchical system, Tange's Plan for Tokyo was in fact less a plausible proposal to realize a city's adaptability to growth and change than an expressive gesture of monumentalizing infrastructure as a means to control the urban process.

Planning the postindustrial city

During the 1950s and the 1960s, when Tange proposed the Plan for Tokyo, the city was undergoing dramatic changes. As Tokyo absorbed more and more people, businesses, and industries, its urban center suffered from severe land shortages and traffic congestion. Paradoxically, the city was also facing the possibility of being dissolved as it continued to expand rapidly and spontaneously. The proliferation of automobiles accelerated the process of urban sprawl and contributed to the chaotic urban scene. It seemed to many that a new sort of order was needed to regulate the urban growth. The inefficiency, confusion, and inequity of the metropolis made a ready case for bold, comprehensive restructuring rather than piecemeal remedies cast within existing parameters. Tange's plan responded exactly to this situation. It represented an innovative undertaking, projecting a future Tokyo based on a linear city principle, and integrating infrastructure, urban space, and architecture into a dynamic system. By so doing, he tried to manipulate the dramatic urban growth and trans-formation, and impose a new pattern on the metropolis.

Aware of the critical role that private automobiles played in the transformation of city life and the making of urban form, Tange organized the whole city based on an innovative system of transportation, and he focused on the essential characteristics of a postindustrial city, namely mobility, openness, and adaptability to change and growth. These had become key issues in Japan's urban development after the Second World War, as the country underwent a fundamental reconstruction of its cities and pursued economic modernization. Tange's observation of the postindustrial city was acute, but the solution he came up with, when considered on a practical base, remains questionable. Why didn't Tange's ideal city come true? Or should his plan be implemented at all? To what extent has this plan influenced Tokyo's city building in the following decades?

Several factors prevented Tange's proposal from being carried out. The first and foremost one lies in his megastructural approach. This ambitious plan set out to establish a new spatial order for human habitats and proposed interventions that made no difference between the scale of city and that of architecture. Reflected on the plan, office buildings along the linear axis and residential blocks on the bay assumed an urban scale while the highway system was turned into a monumental architecture. However, besides the difference in scale, a city is a much more complex entity than a building in terms of its organization. Therefore, various aspects in Tange's proposal, as we can see now, were problematic. The system he envisioned mandated a segregation of pedestrian from automobile transportation on one hand, and a hierarchical organization of spaces according to different speeds of movement on the other. The separation of pedestrians and automobiles often sacrificed the human scale of the city, as manifested in many projects realized in the following decades. The hierarchical transportation system, once built, could be quite efficient, but hardly flexible.

Tange's scheme not only encountered technical problems, it was also entangled by political and economic constraints. Aiming to give the city a new structure, the plan entailed nothing less than a redefinition of its social organization. The reclamation of the bay, the building of the central spine, and the construction of public "artificial land" for residential and business developments, as well as other associated infrastructure were all massive projects that needed to be done before any usable space could be installed. It potentially required an extremely powerful authority to ensure adequate financial sources and smooth implementation, which was only possible with a totalitarian government. In the prewar years, the chance may have existed in authoritarian Japan or its colonies but, after the war, neither Japan's central government nor any corporation and agency possessed such power. Furthermore, the strict hierarchy in Tange's plan implied a social organization of the same structure, which was not only unrealistic under the democratic system gradually established in Japan in the postwar era, but was also in conflict with the values of a contemporary society, namely, democracy and equality, which Tange claimed for his plan.

Tange tried to realize the ideas of mobility, openness, and adaptability to change and growth in this sophisticated scheme. The way he approached these issues, however, was more symbolic than practical. His proposal presented a powerful image to communicate the architect's design and social ideals with professionals as well as the general public, but technically it remained unrealistic as a physical plan. Therefore it is not difficult to detect contradictions between the objectives of the plan and the means to achieve them. The relationship between order and spontaneity, both critical to a contemporary city, was fully represented in the scheme but hardly reconciled. Here, the Metabolist notion of change was combined with the pursuit of monumentality, a quality Tange had developed in his earlier works such as Hiroshima Peace Memorial Park. The result was an ideal city responding to the transformation of culture and attempting to provide a new communal symbol.

Although Tange failed to carry out the plan, his concept proved to have profoundly influenced Tokyo's urban development in the following decades. As a result, several features of his plan were gradually realized, although not in the way Tange expected. Especially, his ideas of a linear form and the expansion of the city into the bay accurately anticipated the transformation of Tokyo.

While Tokyo retained its radiant urban structure and fragmented urban landscape through the rest of the twentieth century, the city was brought into a larger linear urban cluster, later known as "megalopolis" after Jean Gottmann's 1961 study.[70] The fact that Gottmann's book and Tange's plan were published in the same year was not entirely coincidental. They both addressed a global phenomenon of urban geography and demography emerging in this particular period. By 1960, the region along the Tokyo–Yokohama axis housed over thirteen and half million people. By 1970, the once scenic route between Tokyo and Osaka called Tokaido had become a continuous industrial belt, linking together a series of big cities and their metropolitan areas and accommodating around 40 percent of Japan's total population.[71] The Tokaido Shinkansen high-speed rail line served as the spine of this megalopolis, just as the linear highway system in Tange's 1960 plan was the spine of the new Tokyo.[72] In 1970, Tange responded to this new urban agglomeration again in his national vision plan, commissioned by Japanese central government and targeting the twenty-first century. In this plan, the axial structure in his previous Tokyo Bay plan was extended throughout the country to form a network of cities supported by a rapid transportation system.

Ten years after the publication of Tange's Plan for Tokyo, the reclamation of Tokyo Bay was well under way, although not in the systematic manner Tange envisioned. By the end of the twentieth century, there were more than forty projects under construction on several reclamation sites in the bay.[73] In contrast to the waterfront developments in the postwar period, most of which had been designated for heavy industries and ports, many of the recent mega-projects built new business districts, such as the Tokyo Teleport Town and the Minato Mirai 21, or mixed-use residential and entertainment areas, such as the River City 21.

Tange participated in a few projects that developed the Tokyo Bay, including the megastructural tower for Fuji TV Corporation Headquarters. In 1986, the Kenzo Tange Association published a new plan for Tokyo that was as ambitious as the 1960 plan. The new proposal was again based on an axis, consisting of several parallel transportation mainlines connecting Tokyo to the artificial islands on the bay and further to the cities across the bay. The major difference between the 1960 plan and the 1986 plan was that the developments in the bay no longer formed a continuous megastructure. Instead, they were a series of artificial islands. The plan called for a two-phase exploitation of Tokyo Bay. In the first phase, projects planned up to that point and those already under construction would be integrated into a Coastal City of Tokyo, out on the bay from the existing urban center of Tokyo. In the second phase, the axis of development would be extended all the way to Kisarazu on the opposite shore of the Tokyo Bay, and a new city center would be created at the center of the bay. These developments would form a new Tokyo Bay City, covering some 6,600 hectares of land and accommodating 700,000 employees and 2.5 million residents. There would also be a new 1,600-hectare international airport in the bay, operating 24 hours a day. The ultimate objective was to create a new city serving international trade, the information industry, and financial services for the twenty-first century that "Japan could proudly show the world."[74] The movement system, now consisting of a variety of infrastructure for public and private transportations and assuming a more accessible form, still dominated the whole plan as a generator of the new city. Compared to the 1960 plan, the 1986 plan was more practical yet still ambitious. The first phase it envisioned, the Coastal City of Tokyo, has so far effectively guided the developments in Tokyo Bay. Nevertheless the 1960 Plan for Tokyo remained Tange's strongest statement of urbanism, which was more important for the stimulus it provided than for any practical possibility of its realization.

3.23
Kenzo Tange, Fuji TV Corporation Headquarters Building, 1996

3.24
Kenzo Tange, Plan for Tokyo 1986. Model view

Notes

1 Reyner Banham, *Megastructure: Urban Futures of the Recent Past* (New York: Harper & Row, 1976).
2 Hajime Yatsuka, "The 1960 Tokyo Bay Project of Kenzo Tange," in Arie Graafland and Deborah Hauptmann, eds, *Cities in Transition* (Rotterdam: 010 Publishers, 2001), 179.
3 For details of Tokyo's postwar urban development, see Ichikawa Hirro, "Reconstructing Tokyo: The Attempt to Transform a Metropolis," in Carola Hein et al., eds, *Rebuilding Urban Japan after 1945* (New York: Palgrave Macmillan, 2003), 50–67.
4 Noboru Kawazoe, "A New Tokyo: In, On, or Above the Sea?" *This is Japan* 9 (1962): 57.
5 Roman Cybriwsky, *Tokyo: The Changing Profile of an Urban Giant* (Boston: G. K. Hall & Co., 1991), 88.
6 Ibid.
7 Hirro, 55 (see note 3).
8 Ibid.
9 Noboru Kawazoe, "A New Tokyo: In, On, or Above the Sea?" *This is Japan* 9 (1962): 57–58.
10 For details of the development of Tokyo's postwar policy of urban planning, see André Sorensen, *The Making of Urban Japan: Cities and Planning from Edo to the Twenty-first Century* (London; New York: Routledge, 2002), 162–163.
11 Erhard Hursch, *Tokyo* (Tokyo: Charles E. Tuttle, 1965).
12 Kenzo Tange, "A Plan for Tokyo, 1986," *Japan Architect* 367/368 (Nov./Dec. 1987): 8.
13 Hirro, 50 (see note 3).
14 Botond Bognar, *Tokyo: World Cities* (London: Academy Editions, 1998), 49. For a detailed historical account of Tokyo's reconstruction after the 1923 Great Earthquake, see Cybriwsky (note 5), 81–83.
15 Cybriwsky, 82 (see note 5).
16 The reconstruction plans of Tokyo were drawn up under the direction of Hideaki Ishikawa, head of the planning division of the Toyko Metropolitan Government. For details of this plan, see Cybriwsky, 84–88 (see note 5).
17 By 1950, only 1,380 hectares of the 20,000 hectares of land originally slated for mass reconstruction had been rebuilt. Hirro, 55 (see note 3).
18 Japan's gross national product rose from $15.1 billion in 1951 to $51.9 billion in 1962, and to $290 billion in 1972. Edwin Reischauer and Albert Craig, *Japan: Tradition and Transformation* (Boston: Houghton Mifflin, 1978), 286.
19 The Metropolitan Region includes Tokyo and the prefectures of Chiba, Saitama, and Kanagawa. Bognar, 49 (see note 14).
20 Bognar, 50 (see note 14).
21 For details of the 1958 National Capital Region Development Plan, see Cybriwsky, 200–201; (note 5) and the Tokyo Metropolitan Government, *A Hundred Years of Tokyo City Planning* (Tokyo: Tokyo Metropolitan Government Publications, 1994), 56. For Abercrombie's Plan for London, see Patrick Abercrombie, *Greater London Plan 1944* (London: Stationery Office, 1945).
22 Cybriwsky, 201 (see note 5).
23 A detailed discussion of MITI's role in Japan's economic growth is provided in Chalmers A. Johnson, *MITI and the Japanese Miracle: The Growth of Industrial Policy, 1925–1975* (San Francisco: Stanford University Press, 2004).
24 Kano had served as the mayor of Chiba, the prefecture across the bay from Tokyo. Noboru Kawazoe, "The Metabolists, from their Time of Learning to the Present," in Masato Otaka and Noboru Kawazoe, eds, *Metabolism and Metabolists* (Tokyo: Bijutsu shōbansha, 2005), 13.
25 For details of Kano's plan, see Kenzo Tange and Terunobu Fujimori, *Kenzo Tange* (Tokyo: Shin Kenchikusha, 2002), 345; and Noboru Kawazoe, "A New Tokyo: In, On, or Above the Sea?" *This is Japan* 9 (1962): 60.
26 Noboru Kawazoe, "A New Tokyo: In, On, or Above the Sea?" *This is Japan* 9 (1962): 60–63.
27 Ibid.
28 Oscar Newman, ed., *New Frontiers in Architecture: CIAM'59 in Otterlo* (New York: Universe Books, 1961), 7.
29 Ibid, 184.

30 Ibid, 172.

31 Later Tange reorganized his design team into an atelier called "URTEC."

32 Kenzo Tange and Terunobu Fujimori, *Kenzo Tange* (Tokyo: Shin Kenchikusha, 2002), 357.

33 Kenzo Tange Team, "A Plan for Tokyo, 1960: Toward a Structural Reorganization," *Shinkenchiku* (Mar. 1961): 8–38; "Tokyo into Venice?" *Architectural Forum* (Sep. 1961): 142–143.

34 Hajime Yatsuka, "The 1960 Tokyo Bay Project of Kenzo Tange," in Arie Graafland and Deborah Hauptmann, eds, *Cities in Transition* (Rotterdam: 010 Publishers, 2001), 178–191.

35 The World Design Conference opened on May 11 and ended on May 16. The demonstrations protesting the US–Japan Security Treaty became turbulent on May 19, when the ruling Liberal-Democratic Party forced an extension of the parliamentary session to pass the Security Treaty.

36 Kenzo Tange, "Recollections: Architect Kenzo Tange, Part 5," *Japan Architect* (Aug. 1985): 9.

37 Kenzo Tange, "The Future City over the Sea: The Realization of a New Plan for Tokyo," *Syūkan Asahi*, Oct. 16, 1960.

38 "Editorial," *Japan Architect* (April 1961): 7.

39 Kenzo Tange Team, *A Plan for Tokyo, 1960: Toward a Structural Reorganization* (Tokyo: Shikenchikusha, 1961); Banham, 49–54 (see note 1).

40 Kenzo Tange Team, *A Plan for Tokyo, 1960: Toward a Structural Reorganization* (Tokyo: Shikenchikusha, 1961), 6.

41 Ibid, 7.

42 Kenzo Tange, "Geidai daitoshi no chiiki kōzō to kenchiku keitai" (The Regional Structure and Architectural Forms of Contemporary Large Cities) (Dissertation, University of Tokyo, 1959).

43 Kenzo Tange Team, *A Plan for Tokyo, 1960: Toward a Structural Reorganization* (Tokyo: Shikenchikusha, 1961), 9.

44 Le Corbusier, *The Radiant City: Elements of a Doctrine of Urbanism to Be Used as the Basis of our Machine-age Civilization* (New York: Orion, 1967).

45 Tange's concept of core system may also have been inspired by Luis I. Kahn's design of the Richards Medical Laboratory at the University of Pennsylvania, a project Kahn introduced at the 1959 CIAM meeting.

46 Kenzo Tange Team, *A Plan for Tokyo, 1960: Toward a Structural Reorganization* (Tokyo: Shikenchikusha, 1961), 24.

47 Ibid.

48 Louis I. Kahn , "Toward a Plan for Midtown Philadelphia," in Alessandra Latour, ed., *Louis I. Kahn: Writings, Lectures, Interviews* (New York: Rizzoli, 1991), 28.

49 Alison Smithson, ed., *Team 10 Primer* (Cambridge, MA: MIT Press, 1968), 57.

50 Kenzo Tange Team, *A Plan for Tokyo, 1960: Toward a Structural Reorganization* (Tokyo: Shikenchikusha, 1961), 10.

51 Ibid.

52 Ibid, 12.

53 Arturo Soria y Mata, *La cité linéaire: conception nouvelle pour l'aménagement des villes* (Paris: École nationale supérieure des Beaux Arts, 1984).

54 N. A. Miliutin, *Sotsgorod: The Problem of Building Socialist Cities*, trans. Arthur Sprague (Cambridge, MA: MIT Press, 1974). His idea of the linear city was followed by Ernst May's project for Magnitogotsk, a linear town of twenty miles long and one mile wide. See Kenneth Frampton, "Notes on Soviet Urbanism, 1917–32," in *Urban Structure: Architects' Year Book*, ed. David Lewis, v. 12 (London: Elek Books, 1968), 238–252.

55 Studies of linear cities can be found in *Architects' Year Book*s published in the 1950s and 1960s. George R. Collins, "The Linear City," in *Pedestrian in the City: Architects' Year Books, V.11.* ed. David N. Lewis (London: Elek Books), 204–217; C. A. Doxiadis, "On Linear Cities," in *Urban Structure: Architects' Year Books, v.12.* ed. David N. Lewis (London: Elek Books), 49–51.

56 Ebenezer Howard, *Garden Cities of To-morrow* (London: S. Sonnenschein & Co., 1902).

57 Kurokawa was responsible for designing this transportation system.

58 Peter Smithson, "Reflections on Kenzo Tange's Tokyo Bay Plan," *Architectural Design* 34 (1964), 479–480.

59 Kenzo Tange Team, *A Plan for Tokyo, 1960: Toward a Structural Reorganization* (Tokyo: Shikenchikusha, 1961), 13.

60 Christopher Alexander, "A City is not a Tree," *Architectural Forum* 122, no. 1 (1965): 58–62; 122, no. 2 (1965): 58–61.

61 In this essay, Alexander used his mathematical expertise in architectural criticism and applied the set theory to his analysis of the "tree" model and the "semi-lattice" model. Ibid.

62 Hajime Yatsuka, "The 1960 Tokyo Bay Project of Kenzo Tange," in *Cities in Transition*, ed. Arie Graafland and Deborah Hauptmann (Rotterdam: 010 Publishers, 2001), 178–191.

63 Alison Smithson, ed., *Team 10 Primer* (Cambridge, MA: MIT Press, 1968), 68.

64 Ibid.

65 Günter Nitschke was one of the first to look for the origin of Metabolist theory in Japan's traditional philosophy. He wrote about the possible influence of *I Ching*, Buddhism, and Shintoism on Metabolism in the essay "The Metabolists of Japan," *Architectural Design* 34 (Oct. 1964): 509–524.

66 Fumihiko Maki, "*Investigations in Collective Form* (St. Louis, MO: Washington University Press, 1964), 11.

67 Peter Smithson, "Reflections on Kenzo Tange's Tokyo Bay Plan," *Architectural Design* 34 (1964): 479–480.

68 Maki, 11 (see note 66).

69 Maki, 12 (see note 66).

70 Jean Gottmann, *Megalopolis: The Urbanized Northeastern Seaboard of the United States* (New York, Twentieth Century Fund, 1961). Gottmann employed the term "megalopolis" to describe the linear form of dense urban agglomeration in the northeastern seaboard of the United States. It was later applied to other regions. Japan's Tokaido area is widely regarded as another high-density megalopolis.

71 Kodansha International, *Japan: Profile of a Nation* (Tokyo: Kodansha International, 1999).

72 For a detailed discussion of Tokaido megalopolis and the influence of Tange's plan on current mega-projects in the Tokyo Bay area, see Zhongjie Lin, "From Megastructure to Megalopolis: Formation and Transformation of Mega-projects in Tokyo Bay," *Journal of Urban Design* 12 (Feb. 2007): 73–92.

73 Not all of these landfills belong to Tokyo. Some were developed by Yokohama, Kanagawa, or Chiba. For a list of these projects and a detailed description of some important projects in Tokyo Bay, see Cybriwsky, 211–224 (see note 5).

74 Kenzo Tange Association, *Kenzo Tange: Forty Years of Urbanism and Architecture* (Tokyo: Process Architecture Publishing Co., 1987), 72–79.

Chapter 4

Structure and symbol

Kenzo Tange's 1960 Plan for Tokyo and the debates around it betray the architect's utopian notions in urban design. Such utopianism grew from his faith in the continuing progress of modern technology and its role in the development of society at large. The dramatic socio-cultural changes in postwar Japan stimulated the architect's techno-utopian ideas, propelling him to pursue a systematic and futuristic approach to urban design that often involved the reorganization of cities on an unprecedented scale. Two important concepts constituted the foundation of Tange's methodology of urban design: *structure* and *symbol*. Elaborated on in several essays, both concepts stemmed from Tange's understanding of the social meanings of modern technology and both significantly influenced his design approaches. Developed in his early urban projects and theoretical explorations, these concepts were synthesized in the Plan for Tokyo and then blossomed in his subsequent architectural and urban design practice. Therefore it is fundamental to examine what structure and symbol stood for in his theory, and how they informed his urban design. Two projects in the 1960s, the Yamanashi Press and Broadcasting Center in Kofu and the Plan for Reconstruction of Skopje, exemplify Tange's concepts of structure and symbol respectively, and reveal his approaches to urban design.

Technology and humanity

Tange's observations of the relationship between modern technology and social progress were reflected in his 1960 Plan for Tokyo, in which he justified his radical proposal with the emerging phenomena of a technological society such as the proliferation of automobiles and rapid progress in communication technologies. Tange believed technology had fundamentally changed urban life and would inevitably influence city form, and architects' design methodology should address this changing relationship. Tange shared these thoughts about technology with Metabolists and Arata Isozaki, but, regarding its potential impact, his ideas were distinguished from both the Metabolists' optimistic utopias and Isozaki's pessimistic view of ruins. Instead of celebrating the great innovations emerging in the twentieth century, Tange was first concerned about the potential destructiveness of unprecedented technological advance. In his presentation at the 1960 World Design Conference in Tokyo, Tange opened with the following comments:

> As we leave the earlier half of the twentieth century and proceed into the second half, I have the feeling that we are experiencing vital changes in cultural forms, in social structure, and in human environment. There is no way to predict the future, but I believe we can say this much: the current great change is resulting from the development of atomic energy and electronics, and the direction of the change is not toward unregulated expansion of energy, but toward the controlling and planning of its development. Mankind is engaged in a second attempt to gain superiority over scientific techniques.[1]

As a person who had witnessed the devastation of atomic bombing and had been involved in rebuilding cities thereafter, Tange was doubtful about the health of a society increasingly dominated by technology. Soon after the end of the Second World War, Tange led a team working on the master plan for Hiroshima's reconstruction, conducting extensive surveys when the entire city was virtually ground zero. The miserable scenes after the nuclear holocaust struck Tange so deeply that when he designed the Hiroshima Peace Memorial Park a few years later, he placed a cenotaph at the center of the park: a piece of debris of a

nzo Tange,
roshima Peace
emorial Park,
55. Cenotaph

neoclassical dome from the city hall destroyed in the bombing. Tange's concern about the destructive aspects of technology resonated with Fumihiko Maki. The younger architect wrote in his *Investigations in Collective Form*: "We frequently confuse the potential that technology offers with a kind of compulsion to 'use it fully.' Technological possibility can be sanguinely useful only when it is a tool of civilized persons. Inhuman use of technological advance is all too frequently our curse."[2]

Japan's remarkable revival after the war, however, showed the architects the constructive side of technology. Technological advances were among the factors that spurred the explosive growth in Japan's postwar economy and restored the country from near annihilation to one of the world's economic powers in just a decade and a half. Japanese cities, stimulated by both economic growth and technological innovations, were resurrected at a surprising pace. By the 1960s, these cities, including Hiroshima, had become bigger and more prosperous than ever before.[3] Witnessing a bombed Hiroshima and its resurrection made Tange aware that technology is a double-edged sword. He noted that technological advance was changing the physical environment and challenging the prevalent design methods. For instance, large-scale constructions like inner-city highways had become dynamic intrusions into human spaces. Such elements, as products of modern technology, were competing with human-scale elements in the city and there was no effective way to unify them. The result was chaotic urban landscapes and declining environmental quality. In the meantime, individual identity continued to be diluted by mass production and mass communication. As products became more universal and anonymous, people too were becoming more alike. The same thing happened to cities as a whole because buildings and urban spaces tended to become homogeneous and gradually lose their identities.

For Tange, the modern city had become a place of great incompatibilities: human scale and megastructural scale, stability and mobility, permanence and transience, identity and universality. They were reflections of the conflict between technology and humanity. A third party had to be introduced to bridge the chasm between technology and humanity in order to create order out of the confusion in the modern city, and, in Tange's view, only human ingenuity could achieve this goal. He noted: "as science becomes social reality, it will doubtless be mankind which decides whether new discoveries are beneficial or harmful to man and whether they are to be accepted or rejected."[4] In particular, Tange stressed the role of architects and designers in this enterprise, because they are "the only people who stand in the middle ground between technology and humanity."[5] Through their thoughtful design and construction, architects could reconcile the discrepancy between the mass-human scale and the scale of man in both functional and visual terms. To do that, however, they must keep up with technological progress because "it is essential that with the advance of science they manifest more and more creativeness."[6] For Tange, the only way to overcome the potential destructive force of modern technology was to be its master. This paradoxical attitude dominated his urban design practice through the 1960s as he tried to incorporate the latest technologies when establishing a new order for the city.

Tange also contended that, to strike a balance between technology and humanity in the design of cities, architects should not look back. His stance regarding the relationship between historical form and technological creativeness was clear. At the 1959 CIAM conference in Otterlo, he rejected Ernesto Rogers' attempt to associate his projects with Japanese traditional forms, and he declared that he did not wish to be as conservative as "Rogers himself in the case of *Torre Velasca*."[7] Tange argued: "Creative work is expressed in our times in a union of technology and humanity. . . . Tradition can, to be sure, participate in a piece of creation, but it can no longer be creative itself."[8] He thus distanced himself from the regionalists and proposed a different strategy of urban design, centered on the concepts of structure and symbol.

Structure and structuring

Tange saw the year 1960 as the dividing point between two epochs, the first from 1920 to 1960 and the second from 1960 onward. Architecture and urbanism in the second epoch are distinguished from those in the first one because of the "large-scale metamorphoses of the modern civilized society" on one hand and the "rapid advancement of modern communication systems" in society on the other.[9] Both factors were related to the progress of information technology and contributed to the emergence of new patterns of urban development. In Tange's opinion, the period prior to 1960 was dominated by a static and deterministic approach in design, which tended to identify each function with a specific space. He claimed that this rationalist methodology was no longer suitable for contemporary cities because of their constant change and rapid growth. He thus advocated the strategy of structuring in urban design.

Although Tange tried to define the concept of structure in several writings and presentations, its actual meaning remained ambiguous. Nor did he articulate how the structuring process would be carried out in design. Historians often linked his concept of structure to megastructure.[10] According to Tange himself, however, structuring is "a process of coupling the functional units," and a basic theme of urban design which "thinks of the spatial organization as a network of communication and as a living body with growth and change."[11] Although this description was still somewhat unclear, Tange's idea of structure, above all, pointed to a kind of dynamic system, rather than a physical form or singular space. This system should link together spaces of different qualities and regulate growth and transformation of the city. Tange went on to argue that people and things were in a state of flow in contemporary society and, as a result, designers should be engaged in the process of giving structure to space which meant "formalizing the communicational activities and flows within spaces."[12] Apparently, the emphasis of "structuring" was placed on the visual representation of these relationships and movements within the system he described.

Elaborating on the concept of structure, Tange cited Norbert Wiener's cybernetic theory, referring to the spatial organization of a city as a network of energy and information.[13] The components in the network follow certain rules and maintain a certain degree of independence and flexibility. The structural approach to design involves circulatory processes of control, feedback, and reaction in the system; it thus distinguishes itself from the traditional functionalist approach in that the former can result in a dynamic relationship between space and function while the latter represents a static relationship. Along with the biomorphic analogies he often invoked to conceptualize his urban design schemes, Tange's employment of cybernetics to describe design methodology manifested his belief that modern science and technology should participate in the development of new languages of architecture and urbanism.

However, Tange failed to consider another important theory of structure from social sciences which might be more relevant to his design method: structuralism. Pioneered by Ferdinand de Saussure in linguistics and Claude Lévi-Strauss in anthropology, the structuralists examined large-scale systems through studies of relations and functions of the smallest constituent elements within the systems.[14] They were concerned with profound structures within the organization more than phenomenal representations or historical evolutions. Their studies analyzed unconscious patterns underlying cultural phenomena and regarded elements in the system as "relational" instead of independent entities. In the post-Second World War era, structuralism gained a wide audience and was applied in various fields. Team 10 architects were among the first to introduce structuralist ideas to studies of architecture and urbanism.[15] These young theorists, led by Aldo van Eyck and Alison and Peter Smithson, were engaged in the search for a relationship between elements in the built environment. Seeking to define their profound organization, they were interested in social structures and mental processes that contributed to the design process. In urbanism, they called for establishing various scales of "human associations," developed from sociological relationships, to replace functional divisions of the *Athens Charter*.[16] Van Eyck later became the leader of Dutch Structuralism in architecture, which also involved Piet Blom and Herman Hertzberger, among other Dutch architects. In 1967, when Alison and Peter Smithson published a collection of their essays on urban theory, they used the title *Urban Structuring*.[17]

Tange became familiar with Team 10 members and their design ideas at the 1959 CIAM meeting in Otterlo, which was organized by Team 10. In fact, his concept of structure demonstrated similarities to the Smithsons' concept of urban structuring. Both opposed functionalism in city planning, both recognized mobility and communication as keys in restructuring the modern city, and both stressed the comprehensibility of organization. Despite their shared idea of urban structuring, Tange and the Smithsons divided on which relationships were intrinsic to the urban system and thus took different approaches to design. The Smithsons' concept of association comprehended the patterns of human society in terms of the particular environment and the "scale of complexity." Instead of the analytical technique characterized by the *Athens Charter*, they based their urban studies on a hierarchy of associations composed of house, street, district, and city. Each would be defined by the characteristic of its respective sub-divisions or "appreciated

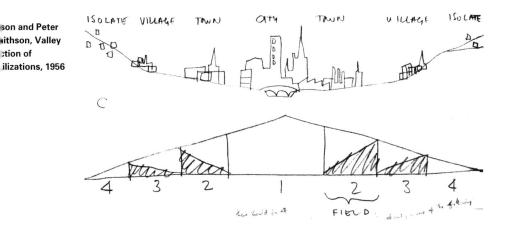

son and Peter
ithson, Valley
ction of
ilizations, 1956

units."[18] A large city could not simply evolve from a small town, and a small town should not copy the pattern of the large city. Each level of association must invent the structure of its subdivision. Leaning on the sociological aspects of the built environment, the Smithsons were concerned with the interrelated issues of density, scale, and identity. In contrast, Tange's study of structure emphasized the visual representation of organization. The formal principle of structure, to him, should be free from the scale and nature of its subject, whether it is a city or a building. He thus looked for a general system that would govern urban constructions on all scales consistently. This notion of scalability informed his design approach, and was manifest in his design of the Yamanashi Press and Broadcasting Center in Kofu. In this project Tange introduced a three-dimensional system, differentiating structural and inhabitable spaces, to serve as a framework for not only the composition of various programmatic components in the complex but for its future growth as well. The same operation could also be applied to urban projects on a larger scale.

Symbol and symbolism

In addition to the city's internal structure, Tange extended his exploration of urban form and urban space to their metaphysical meaning, and called for consideration of symbolism in the design process. He argued that urban spaces should be conceived as communicational fields. Symbolism is significant in urban design because it serves to balance technology and humanity. Tange was struck by the fact that traditional urban spaces, like Italian agoras and forums, were often filled with symbolic meanings and metaphors, and he worried that contemporary design had lost such characteristics. He thus contended: "I venture to say we need a symbolic approach to architecture and urban space in order to secure humanity, human meaning and human value in architecture and urban space." Architects should consider "what is the symbol of the day, where the symbol reveals itself, and how the symbol is created."[19]

Tange first raised the issue of symbolism at the eighth CIAM conference in 1951. The meeting assumed the theme of the "Core of the City," representing a conscious revision of the Functional City principles that had dominated most previous conferences. This theme also expanded CIAM's discourse on urbanism into the domain of sociology and psychology, and responded to problems arising from recent reconstructions of city centers destroyed in wartime bombardments as well as the disintegration of urban life caused by accelerating suburbanization. Echoing Le Corbusier's call for the "moral value" in city building, the discussions involved such issues as monumentality, collective value, symbolic representation, and the relationship between modern architecture and historic artifacts.[20] At the meeting Tange introduced his Hiroshima Peace Memorial Park, which responded in a particular way to the issue of reconstruction of urban core. Moving away from a functionalist planning approach, Tange employed a classical layout and a monumental scale in order to arouse the urban dignity characteristic of traditional city centers. The scheme featured an axial and hierarchical composition of buildings and landscape centered on the cenotaph to create a unique ethos that would inspire the city's reconstruction.

Tange's symbolic attitude was also reflected in his Plan for Tokyo 1960, where it was taken to a greater scale. The spectacular linear spine not only served as a structure to generate the city form, but also provided an unmistakable icon of the postindustrial city characterized by speed and mobility, free communication and continuing growth. Symbolism became a prevailing feature in Tange's 1965 plan for the reconstruction of Skopje. The whole city was to be bound together with the images of "city gate" and "city wall." Through such metaphors of traditional urban elements, Tange hoped to establish a new order for the city destroyed by a severe earthquake. For him, giving symbolic significance to urban structures was useful both in elaborating a design and in making the design more comprehensible to society.

What Tange exactly meant as symbol remained somewhat ambiguous in his writing, but his design projects demonstrated a clear inclination toward the creation of iconographical reference rather than philosophical connotation. It is also evident that Tange's concept of symbol constituted certain continuity with his idea of structure because, for him, organization and representation should be consistent. A city not only needs an articulated structure to regulate the internal spatial relations, but that structure should reflect the city's function, organization, and epoch.

Tange anticipated that the symbolic approach would play a key role in bridging the gap between technology and humanity. He wrote:

> Can modern technology restore humanity? Can civilization find the channel linking itself and a human being? Can modern architecture and urban space be again the place for building up human character? My experiences seem to answer "yes" to these questions. But we can say "yes" only when modern technology has succeeded in creating in a space a symbol of the spirit of the times. And I am also convinced of this possibility.[21]

Apparently Tange was against the notion that a symbol could be attained from traditional architectural language. Rather, he stressed the role of modern technology, which embodied the "spirit of the time."

To some critics, such a notion of symbolism was problematic. A few years later, when Robert Venturi, Denise Scott Brown, and Steven Izenour published their *Learning from Las Vegas*, the authors differentiated two types of symbolism in architecture: one is called the "duck," and the other the "decorated shed."[22] The former refers to the case in which a building becomes a symbol in itself through its formal or spatial features, while the latter refers to a building to which symbolism is applied. Tange's symbolism, presented in his monumental projects, fell in the first category, which Venturi and his coauthors criticized.

The Yamanashi Press and Broadcasting Center

In 1961 when Kenzo Tange was working on the National Olympic Stadium project, he received a commission from the Yamanashi News Group to design a new office building in Kofu. The architect took advantage of this opportunity to test his structuralist idea of the "three-dimensional space network" in architecture, which he had in principle elaborated in the 1960 Plan for Tokyo.[23] Although it is the capital of Yamanashi prefecture, Kofu is a much smaller city than Tokyo, with only around 100,000 residents in 1960. It lies in Japan's mountainous inland area near Mt. Fuji. The proposed building for a 4,000 square-meter site would house the installations of three media firms serving the region: Yamanashi News, Yamanashi Broadcasting Co., and a new printing company. The compositeness of the building program encouraged the concept of a building as a small city, as it comprised a variety of functions, including broadcasting studios, a printing plant, and offices for all three companies. In addition, there would be a cafeteria and shops on the ground level, linking the building to the town. Expecting the growth of these relatively young firms, the architect was also expected to take possible expansion into account. Such expansion would no doubt occur, but it was difficult to foresee how it would occur.

Tange's design strategy involved a two-step operation. First, he sorted the spaces of the three firms by function, such as offices, production areas, and studio spaces, and organized them in program-based units to allow firms to share common facilities. Subdivision of firms was subordinate to the organization of units. Then the architect stacked these units one upon another, so the overall arrangement appeared vertical. This vertical organization was not only a response to the relatively small site, but also the result of respective demands of different units: installations of the printing plant sit on the ground floor, providing direct connections to the street via ramps for convenient loading and transportation; studios are housed in sealed boxes on upper levels so that the environmental interference would be minimized; offices of all three companies are located in the middle of the building, wrapped by balconies to provide optimal natural lighting.

In the second step, all service spaces including elevators, stairs, piping, equipment rooms, and sanitary rooms, were grouped and loaded into

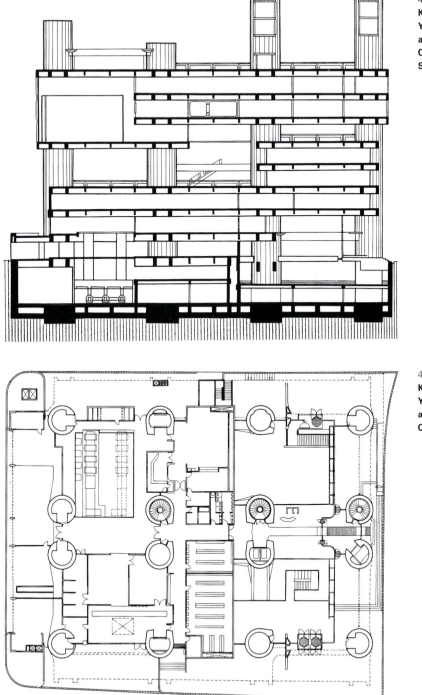

4.3
**Kenzo Tange,
Yamanashi Press
and Broadcasting
Center, 1964.
Section**

4.4
**Kenzo Tange,
Yamanashi Press
and Broadcasting
Center, 1964. Plan**

sixteen reinforced-concrete cylindrical towers with identical diameters of five meters. Serving as the structural framework of the whole building, these towers were arranged on a gridiron plan. Tange then inserted the functional units of studios, offices and workshops onto different levels within this framework. The result is a three-dimensional lattice made up of the vertical cores carrying people, material, energy, and information up and down, and the horizontal containers housing various usable spaces. The containers were conceived as elements independent from the structure, just like drawers in relation to a cabinet, to maintain maximum flexibility in utilization and permutation.

The division between "servant" spaces and "served" spaces inevitably recalled Louis Kahn's design of Richards Medical Research Laboratories.[24] Indeed, the combination of monumental service towers and open floor plans became a popular architectural motif in the 1960s. What distinguished the Yamanashi Press and Broadcasting Center from other Kahn-inspired designs was Tange's conception of the building as a structure fully amenable to change and expansion. Here, the "servant" and "served" spaces were not only distinguished by the roles they played spatially, but also characterized by their different durations according to the Metabolist principle. The sixteen vertical shafts, constituting the structural framework and providing access to every part of the building, were considered permanent constructions, while horizontal inhabitable units should be amendable and open for any given functions. The largest span between the towers was seventeen meters, and the absence of auxiliary supports in between ensured the spatial flexibility of floor plans. Furthermore, the reinforced concrete units did not fill up the three-dimensional lattice. Instead, a few "voids" were left. These open-air spaces provided pedestrian areas on different levels and separated the functional units visually. They were also potential spaces for future expansion. Not only were there spaces for infill, the structure itself could grow too. The sixteen cylindrical towers terminated at different heights in the air, implying the capacity of infinite growth in the vertical dimension.

The same notion of open-endedness was evident on the building façades: horizontal members were clipped on the towers with large beam joints similar to wood structures – but made of concrete. On the periphery of the building, some joints were left deliberately on the towers, implying that more inhabitable containers could be added to the complex and more towers could be constructed based on the pre-established pattern. Tange anticipated that such organic expansion would happen. Once opportunities were provided, the generative system could grow and take over the whole town.

This generative system, articulated with the core and truss combination, evolved from the "pilotis and core" system in the design of the central business axis in the 1960 Plan for Tokyo, which in turn made reference to Isozaki's Joint-Core System. Through this development, Tange continued to refine his design vocabulary, making the form more concise. Persistent was his faith that this structural approach would generate a basic pattern to elicit an orderly growth of the entire city. The architect had made this ambition explicit

4.5
Kenzo Tange,
Yamanashi Press
and Broadcasting
Center, 1964

4.6
Photo taken in the
1970s indicated
infill and
expansion in the
building

when he applied the same principle in the planning of the new headquarters complex of the Dentsu Corporation in the Tsukiji District of Tokyo, a project preceding the Yamanashi Building. The complex was characterized by an enormous space lattice: numerous rectangular cores soaring up and lifting gigantic horizontal trusses of similar formation, interconnecting in the air. These inhabitable trusses extended outward in different directions. Along with multi-level highways underneath, they demonstrated the tendency for growth into the rest of the city. Recalling the design process of this project, Tange later wrote:

> After we had made public our Tokyo Plan 1960, and just as I was hoping for an opportunity to design an office building with a three-dimensional network based on the civic axis set forth for that plan, Mr. Hideo Yoshida, president of Dentsu, the largest advertising company in Japan, commissioned me to design headquarters offices for his firm. . . . I felt that the site, located in the Tsukiji district of Tokyo, along Express Highway No. 1, had been selected with a view to future development. Convinced that Dentsu itself would develop too, I began considering the optimum nature of an enterprise founded on informational services and the influence it would exert on the surroundings. The design I proposed consisted of widely spaced vertical cores connected by means of horizontal spaces free of posts. The design was based on the idea that extending the core system right and left and forward and rearward with these horizontal spaces would enable the building to conform to all kinds of future development. . . . Mr. Yoshida was so happy when he saw the proposal that he began talking of the likelihood of a similar kind of redevelopment for the entire Tsukiji district.[25]

What followed, however, was a quite unexpected reversion. Yoshida passed away when the construction was about to start, and the succeeding president of Dentsu, a pragmatic person, abandoned Tange's plan. He turned to a new scheme which, in Tange's point of view, was "perfectly ordinary."[26] Tange was extremely disappointed by this change and regretted to see that, as Dentsu Corporation continued to grow in the following years, its buildings spread all over the neighborhood but failed to form a coherent complex as he had expected.

Although his Dentsu project was not realized, Tange gained confidence in the "technical feasibility of the three-dimensional network," which he soon applied in the design of the Yamanashi Press and Broadcasting Center.[27] Despite the drastic differences between these two projects in terms of their scales and urban contexts, the architect conceived of their designs in a way similar to the planning of a Metabolist city. He wrote of the Yamanashi project: "The building is at once a single spatial type capable of change and growth, and a space established within a three-dimensional communications grid. This is a proposal for both a single building and for urban design."[28] The capacity for accommodating future growth and change was achieved through the

4.7
**Large beam joi••
clipped on the
towers of the
Yamanashi
building**

differentiation of structural and non-structural elements. The structural elements in the system, comprising sixteen cylindrical towers in the case of the Yamanashi Press and Broadcasting Center, were the "vertical streets" of a city, providing necessary infrastructure for all sorts of developments, and "the horizontal spaces connecting them are like the buildings along streets in a city."[29] Various types of spaces were placed at the spots most suitable for their functions. "The result is that the vertical roads are built, but unoccupied voids remain here and there. These will provide the extra space needed for expansion."[30] Tange compared this three-dimensional urban system to a conventional two-dimensional urban layout: "Some plots of land in a city are vacant; others are scheduled for the expansion of existing buildings. We made it possible for people to have the spaces

zo Tange,
ıanashi Press
Broadcasting
ter, 1964.
et view

they require within a multidimensional composition. . . . Though it seemed incomplete, the building had an organic unity."[31]

Tange was proud to note that the users of the Yamanashi Press and Broadcasting Center "seemed able to employ the building successfully," and that the building started to generate itself.[32] In fact, a few infill constructions were done within the three-dimensional lattice in a few years, and some of the office spaces were expanded. Tange recalled later: "Before a decade had passed, various additions were made in the void spaces without the local people being aware of how. And there is still leeway for further expansion within the composition."[33]

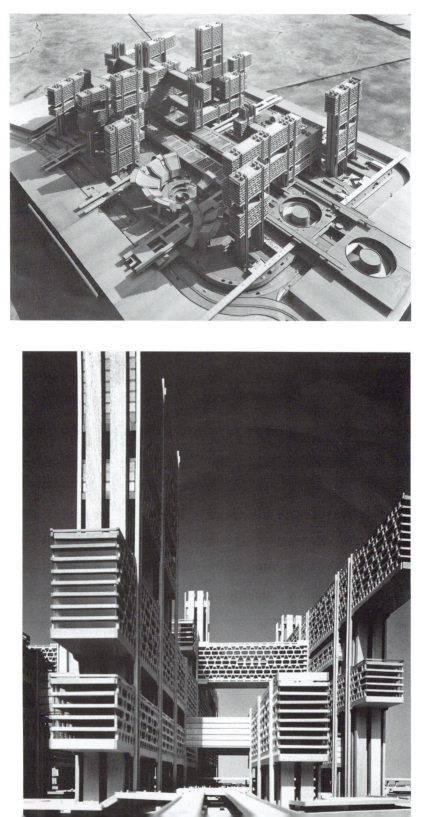

4.9
Kenzo Tange, Tsukiji District Redevelopment Plan, 1963. Model view

4.10
Kenzo Tange, Tsukiji District Redevelopment Plan, 1963. Model detail

Despite these successful infills, the building's three-dimensional lattice did not expand into its urban context as Tange had expected; nor did it catalyze similar megastructural development in the surrounding area. The building stood alone like an alien within Kofu's nearly medieval urban texture dominated by low-rise tile-roof houses. It also seemed unlikely that the towers and containers could continue to expand as they were constructed onsite in

1
nzo Tange,
izuoka Press
d Broadcasting
nter, 1967

conventional reinforced concrete. The result, as Reyner Banham later noted, was "a monolithic statue commemorating an ideal of adaptability that was practically impossible to realize in built fact."[34] Other historians also criticized Tange's emphasis on adaptability and extensibility of physical structure, noting that it would undermine the actual use of the building on human terms as its program was treated as subordinate to such an urban gesture. Paolo Riani wrote in his monograph on Tange: "The possibility of giving form to a particular moment of a process of development is a very enjoyable experience for an architect, but the human element of his architecture may suffer as a result."[35] Banham and Riani's criticism summed up most historians' skepticism about the technical and humanist aspects of Tange's idea.

Despite questions of its feasibility, Tange insisted that the "three-dimensional space network" would create order out of urban chaos, and should become the universal method for urban design, whether the site was located in a big city or small town, in Japan or another country. He continued to experiment with this concept in projects in various geographical and cultural settings. Not long after the completion of the Yamanashi building in 1966, Tange designed a building for another media company, the Shizuoka Press and Broadcasting Center, located at a small street-corner site in Tokyo's bustling Ginza business district. Tange managed to apply the same formal elements as in Kofu, using only one cylindrical shaft. No office space is located on the first and second floor. From the third floor, office spaces in the form of steel-and-glass boxes radiate from the central core. Every three or four floors there is a balcony level separating the office levels, articulating the cantilever structure and making the distinction of structural space and inhabitable space explicit. Similar compositions of the "core and bridge" system were also used in a few projects overseas, including the Plan for Skopje (1965), the plan for a sub-center in Bologna, Italy (1975), and the campus of Nanyang Technological Institute in Singapore (1981).

Reconstruction plan for Skopje

In January 1965, Tange received a telegram from the United Nations asking if he would be interested in participating in an international planning competition for the reconstruction of Skopje, the regional capital of the Yugoslav Republic of Macedonia. A severe earthquake hit the city in July 1963, killing more than 2,000 people and destroying roughly 65 percent of the buildings in the city. Reconstruction following the earthquake was carried out by the Yugoslavian government with support from foreign countries and international organizations. The United Nations set up a special fund for preparing a master plan for the city. The Greek architectural firm Doxiades Associates and Polish architect Adolf Ciborowski drew up a regional plan for Skopje in 1964, but they left its center city – an approximately two-square kilometer area – open, with the intention of undertaking a more detailed study through an international competition.[36] Tange considered this project significant not only for its international influence, but also because it would make "a model case of urban reconstruction," so he accepted the invitation.[37]

The competition involved eight design firms, four of them from Yugoslavia and one each from Holland, Italy, Japan, and the United States.[38] The jury awarded the first prize to Tange and the second prize to Yugoslavian architects Radovan Mischevik and Fedor Wenzler, but proposed that the two winning firms work together to develop a final plan. Therefore a design team was formed, consisting of both Japanese and Yugoslavian architects as well as engineers. Arata Isozaki led the architects' team from Tange's office.[39]

Tange's proposal was based on two metaphorical concepts, the "City Gate" and the "City Wall." They referred to the two major elements of the new city with distinct characters. The City Gate, literally a gate into the city, would be put in the area where a new train station and a gateway structure for highway entries to the city would be built. Similar to the composite transportation center in Le Corbusier's *Ville Contemporaine*, the City Gate was characterized by the convergence of all traffic systems – rail, car, bus, and pedestrian movements – and served as the point of transition between regional traffic and local traffic. The railway terminal was designed as an underground structure. Occupying different levels above it were automobile parking decks, transit terminals, and pedestrian zones.

The transportation center was joined by a central business district, known as the City Gate Center, to form the city's main axis. Along the axis were clusters of buildings including a number of office towers, a library, banks, exhibition halls, cinemas, hotels, shops, and restaurants – all connected to the railway and bus terminals with elevated motorways. In the middle of this stretch was the gigantic gateway structure receiving incoming traffic from regional highways. The axis ended at Republic Square, Skopje's principal civic space on the River Vardar and surrounded by state and municipal facilities. An elevated pedestrian system tied the entire City Gate area together and moved people across the river to the neighborhoods on the other side.

The second element defining new Skopje was the City Wall, which was made up of high-rise apartment slabs. These residential buildings, fifteen or sixteen stories on average including five-story bases, were arranged on the perimeter of the center city. Forming an obtuse angle with the City Gate axis and extending in both directions, the City Wall resembled the ramparts of the medieval walled city to symbolically protect the historic city blocks that had survived the earthquake. By adding the City Wall to his plan, Tange integrated residential use with the city center and lent it architectural significance. The proximity of residential areas to the business district was expected to bring vitality back to the city.

The plan for Skopje demonstrated the remarkable continuity of Tange's approach to city design. The concept of the City Gate was based on a linear axis concentrating all urban functions related to communications and business operations, a fundamental idea in the 1960 Plan for Tokyo. Skopje's linear axis started from its transportation terminal and linked the central business district and civic square that formed the backbone of the city. Like Tange's previous urban projects, the plan for Skopje granted the city's infrastructure

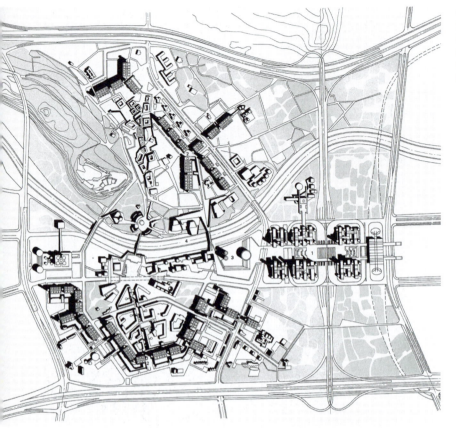

4.12
**Kenzo Tange,
Plan for the
reconstruction of
Skopje, 1965.
Master plan**

monumental scale and sophisticated details, organizing various transportation modes on a three-dimensional system. Following the prototype developed in Kofu, architectures in both the City Gate and the City Wall were characterized by the repetitive pattern combining cylindrical towers housing circulations and services and horizontal inhabitable spaces for residential or business uses. What distinguished the Skopje projects from Tange's earlier schemes, however, lay in the symbolic meaning of the urban structures, which the architect had started to explore in his Tokyo Bay project but had not fully developed until the Skopje project. The entire city was bound together with the symbolic concepts of its "gate" and "wall," serving both as programmatic features and metaphors for the urban form. In fact, these metaphors constituted the springboard for the whole design. Tange recalled:

> We made ample use of this [symbolic] attitude at Skopje. For instance, in applying the name City Gate we not only gave ourselves the hint that we should use something physically gate-like in this area, but we also planted in the mind of the people the understanding that this

3
nzo Tange, Plan for the
construction of Skopje,
65. "City Gate"

4
nzo Tange,
n for the
construction
Skopje, 1965.
ity Wall"

is the gate through which one enters the city of Skopje. If the design is false to the name, the citizens will reject it.

The City Wall, too, gained fame, and even though at one point the opinion emerged that perhaps the Wall was an obstacle that we should abandon, the people of the city were opposed to doing away with it. They understand the city wall, and it became the center of our image of what symbolizes the city. Now we are told that we definitely should not abandon the Wall. We learned through experience that it is necessary for a variety of symbolic processes to emerge during the operation of structuring.[40]

Tange contended that, through the metaphors of a city with traditional constituents, his plan conveyed meaning beyond the level of physical form and enabled communication with residents and visitors in order to recover the vitality and humanism of the city.

Tange's symbolic return to the classical vocabulary of urban form recaptured some characteristics of Louis Kahn's 1961 plan for Center City Philadelphia. Kahn called his project "Viaduct Architecture."[41] The plan developed from his studies of traffic patterns and earlier projects for Philadelphia, and it envisioned that the whole city would be surrounded by a multilevel highway loop (the "viaduct"). The concept of viaduct reflected an abstract mastery of Roman forms, as Kahn wrote: "This architecture of movement may be compared to the Viaduct architecture of Rome which was of a scale and consistency different from the architects of other useful buildings."[42] The viaducts in his plan for Philadelphia, carrying high-speed automobile traffic, defined the boundary of the modern city while allowing unencumbered connection between areas on both sides of the boundary. Several gigantic parking towers standing beside the viaducts served as gateways to the city. Kahn believed that the city would flourish with the viaducts serving automotive traffic and protecting downtown from the invasion of incoming traffic flows. Like Kahn, Tange used the metaphors of classical form to reinterpret modern infrastructure, providing those large-scale constructions with legibility and cultural significance.

Transitions in Tange's attitudes toward historical context and locality can be detected between his two monumental plans: the 1960 Plan for Tokyo and the 1965 Plan for Skopje. The Tokyo project was dominated by a strong forward-looking aspiration. Tange criticized the city's existing organization as a "closed structure" which belonged to a "medieval town," obsolete and dysfunctional for a city of Tokyo's magnitude.[43] In Skopje, the architect turned to the construction of a "City Gate" and a "City Wall," seeking to recover the meaning of a traditional town. The urban scene in Skopje after the violent earthquake could not be less chaotic than the urban scene in Tokyo in 1960. However, instead of rebuilding the city, Tange tried to preserve the remaining structures in Skopje and used the City Wall to frame the historic areas. He also treated the city's geographical characteristics in a delicate manner.

In fact, the competition jury applauded Tange's scheme for its successful "incorporation of Kale Hill into the composition of the center" and the "integration of the left and right banks of the Vardar [River] by their development with public buildings, shops, bridges, and pedestrian squares and platforms."[44] Tange's transition to a more sophisticated approach to history and local conditions could be justified by the fact that the Skopje plan was proposed for actual implementation, rather than being a theoretical project like the Tokyo Bay Plan. It was also certain, however, that by turning to historical metaphor and localism, Tange demonstrated his awareness of the cultural implication of urban structures and attempted to expand his language of urban design through employment of metaphorical and symbolic elements.

In Tange's vision, Skopje remained a planned city under an architect's complete control. He later recalled that, when working on the Skopje project, he had to make a decision between two approaches to formulating the building guidelines. The first approach would "lean strongly in the direction of allowing the city to grow and alter in a dynamic and recurrent pattern;" the planner's responsibility would mainly involve "establishing space usage and wall lines that guarantee open spaces and flow," leaving other things for free construction and urban growth. With the second approach, "an ultimate form for the whole is designed on a virtually constitutional basis and all development is made to agree with this form;" this method would "make it possible to produce a total image."[45] Tange chose the second approach because he felt that the Skopje project was less about stimulating the growth and redevelopment of a living city than it was about establishing a total image around which a devastated city could be resurrected.

Political factors in Skopje also influenced Tange's decision. The architect later wrote: "Yugoslavia is a Socialist country in which land is not privately held, the city government had sufficient power to make it possible to introduce our total plan."[46] He believed public land ownership was on his side in realizing his grand plan. Tange's comment to a certain extent echoed Le Corbusier's admiration of the authority of the Soviet Union in the interwar period, to which he dedicated his *Ville radieuse*.[47] In Japan, dispersed private land ownership made it difficult to carry out large-scale urban redevelopments within

15
Louis I. Kahn,
Viaduct
Architecture, 1962.
Sketch

4.16
**The revised desig
of the "City Wall"
in a later phase o
planning**

existing political parameters. Tange's and the Metabolists' urban projects thus remained theoretical speculations. Just as Le Corbusier had turned to Soviet Russia, Tange found Skopje a promising land to realize the ideas of a total plan that he had put forward in theoretical proposals for Tokyo.

Tange's concepts of City Gate and City Wall persisted in all three phases of planning – the master plan, the development plan, and the detail plan. Constructions also proceeded according to his choice of the second approach to "produce a total image." Tange noted that the urban planning authority of Skopje required architects of individual buildings to abide by the master plan and the building guidelines "even in matters of detail where it is unnecessary to require them to do so."[48] The outcome of implementation, however, did not live up to Tange's expectations, despite the effort of the authorities. His spectacular vision, when turned into concrete construction, suffered from various compromises. There were numerous modifications in the design and construction process due to technical and financial constraints. Furthermore, the buildings were designed by various architects with different understandings of the master plan. According to Ian Davis, although the City Wall was built up, buildings forming the "wall" lacked a coherent architectural expression. The "wall" was also "breached" by a few tower-shaped structures in various locations.[49] The "city gate," on the other hand, was simply too grandiose to be realized, and the axis has never come into being. The only major structure erected somewhat to the master plan's specification was the transportation center, which happened to be the only building designed by Tange. This gigantic building included a railway station with a vast elevated platform fifteen meters above the ground. Underneath was a bus station. It became a landmark of the new Skopje, but it was often criticized for being too grand for a relatively modest city of only 430,000 residents.[50]

Nevertheless, Tange's plan played an important role in guiding the process of Skopje's reconstruction, which was a remarkable success in terms of its efficiency and international cooperation. The city soon regained its vitality and enjoyed an economic boom. Under the guidelines framed by the planning team, the new buildings tended to be "progressive" in design style, a tone set by Tange's response to the demand of "a new architecture for a new revolutionary society."[51]

Tange's techno-utopia

The Yamanashi Press and Broadcasting Center and the Plan for Reconstruction of Skopje exemplified Tange's urban design concepts developed in the 1960s: structure and symbol. The Yamanashi project provided a model of his three-dimensional generative planning system made up of a matrix of structural shafts and horizontal infill units. Applying it to an individual building project, Tange anticipated that this generative system could expand into the whole city based on the predetermined pattern. Unlimited growth and expansion was guaranteed by the progress of technology and the desire of spatial flexibility in contemporary urban development. In Skopje, although the distinction of structural elements and inhabitable spaces remained the theme of the megastructural project, the architect shifted the emphasis to the symbolic representation of the "city gate" and the "city wall." These concepts above all conveyed a sense of containment and consolidation, and reflected Tange's thinking about humanity, a domain that he wished to preserve in order to protect people physically and psychologically from both natural forces and negative effects of technology.

From the somewhat contradictory concepts of structure and symbol, it is evident that Tange tried to strike a balance between technology and humanity in order to formulate a design paradigm for the postindustrial city. Unlike traditionalists who tended to copy pre-industrial urban forms and spaces, Tange believed that a new urban order could only be achieved with up-to-date technologies. Thus he claimed: "Order is not something we are given; it is something we must create."[52] Meanwhile, moving away from the young Metabolists' unflinching faith in technological and social progress, Tange contended that technology was not the aim in itself and its force had to be controlled and channeled to human benefit. This sophisticated idea led to his technocratic notion that contemporary society must be extensively planned in order to reconcile technology and humanity.

Tange claimed: "Architects and urban designers are men who have the responsibility of creating the channel between the physical environment and the metaphysical world, of building a bridge between technology and humanity, and of restoring human significance to man's environment."[53] His belief that an architect was the natural mediator between a passive humanity and potentially disruptive technology inevitably cast him in this role. Tange's architecture reached out to both sides of social values: authority and freedom, organization and individuality, planning and spontaneity. He held tenaciously to the belief that reconciling these contradictions was imperative, thus his urban projects tended to combine a Cartesian order with a representation of contingency.

Tange was not alone with such technocratic notions among architects in the 1950s and 1960s, when large-scale urban intervention was the norm. Architectural critic Terence Farrel commented, "the way in which Kenzo Tange has reconciled the individual role of the architect with the needs of society is typical of him and our society."[54] In particular, Le Corbiusier's faith in technocracy and authoritarianism, along with his sociological naïvety, had profoundly influenced Tange's work. Both architects believed that the acceptance of responsibility for the future presupposed total planning, which was inconceivable without a vision of what the future might look like.

Hajime Yatsuka traced the origin of both Le Corbusier and Tange's technocracy to the ideology of constructivism of the twentieth century. By constructivism, he not only referred to the Russian avant-garde artistic and architectural movement in the 1920s, but also the socio-economic thoughts of constructivism. He cited the definition by Friedrich Hayek, an economist and Nobel Prize laureate, that constructivism was the technocrats' belief in the capacity to control the total economy of a country.[55] Such a notion was evident in Russian constructivist architects' utopian projects for socialist cities and Le Corbusier's Radiant City designed for a syndicalist society.[56] The same techno-utopian notion persisted in Tange's urban projects through the 1960s. The architect believed rational planning would control undesired urban sprawl, bring order to city landscapes, and protect human beings from natural disasters like earthquakes as well as technological catastrophes like atomic bombings. His works summoned up an uncommon scale of design and entailed nothing less than a total redefinition of society. The synthesis of high technology and symbolic expression that Tange advocated became a recurrent slogan in architectural debates in the 1960s. His urban projects, characterized by open form and a systematic approach, explored new dimensions in both buildable form and utopian ideas, and constituted his central contribution to these debates.

Notes

1 Kenzo Tange, "Technology and Humanity," *Japan Architect* (Oct. 1960): 11–12.
2 Fumihiko Maki, *Investigations in Collective Form* (St. Louis, MO: Washington University, 1964), 9.
3 The population of Hiroshima returned to the prewar level in 1955. Isozaki wrote in 1966: "Take Hiroshima as an example. It was virtually completely annihilated. But not long after the atom bomb, its urban entities began to reemerge. Today it is a bigger city than ever before." Arata Isozaki, "Invisible City," in Joan Ockman, ed., *Architecture Culture, 1943–1968: A Documentary Anthology* (New York: Rizzoli, 1993), 403.
4 Kenzo Tange, "Technology and Humanity," *Japan Architect* (Oct. 1960): 11–12.
5 Ibid.

6   Ibid.
7   Oscar Newman, *New Frontiers in Architecture: CIAM'59 in Otterlo* (New York: Universal Books, 1961), 172.
8   Ibid.
9   Kenzo Tange, "Function, Structure and Symbol," in Udo Kultermann, ed., *Kenzo Tange 1946–1969: Architecture and Urban Design* (Artemis Zurich: Verlag für Architektur, 1970), 240.
10 Reyner Banham, *Megastructure: Urban Future of the Recent Past* (New York: Harper & Row, 1976).
11 Kenzo Tange, "Function, Structure and Symbol," in Udo Kultermann, ed., *Kenzo Tange 1946–1969: Architecture and Urban Design* (Artemis Zurich: Verlag für Architektur, 1970), 241.
12 Ibid, 242.
13 Ibid, 241. Wiener's pioneering writings on the cybernetic environment were based on his research on feedback-based weaponry during the Second World War, and was first published in 1948. Norbert Wiener, *Cybernetics: Or Control and Communication in the Animal and the Machine* (New York, Wiley, 1948).
14 Ferdinand de Saussure, *Course in General Linguistics*, trans. Wade Baskin (New York: Philosophical Library, 1959). Claude Lévi-Strauss, *Structural Anthropology*, trans. Claire Jacobson and Brooke Grundfest Schoepf (New York: Basic Books, 1963).
15 In the United States, structuralism also influenced Christopher Alexander in his studies of "pattern language" in architecture and urban design. Christopher Alexander et al., *A Pattern Language: Towns, Buildings, Construction* (New York: Oxford University Press, 1977), and Christopher Alexander, *The Timeless Way of Building* (New York: Oxford University Press, 1979). For a historical investigation on structuralism in architecture, see Alan Colquhoun, "Postmodernism and Structuralism: A Retrospective Glance," in Alan Colquhoun, *Modernity and the Classical Tradition, Architectural Essays 1980–1987* (Cambridge, MA: MIT Press, 1989), 243–255.
16 For details for Team 10's urban theory, see Alison Smithson, ed., *Team 10 Premier* (Cambridge, MA: MIT Press, 1968).
17 Alison and Peter Smithson, *Urban Structuring: Studies of Alison and Peter Smithson* (New York: Reinhold Publishing Corporation, 1967).
18 The Smithsons criticized modernist cities: "The planning technique of the *Charte d'Athene* was an analysis of functions. Although this made it possible to think clearly about the mechanical disorders of towns it proved inadequate in practice because it was too diagrammatic a concept." The Smithsons' ideas of the hierarchy of human association and its relationship to environment were influenced by Patrick Geddes. They appropriated Geddes's Valley Section diagram to illuminate the structures of human agglomeration with different density and in different settings. Ibid, 18–20.
19 Kenzo Tange, "Function, Structure and Symbol," in Udo Kultermann, ed., *Kenzo Tange 1946–1969: Architecture and Urban Design* (Artemis Zurich: Verlag für Architektur, 1970), 243.
20 Le Corbusier wrote: "The spirit which prevails in the oldest part of the city is built up over the years; ordinary buildings acquire an everlasting significance insomuch as they come to symbolize collective consciousness; they provide the skeleton of a tradition, which without attempting to limit future progress, nevertheless conditions and forms individuals in much the same way as do climate, country, race or custom. Such cities, and especially historic town centers, are nations unto themselves, there is a sense of moral value that holds a meaning and to which they are indivisibly linked." Le Corbusier, *The Athens Charter* (1933), trans. Anthony Eardley (New York: Grossman Publisher, 1973), 28. For discussion about the CIAM VIII and Tange's design of Hiroshima Peace Memorial Park, see David B. Stewart, *The Making of a Modern Japanese Architecture: 1968 to the Present* (Tokyo: Kodansha International, 1987), 173–175.
21 Kenzo Tange, "Technology and Humanity," *Japan Architect* (Oct. 1960): 11–12.
22 Robert Venturi, Denise Scott Brown, and Steven Izenour, *Learning from Las Vegas: The Forgotten Symbolism of Architectural Form* (Cambridge, MA: MIT Press, 1972).
23 Kenzo Tange, "From Architecture to Urban Design," in *Japan Architect* (May 1967): 25; and Kenzo Tange, "Recollections, Architect Kenzo Tange, no.7," in *Japan Architect* 8510 (Oct. 1985): 6.
24 Kahn talked about this design at the 1959 CIAM meeting in Otterlo: "Every space must have its own definition for what it does, and from that will grow the exterior, the interior, the feeling of

spaces, the feeling of arrival. The serving areas of a space and the spaces which are served are two different things. It is very likely that a plan starts this way." Louis I. Kahn, "New Frontiers in Architecture: CIAM in Otterlo 1959: Talk at the conclusion of the Otterlo Congress," in Alessandra Latour, ed., *Louis I. Kahn: Writings, Lectures, Interviews* (New York: Rizzoli, 1991), 89.

25   Kenzo Tange, "Recollections: Architect Kenzo Tange, no. 7," in *Japan Architect* 8510 (Oct. 1985): 6.

26   Ibid.

27   Ibid.

28   Kenzo Tange, "Function, Structure, and Symbol," in Udo Kultermann, ed., *Kenzo Tange 1946–1969: Architecture and Urban Design* (Artemis Zurich: Verlag für Architektur, 1970), 243.

29   Kenzo Tange, "Recollections, Architect Kenzo Tange, no.7," *Japan Architect* 8510 (Oct. 1985): 6.

30   Kenzo Tange, "From Architecture to Urban Design," *Japan Architect* (May, 1967): 26.

31   Kenzo Tange, "Function, Structure, and Symbol," in Udo Kultermann, ed., *Kenzo Tange 1946–1969: Architecture and Urban Design* (Artemis Zurich: Verlag für Architektur, 1970), 243.

32   Kenzo Tange, "Recollections, Architect Kenzo Tange, no.7," *Japan Architect* 8510 (Oct. 1985): 7.

33   Ibid.

34   Reyner Banham, *Megastructure: Urban Futures of the Recent Past* (New York: Harper & Row, 1976), 55.

35   Paolo Riani, *Kenzo Tange* (London: Hamlyn, 1969), 46.

36   Earnest Weissman, head of Social Affairs for the United Nations, took charge of the planning committee supervising Skopje's reconstruction. Weissman was a student of Le Corbusier and had visited Japan several times for surveys of the reconstruction of Japanese cities. Kenzo Tange, "Recollections: Architect Kenzo Tange, no.6," *Japan Architect* (Sept. 1985): 15. Ciborowski had been in charge of the reconstruction of Warsaw after the Second World War. Ian Davis, "Skopje Rebuilt: Reconstruction following the 1963 Earthquake," in *Architectural Design* 45 (Nov. 1975): 660.

37   Kenzo Tange, "From Architecture to Urban Design," *Japan Architect* (May 1967): 26.

38   The architects were Kenzo Tange (Japan), Van den Broek and Bakema (Holland), Luigi Piccinato (Italy), Maurice Rotival (USA), Aleksandar Dordevik (Yugoslavia), Eduard Ravnikar (Yugoslavia), Radovan Mischevik and Fedor Wenzler (Yugoslavia), and Slavko Brezorski (Yugoslavia). Davis, 660–663 (see note 36).

39   The other architects from Tange's office included Sadao Watanabe and Yoshio Taniguchi.

40   Kenzo Tange, "From Architecture to Urban Design," *Japan Architect* (May 1967): 27.

41   The term "Viaduct Architecture" came from his 1960 essay "Form and Design." He concluded the essay with his unified vision of the city: "The motor car has completely upset the form of the city. I feel that the time has come to make the distinction between the viaduct architecture of the car and the architecture of man's activities. . . . The viaduct architecture includes the street which in the center of the city wants to be a building. . . . The distinction between the two architectures, the architecture of viaduct and the architecture of man's activities, could bring about a logic of growth and a sound positioning of enterprise." Louis I. Kahn, "Form and Design," in Alessandra Latour, ed., *Louis I. Kahn: Writings, Lectures, Interviews* (New York: Rizzoli, 1991), 115–116.

42   Ibid.

43   Kenzo Tange, *A Plan for Tokyo, 1960: Toward a Structural Reorganization* (Tokyo: Shikenchikusha, 1961), 12.

44   "International Competitions, 1965," *UIA: revue de l'Union international des architects* 37 (Feb. 1966): 9–30.

45   Kenzo Tange, "Past Lineage and Future Vector of Urban Design at the Tange Studio," in *Japan Architect* (Sep. 1971): 45.

46   Ibid.

47   On the dedication page of *Ville radieuse*, Le Corbusier wrote: "To Authority." Le Corbusier, *The Radiant City: Elements of a Doctrine of Urbanism to be Used as the Basis of our Machine-age Civilization, 1933* (New York: Orion Press, 1967).

48   Kenzo Tange, "Past Lineage and Future Vector of Urban Design at the Tange Studio," in *Japan Architect* (Sep. 1971): 45.

49 Ian Davis, "Skopje Rebuilt: Reconstruction following the 1963 Earthquake," *Architectural Design* 45 (Nov. 1975): 660–663. Davis's article provides a historical account of Skopje's post-earthquake reconstruction up to 1975.

50 Ibid. The projected population of Skopje in the 1965 reconstruction plan was 310,000. Statistics of 1975 indicated that 430,000 people lived in the city.

51 Ibid.

52 Kenzo Tange, "Aestheticism and Vitalism," *Japan Architect* (Oct. 1960): 8–10.

53 Kenzo Tange, "Function, Structure and Symbol," in Udo Kultermann, ed., *Kenzo Tange 1946–1969: Architecture and Urban Design* (Artemis Zurich: Verlag für Architektur, 1970), 245.

54 Paolo Riani cited Terence Farrel in the RIBA Journal (February, 1969). Paolo Riani, *Kenzo Tange* (London: Hamlyn, 1969), 40.

55 Hajime Yatsuka, "The 1960 Tokyo Bay Project of Kenzo Tange," Arie Graafland and Deborah Hauptmann, eds., *Cities in Transition* (Rotterdam: 010 Publishers, 2001), 179–180.

56 For Le Corbusier's Radiant City as expression of Syndicalism, see Robert Fishman, *Urban Utopias in the Twentieth Century: Ebenezer Howard, Frank Lloyd Wright, Le Corbusier* (Cambridge, MA: MIT Press, 1982).

Chapter 5

Expo '70

As spectacular as Kenzo Tange's Tokyo Bay project was, it was never realized; it remained a scheme on paper and a much-published model. In Skopje, although his ambitious plan had a significant impact on the initial stages of the city's reconstruction, delineating a powerful vision for the city's resurgence after the devastating earthquake in 1963, Tange was forced to withdraw from the commission in 1967. Apparently such a large-scale international urban redevelopment project was not beyond the influence of politics, and he gradually lost control of the project. Tange had to be content with realizing his mega-structural ideas in individual building projects such as the Yamanashi Press and Broadcasting Center and the Shizuoka Press and Broadcasting Center. It was not until the end of the 1960s that a unique opportunity emerged for him to implement his urban concepts on a greater scale: Tange was named master planner for the 1970 World Exposition in Osaka, a position responsible for coordinating all construction involved with the event. This commission confirmed his status as Japan's "national architect," a reputation already earned for monopolizing the country's most high-profile projects, including Hiroshima Peace Memorial Park, Tokyo City Hall and the Tokyo Olympic Stadium. More importantly the exposition allowed him to explore the urban form of the future with the structuralist approach that he had developed in his earlier works.

In fact, Expo '70 turned out to be an unprecedented opportunity not only for Tange but for all of the Metabolist architects. Under Tange's direction, they built a number of impressive pavilions and fantastic objects, using them to test their radical ideas about architecture and city design. Expo '70 thus pushed the Metabolist movement to its climax. The event was dominated by the Metabolists' iconic forms of megastructure and capsule, and brought great international visibility to their work. However, the crisis of techno-utopia also became evident in this grand show. The social ideals that had been associated with the Metabolists' urban schemes fell through, giving way to a commercialism that took complete control of the event. Technology, originally intended as an essential means to stimulate social change, turned out to be no more than an instrument of exhibitionism and objects of popular entertainment. In this sense, Expo '70 was the swansong of the Metabolists' heroic urban speculations. It also signified the conclusion of utopianism in city building in the wake of the "shocking economic depression, cultural crisis, and the decline of the symbolic realm" that swept the world in the early 1970s.[1]

The Japanese Miracle and the development of Metabolism

The 1970 World Exposition in Osaka was one of the largest and best-attended world's fairs in history. It was another significant event following the successful Tokyo Olympic Games in 1964. The country's dramatic economic surge after the Second World War played an important role in bringing such events to Japan, and, in turn, the international exposure created by the Olympics and the World's Fair allowed Japan to showcase its achievements in technology, helped boost its export-oriented economy, and promoted innovative ideas of architecture and city building.

Under the leadership of Prime Minister Hayato Ikeda, the Japanese government launched an ambitious "Income-doubling Plan" in 1961. Spurred by the government's strong pro-industry policies, Japan entered a period of record economic growth later known as the Japanese Miracle, maintaining an annual double-digit increase of Gross National Product (GNP) for over a decade. In addition to motivating individual spending and providing low-interest loans to economic sectors designed for growth, the Ikeda cabinet drastically expanded the country's investment in infrastructure: highways, high-speed railways, subways, airports, port facilities, and dams. In the meantime, the country as a whole was effectively organized to support an export economy. The Ministry of International Trade and Industry (MITI) coordinated a variety of economic sectors to facilitate their development and guarantee their reciprocal support.[2] One distinctive characteristic of Japan's economy during this period was the formation of *keiretsu*, coalitions of manufacturers, suppliers, distributors, and banks that held common interests and shareholdings.[3] Keiretsu allocated resources efficiently and streamlined the processes of financing, procurement, production, and distribution, making associated companies more competitive in the international market. These coalitions enjoyed close relationships with government bureaucrats, who promoted the creation of robust trade corporations that could withstand intensified trade competitions in the world. MITI formalized cooperation between the Japanese government and the private sectors, and also coordinated industries, including the emerging keiretsu, to reach national production goals and protect private economic interests.

Stimulated by the government's growth-first policies, the Japanese economy expanded steadily. Its GNP rose by 420 percent from 1960 to 1970. At the beginning of the 1960s, Japanese domestic product was worth a little more than half of the prosperous European countries like West Germany and Britain, and a mere 7.7 percent of the United States' economy. By 1970, however, Japan had overtaken all European economies, and represented over

20 percent of the United States' GNP.[4] The rapid growth brought an unpre-cedented boom in economic and cultural life, and led to the first "golden age" in Japan's postwar architecture. As Botond Bognar put it, the 1960s witnessed "the most interesting, most dynamic, and fastest-developing period in the history of Japanese architecture."[5] He continued:

> In the course of approximately ten years Japan overwhelmingly scraped away the damage inflicted by the war to become the world's third industrial power. . . . With almost unlimited industrial and financial investment, many new technologies were experimented with and numerous large-scale projects and complex were built – and most of them with various megastructures; without such industrial and financial back-up none of this would have been possible. The process was pervaded by the keen and receptive spirit of testing and applying everything new, a spirit that – beside the respect for tradition – has always characterized the Japanese.[6]

It was no surprise that Japan was accordingly optimistic about economic and social progress as well as the power of modern technology.

In this atmosphere of progress and affluence Metabolists found more opportunities to carry out their radical design concepts. Their utopian ideas, however, underwent subtle yet definitive changes in this economic and social climate. Early Metabolist projects had been presented as idealistic plans with strong social agendas. Based on concepts of artificial land and megastructure and intended for drastic reorganization of high-density urban areas, these projects sought to overthrow rigid laws governing land division and property ownership in Japanese cities. They offered new types of physical and social environments from which a new model of communal society would emerge and thrive. As they developed, however, the revolutionary concepts of urban form and building systems were divorced from their initial social intent. With this transition, Metabolists found their novel design ideas suited for the prevalent faith in technology and industrial power, and the appetite for new technology in the society in turn justified the Metabolist schemes. Just as Wilhelm Klauser observed, "it was indeed technology – and directly associated with it, industry – that lent these projects a convincing quality of realism which subsequently and with increasing clarity became the motive force behind the architecture of Metabolism."[7] Technology became both the means and the end, and the spirit of the age was right for it. By employing and showcasing the most up-to-date technologies in their projects, architects were assured of public attention and fame.

The mania for technology, among other characteristics of Metabolist projects, was manifested by an overwhelming use of megastructural form. One project indicating this trend is Kikutake's Miyakonojo Civic Center (1966), erected in a quiet medium-sized town. This 1,400-seat performing arts center is a gigantic fan-shaped building with radial steel frames. Its massive asymmetrical form and

onori Kikutake,
akonojo Civic
ter, 1966

5.2
Kisho Kurokawa,
Cannery of Nitto
Food Company,
1964

huge steel structural members clearly pronounced itself as a product of modern technology and industrial production. Besides megastructure, Metabolists extensively employed the technologies of prefabrication in their projects. Such designs reflected industrial aesthetic and often pursued structural flexibility based on interchangeable components. Typical of this aesthetic was the work of Kurokawa. Kurokawa was particularly fascinated by the idea of capsule architecture, which he regarded as fitting perfectly with the spirit of Metabolism. Kurokawa left Tange's studio in 1962 to set up his own practice. He started out with a few small commissions, applying the concept of capsules in these buildings. One example was Odakyu Drive-in, a small roadside restaurant in Hakone, a famous resort area in Kanagawa Prefecture. The architect placed the box-shaped restaurant within an independent steel-tube space frame. Its overwhelming structure was further emphasized by the frame's joints, which were conspicuously exposed to suggest further extension and easy disassembly. The project's small size made this solution appear quite forceful; it nevertheless became the forerunner of more genuine capsule projects he was to design at the Osaka Expo. Another early building by Kurokawa, the Cannery of Nitto Food Company, was also based on his concept of module construction and an aesthetic of incompleteness. Built from a prefabricated steel tube structure, the factory consisted of eight identical square units of production space. These units were supported by large steel composite columns designed as nodes to connect the modules. Steel panel beams extended from column heads on the periphery of the building, suggesting the possibility of adding more modules to the composition.

Yamagata Hawaii Dreamland, a resort center in an inland city, was another miniature megastructure by Kurokawa. The design concept evolved from the architect's theoretical project Metamorphosis (1965), which envisioned an organic city consisting of a number of interlocking loops, each forming a self-contained urban quarter. When the city expanded, it would grow simply by adding more loops, mimicking the duplication of cells. As a result, the city would stretch out in a natural linear pattern distinct from both the radial form of most existing cities and the rigid linear configuration of the earlier mega-forms like Tange's Tokyo Bay project. Metamorphosis confirmed Kurokawa's commitment

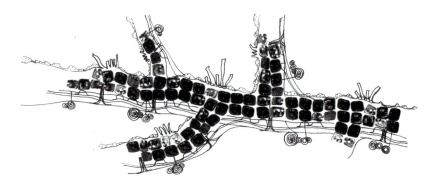

5.3
**Kisho Kurokawa
Metamorphosis
1965. Diagram**

5.4
Kisho Kurokawa, Yamagata Hawaii Dreamland, 1967. Model showing the architect's concept of its future expansion

ho Kurokawa,
nagata Hawaii
amland, 1967

to the "architecture of life."[8] The loop was first employed in a master plan for Hishino New Town in Aichi, which was organized into three loop-shaped residential districts with civic and commercial facilities located along their interfaces. In Yamagata, Kurokawa built only one loop, although he was expecting the resort center to expand in the future, at which time more loops would be added. Forming the loop was a two-story building that housed a hotel and restaurants, with a large swimming pool at the center. Between the building and the pool were a few concrete towers of different heights providing circulation and services for the complex. Comparing these towers to Kikutake's cylindrical megastructure in the Ocean City project, Reyner Banham ridiculed Kurokawa's building: "Ocean City was among the Metabolist visions that achieved built form at a drastically reduced scale and in mild travesty as leisure installations – here, a swimming pool."[9]

      Increasingly preoccupied with technological languages in design and less concerned with their social implications, Metabolists began a honeymoon with the country's leading industrialists, whose rapidly growing economic power made them potential clients of large-scale architectural and urban design projects. For instance, Tange was often invited to seminars sponsored by industrial organizations, such as the Industrial Planning Committee that was responsible for a number of reclamation projects in Tokyo Bay.[10] He also maintained a close relationship with the media and advertising industries and received commissions from both national leaders like the Dentsu Corporation and local companies such as Yamanashi News Group and Shizuoka News Group. Young Metabolists also turned to industrialists to realize their design concepts. Since 1961, Kurokawa, Kikutake, and Otaka had served as architectural advisors to the Nippon Prefabrication Corporation, a consortium of leading construction firms devoted to the development of mass housing.[11] It was with

5.6
**Kiyonori Kikutake
Pear City, 1965.
Model view**

this collaboration that Kurokawa developed his concepts of prefabricated housing. One of his early projects was an apartment building composed of prefabricated concrete module units. It appeared to be a premonition of his capsule buildings a few years later. The emerging keiretsu also became outstanding clients for Japan's avant-garde architects. In 1965, Tokyu Group, a large private railway corporation in Tokyo responsible for a number of ambitious real estate developments, hired Kikutake to produce a master plan for the area along the company's new Denen Toshi rail line. The company anticipated that the area could house a population of around 400,000. Kikutake's plan, known as the Pear City, proposed a linear strip of infrastructure, public service, and greenery to link a series of new towns. Town centers would be located adjacent to railway stations, and feature an extraordinary composition of business skyscrapers, housing slabs, and commercial complexes. Although this spectacular plan was not realized, it demonstrated the promising liaison between the ambitious Metabolist architects and rising industrial elites in reshaping the urban landscape. It was thus not a surprise that Tange and the Metabolists would fully embrace industry and technology at Expo '70.

Nishiyama's Conceptual Plan

The Osaka Expo provided Tange and the Metabolists with an opportunity to apply their urban concepts systematically in the building of a "city." World's fairs had long served as laboratories of new technologies and novel design ideas. Some of the great expositions had kindled creative energies that significantly impacted world architecture and city planning, prominently among them the first World Exposition in London in 1851, the World's Columbian Exposition in Chicago in 1893, and more recently, the 1967 World Exposition in Montreal. Tange and the Metabolists realized the opportunity the 1970 Osaka Expo could offer them: they could apply their urban concepts to the creation of the Expo ground, which might potentially become the core of a new city. Expecting 400,000 visitors daily, the Osaka Expo consisted of a variety of urban components including exhibition pavilions, dining areas, accommodations, commercial facilities, and transportation. Because of its temporary nature – the exposition would last six months, from March 14 to September 13; after that most of the structures would be torn down – it also seemed to comply with the Metabolist notion of the city as an ever-changing entity.

Osaka was the first city in Asia to host a world's fair. Japan had wanted to host an exposition in Tokyo in 1940 to celebrate the 2600th anniversary of the Tenno imperial regime, with a theme called the "Fusion of the Eastern and Western Cultures." This exposition was scheduled along with a proposed Olympic Games in the same year.[12] Though the outbreak of the Pacific War prevented both events from taking place, Tokyo did eventually host the Olympic Games in 1964, which became a milestone in Japan's postwar history. The Olympics not only boosted the country's economy, signaling its recovery after the war, but also substantially improved urban conditions in Tokyo. Public facilities and new infrastructures were built to support this event, including several thoroughfares, parks, and the first section of the Shinkansen express train system between Tokyo and Osaka. With his design of the Tokyo Olympic Stadium, Tange established himself not only as the "national architect" but also the "West's favorite Japanese architect."[13] He ingeniously incorporated the image of a traditional Japanese roof into gigantic suspended structures on the buildings, making a powerful assertion of Japanese identity.[14] The success of the Tokyo Olympics helped Osaka win its bid to host the 1970 World Expo. For governments and industries in Osaka and cities around it, the exposition was expected to promote the entire Kansai region internationally and boost its economic and cultural development, just as the Olympics had done for Tokyo.[15]

In September 1965, a planning committee for Osaka Expo was formed, including Tange and Uzo Nishiyama among its sixteen committee members.[16] Prior to that, Nishiyama had led a Kyoto University team to conduct primary studies for the event, investigating expositions in history and exploring potential sites in Osaka. The team submitted a report to the planning committee in February 1966. When it was time to appoint a chief planner for the Expo, the committee members found themselves in a dilemma. The municipal government of Osaka nominated Nishiyama because he represented architects and designers of the Kansai region. The industrialists and bankers, who were major sponsors of the event, preferred Tange on the basis of his success in such projects as the Hiroshima Peace Memorial Park, the Tokyo Bay Plan, and the Tokyo Olympic Stadium.

Tange and Nishiyama represented different types of architects in postwar Japan. Their ideologies differed more than their design approaches: Tange was the champion of technocrats, whose projects expressed the ambition of Japan's rising elite and big corporations; Nishiyama, a Marxist, was known for his studies of worker housing in Japan, and his work embodied strong social concerns for the low-income classes. The competition between Tange and Nishiyama could be traced back to the 1942 design competition for the Greater East Asia Co-Prosperity Sphere Memorial, to which both had submitted entries. The program of this competition was apparently reactionist in nature, but save only a rare occasion during the war, Nishiyama remained a consistent leftist. He often criticized the government's policies for neglecting the needs of the working class, and he was skeptical of Tange's grand projects. To counter Tange's 1960 Plan for Tokyo, he proposed a Plan for Kyoto in 1964 with the assistance of his students at the Kyoto University.

Nishiyama's Plan for Kyoto integrated two key planning concepts that he had developed in the postwar decades, namely "image planning" and "home city." He used image planning to advocate a comprehensive approach to city design. According to him, image planning was "the planning of an existing vast object that continues to develop an environment, or we could also call it the surface of the earth, that is an entire body, in opposition to the separate designing of the minute tools, equipment, and architecture that make up everyday life."[17] He claimed that planners should not deal with models of individual "parts;"

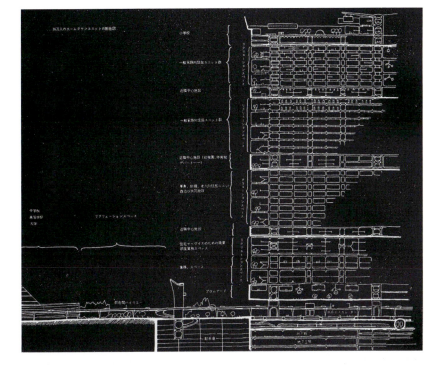

rather, the central concern was the design of "structures containing all these elements in a whole," which provided a synthesized "future image" as a spatial plan to guide the process of urban transformation.[18] The concept of image planning indicated his interest in super-scale integrated environments similar to the megastructures that Metabolists proposed. Unlike the Metabolists, who used megastructures to replace the existing urban patterns of industrial cities, Nishiyama took on the challenge of providing an "image" for Kyoto, the ancient capital with a tremendously rich cultural heritage which people had managed to save from destruction during the Second World War.

Nishiyama had no interest in designing a separate, new city to decentralize Kyoto. He contended: "In Japan, it is impossible to set an old city apart to preserve it and build a separate new city, as is done in Europe."[19] Instead, he tried to consolidate the core of the city and incorporate the beauty of the historic city in its transformation to a modern city. Thus came his concept of *iepolis*, or "Home City," introduced as a critique of American-style suburbanization centered on the automobile.[20] He explained with a metaphor:

> It is an old custom in Japan to take off shoes before entering a house. . . . The indoor life without footwear has its own atmosphere. Likewise, a Japanese city should be considered as a "home" or a "building" which people enter, taking off their shoes, named motorcars. A promise must be made not to let motorcars enter a "home."

. . . In the "home," there are to be built high-speed transportation facilities which correspond to elevators and escalators.[21]

To Nishiyama, cars should be left outside the Home City; people should be able to walk or use mass transportation. Therefore, *iepolis* would become a city for high-density living supported by public transit, pedestrian systems, and mechanized systems like elevators, escalators, and moving walkways. This concept echoed the call for a "Core of the City" voiced at the eighth CIAM Congress, which had advocated the revitalization of traditional urban forms and highlighted the civic functions of a city. To a certain extent, Nishiyama's proposal resembled Kahn's plan for Philadelphia in that both architects valued a traditional city center and tried to keep automobiles from disrupting it. Kahn's plan was characterized by a series of gigantic cylindrical parking towers arranged along the periphery of the city to control incoming traffic. Nishiyama proposed intervention on an even greater scale.

Nishiyama's Plan for Kyoto mainly consisted of a belt-shaped megastructure five street blocks wide and thirteen kilometers long, running parallel to Kyoto's north-south axis and flanked by several primary historic sites including the Imperial Palace, Nijo Castle, and Nishi Honganji Temple. The entire belt would sit on an enormous "artificial land" elevated above the ground, divided into five linear sections of equal width. The central band was reserved for a pedestrian street, open spaces, and low-rise commercial buildings. On either side there were two strips of high-rise residential buildings, all 100 meters high and arranged in a checkerboard pattern. Each building was conceived as a self-contained neighborhood and occupied an entire block. Every few stories in the building there would be a public level, or so-called "Neighboring Space." A primary school and a garden would be located on the rooftop. Skyways, containing a few residential units, connected residential buildings in the air. Highways and monorails would run right beside the artificial land, linking the new linear district to national expressways and railways on either end of it. The space under the artificial land but above the street grid would be used for parking; so would the underground levels.

Nishiyama's ambitious plan resembled Tange's Plan for Tokyo in several aspects, most obviously in its linear urban form. Nishiyama introduced the thirteen-kilometer linear megastructure to guide Kyoto's future development in a similar way as Tange's thirty-kilometer central spine that provided a vision for Tokyo's growth. Both planners rejected the cities' medieval patterns and existing planning perimeters, and they called for a radical reorganization. Nowhere in his essay for the Plan for Kyoto did Nishiyama mention Tange's project, but its influence was evident. However, a few significant characteristics in Nishiyama's linear form indicated fundamental distinctions of his concept of a modern city from Tange's idea. While Tange's spine was intended to decentralize Tokyo's business and administrative functions away from the city and to direct activities of urbanization to Tokyo Bay, Nishiyama embedded his megastructure in the historic center of Kyoto and anticipated the consolidation and growth of the urban

core. Tange's linear form was characterized by a futuristic highway system, celebrating the age of the automobile. Nishiyama was in favor of mass transit systems like monorail, and prohibited automobiles along the linear city. Finally, in Tange's Plan for Tokyo, the central spine was reserved for the city's "brain" and "nerves," that is, the business functions and transportation which constituted the essence of a modern city; the residential activities were regarded as secondary and located along roads branching off from the center. In contrast, Nishiyama placed great importance on residential uses, putting them in imposing high-rise buildings along the central axis. Emphasis was also placed on open spaces in his Plan for Kyoto; they provided connections to the historic city. In particular, the architect designated several blocks on the axis adjacent to the Imperial Palace of Kyoto as a people's square for uses like mass gatherings or everyday entertainments. The square not only tied the new district to the historic city, but it was also a political gesture: democracy could develop in a setting that welcomed open expression and assembly. The hierarchy of urban functions and arrangement of urban spaces in Tange's and Nishiyama's respective plans indicated their different social ideas: Nishiyama's populist project represented an alternative to Tange's technocratic Tokyo Bay Plan.

The two rivals competed again for the planning of the Osaka Expo. The decision involved complex political battles and, in the end, the planning committee compromised by appointing both Nishiyama and Tange as chief planners of the Expo, but dividing their duties. Nishiyama was responsible for the first stage of the project to create a conceptual plan of the Expo site, and Tange was in charge of the second stage to produce a final layout for the facilities. Although the planning whirl seemed to proceed smoothly, the tension between the two architects made it an uneasy collaboration for both sides. As Nishiyama admitted later, he seldom talked to Tange although they met on several occasions.[22]

Nishiyama's conceptual plan for the Osaka Expo extended his vision of urban core as encapsulated in the Plan for Kyoto. He conceived of the Expo site in northern Osaka not as a temporary site for a six-month event, but as a "model core of the future city."[23] His plan thus focused on establishing an infrastructure system that would allow the "city" to continue to grow even after the Expo. This system would integrate human mobility, information flow, public services, and open spaces in a central core. Nishiyama called it *konbinato,* a transliteration of "kombinat" in Russian, meaning combination or union.[24] The idea of creating such a system took shape in his first draft of the conceptual plan as the "Symbol Zone," a rectangular area at the center of the Expo site. The zone intersected with regional expressways, serving as a hub to receive visitors and distribute them to different zones of the Expo campus through various means of mass transportation. Nishiyama continued to develop details of this concept in the following phases. The third draft of his plan indicated a large parking deck on the lower level of the Symbol Zone to contain incoming automobiles, an idea similar to his Plan for Kyoto.

The primary component in the Symbol Zone was a plaza for 150,000 people, which Nishiyama called *Omatsuri hiroba* or Festival Plaza. Noting that the theme of this exposition was "Progress and Harmony for Mankind," Nishiyama argued that the event should be a grand gathering of people from all over the world. He thus suggested including a collective space for events, featuring folk

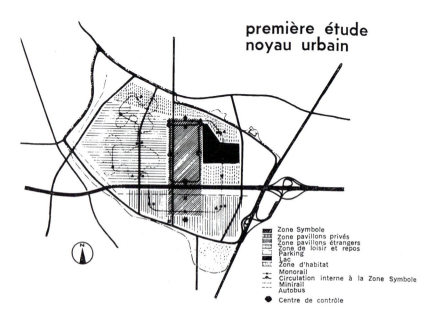

première étude noyau urbain

Zone Symbole
Zone pavillons privés
Zone pavillons étrangers
Zone de loisir et repos
Parking
Lac
Zone d'habitat
Monorail
Circulation interne à la Zone Symbole
Minirail
Autobus
Centre de contrôle

5.9
Uzo Nishiyama, conceptual plan for the Osaka Expo, 1966. The first-phase plan, showing Festival Plaza at the cent

Nishiyama,
ceptual plan
the Osaka
o, 1966. The
d-phase plan,
wing Festival
za at the center

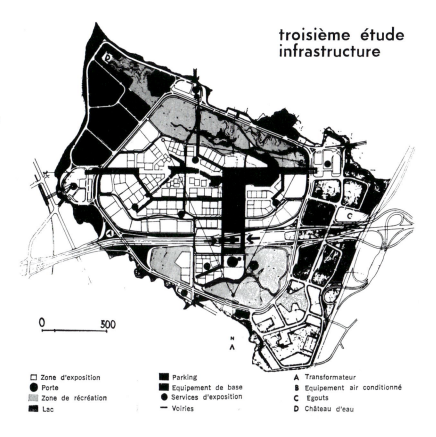

troisième étude
infrastructure

0   500

N
∧

☐ Zone d'exposition   ■ Parking   A Transformateur
● Porte   ■ Equipement de base   B Equipement air conditionné
▨ Zone de récréation   ● Services d'exposition   C Egouts
▨ Lac   — Voiries   D Château d'eau

arts and performances that would involve visitors just like traditional festival parades in Japanese cities. The Festival Plaza concept confirmed his populist notions of the city and indicated his intentions to downplay the commercialism of the exposition and to make it as a culture-oriented event. When the Expo ended, the Festival Plaza would function as the core of the new city that would grow around the Expo site.

Arata Isozaki acknowledged that the idea of the Festival Plaza constituted Nishiyama's most important contribution to the planning of Expo '70. Initially Isozaki was unimpressed by the name "Festival Plaza," calling it a "cheesy term one would even hesitate to pronounce."[25] He also argued that "festival" and "plaza" were urban elements belonging to different cultures: while the plaza was completely a Western concept, the festival was itself and alone the most elaborate and conscious generator of urban events in the cultural context of Japan. In the study "Japanese Urban Space," Isozaki contended that Japanese cities did not have plazas; rather virtual and temporal urban elements like symbols and events helped turn utilitarian spaces such as streets and temple precincts into temporary public spaces.[26] In Nishiyama's proposal, the Western concept of plaza and the Japanese concept of festival were combined to delineate the core of Expo '70 as a model for the future city. It surprised Isozaki that the term "Festival Plaza" turned out to be a "hit" of the event, and since 1970, many Japanese expositions have adopted the *Omatsuri hiroba* as their core element.[27]

In spite of his contribution to the Expo, Nishiyama's progressive political stance and polemical personality often left him unappreciated in the planning committee. He even questioned charging an entry fee to the Expo, arguing that people should have free access since it was a public event.[28] Such socialist notions put him at odds with the industrialists and bankers sponsoring the Expo. As the planning of the Expo entered its later phases, Nishiyama withdrew from the project. Tange and his team revised the master plan and took control of the design and construction of the pavilions. The Metabolist architects were brought in to design the facilities, featuring megastructures and high-tech buildings. The competition between Nishiyama and Tange offered a prelude to the larger battle between utopianism and commercialism at the Expo, which in turn reflected the changing social climate in Japanese society as the 1970s began. The outcomes of these architectural and ideological debates indicated that, with the shift of socio-cultural context, progressive utopian ideas found no place either at the Expo or in Japanese society at large. This trend was manifest in Tange's and the Metabolists' designs.

The plan and pavilions

Expo '70 set a grand stage for the Metabolists. In addition to his post as the chief planner, Tange designed the main pavilion called the Festival Plaza. Kurokawa, Kawazoe, and Maki designed the experimental capsules installed in the roof over the plaza. Kikutake was the architect of the Expo Tower; Otaka designed the main gate; Kurokawa designed two of the most eye-catching pavilions, Takara Beautilion and Toshiba IHI Pavilion; and Isozaki created the giant robots on the Festival Plaza. Moreover, Sumitomo Pavilion was designed by Sachio Otani, Tange's colleague at the University of Tokyo who had also been influenced by Metabolism. Ten years after the founding of Metabolism, these architects gathered again to show the world Japan's creative energy. As the Osaka Expo opened, articles about its master plan and the pavilions appeared in leading architectural journals throughout the world, and many journals covered the event with an entire issue.[29] These articles brought tremendous international visibility to the Metabolists' works.

The master plan for the 330-hectare site completed under Tange's supervision demonstrated the structuralist approach to planning that the architect had developed in the plans for Tokyo and Skopje. It provided a basic structure and allowed individual constructions to happen in an autonomous manner. The infrastructure and main facilities of the Expo were organized around a linear axis known as the Symbol Zone. Running north-south across the entire site, the Symbol Zone consisted of two sections connected by the Main Gate plaza. The northern part of Symbol Zone included the Festival Plaza, the Museum of Fine Arts, and a Japanese Garden in the north end. The southern part extended to the Expo Club and terminated at Kikutake's Expo Tower and the South Gate.

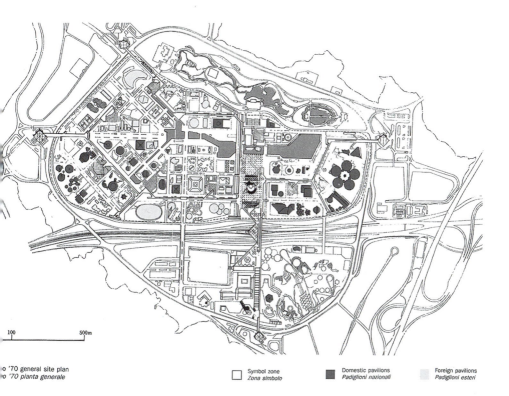

o '70 general site plan
o '70 pianta generale

☐ Symbol zone
Zona simbolo

■ Domestic pavilions
Padiglioni nazionali

Foreign pavilions
Padiglioni esteri

zo Tange,
ka Expo, 1970.
ster plan

The entire zone was bound together with spacious promenades and moving walkways, forming the spine of the Expo city. Reiterating Nishiyama's concept of an urban core, which had been included in the official document of Osaka Expo, Tange claimed that this spine would become the heart of a future city that would eventually grow from the Expo site. He articulated this vision at an interview with Kawazoe:

> I imagine that the trunk elements can remain and that a new city can grow up in the areas where the pavilions now stand. When this happens, what is now the Expo site will become either the heart of a city with a population of 500 thousand or will become that city in its entirety. Some of the factors contributing to the future usefulness of the site are its proximity to Osaka, Kyoto, and Kobe; its direct connections with the express highway running from Tokyo to Kobe, and its position as the starting point of the new *Chugoku* through highway.[30]

To Tange, the northern section of the Symbol Zone, an area about 1,000 meters long and 150 meters wide also known as the Trunk Facility, would serve as the "trunk" of the whole Expo site, which he conceived of as a "tree." He elaborated on this organic analogy:

The trunk facilities organize the entire grounds in the master plan. If we compare them to a tree, the Symbol Zone, located in the center of the grounds, is the trunk. The moving walkways, leading in four directions from the Symbol Zone, and the service areas, or Sub-plaza, at the end of each walkway, can be compared to branches and leaves; and the pavilions grouped around the seven Sub-plazas, to the individual and colorful flowers blooming on the tree.[31]

This made clear Tange's Metabolist strategy in planning. The trunk and the branches set a basic pattern and provided a structure of growth for a "city with a daytime population of 400,000." From the trunk, the circulation system branched out in different directions with escalators, moving walkways, and monorail lines connecting individual pavilions to the trunk. With this structure fixed, a variety of pavilions should be able to "grow" freely and provide sufficient room for individual creativity. In fact, there was hardly any restriction on building design. Even the height control of 100 meters was in the end ignored by architects designing the pavilions, such as the Soviet Union Pavilion. The result was a great variety of structures and forms that Tange described as "colorful flowers."

The layout of Osaka Expo bore similarities to the pattern of Tange's Plan for Tokyo. They both featured a linear axis that accommodated the

5.12
Osaka Expo '70
Aerial photo

circulation spine and the public urban components. Where there had been the "gate" to Tokyo Bay City – the port – there was the main entrance to the Expo. Residential blocks spreading randomly in Tokyo Bay were replaced by a variety of national and corporate pavilions on the Expo site. Monorail lines and moving walkways connecting the Trunk Facility to individual pavilions at the Expo played the same role as the freeways that linked the central spine to residential blocks in the Tokyo Bay Plan. In both cases, all the elements were organized in a hierarchical manner, and both layouts testified Tange's faith that centralized power could foster individual freedom and creativity.

The focal point of the entire Expo site was the Festival Plaza designed by Tange and his associates Isozaki and Koji Kamiya. Reflecting the theme "Progress and Harmony for Mankind," it served as the main space for exhibitions or major events for up to 30,000 people. Tange echoed Nishiyama's original idea about the plaza in his statement:

> The Expo must be more than a display of past traditional achievements and present technological progress of the people of the world. It must also be a festival where human beings can meet, shake hands, and accord minds. Furthermore, the entire exposition ground must be a plaza contributing to the development of this festival of human harmony.[32]

To build such a place for mass gatherings and great events, Tange employed one of the most recent technologies: the space frame construction. An engineering marvel of the twentieth century introduced to architecture by Buckminster Fuller, the space frame and its structural potential were well explored by German-born American architect Konrad Wachsmann, who invented a system using prefabricated elements for large-span buildings like aircraft hangers. The tetrahedral frame and universal joint details of the hanger that Wachsmann designed for the US Air Force circulated widely and inspired many avant-garde architects including the Metabolists. In 1958 Wachsmann offered a two-week seminar at Tokyo Institute of Technology, which informed the Japanese architects of the recent development of space frame structure.[33] The seminar was organized by Takashi Asada, and among the participants were Isozaki and Keiichiro Mogi, both from Tange's laboratory. Tange used a steel space frame structure in the design of a stupendous roof over the Festival Plaza. This roof measured 290 meters long and 110 meters wide, and was lifted 38 meters above the ground by four gigantic posts also built as space frame structures. With the long span of nearly 300 meters, the roof was hailed as the largest single structure in the world. It could alone shelter exhibits and activities of an international exposition. And, theoretically, the structure was capable of infinite extension to cover an even larger area, making possible a miniature city under a single roof.

For visionary architects, the space frame's capacity of expansion, usage of a modular system, utmost flexibility, and openness to programs made it a perfect tool for creating a universal environment. French architect Yona

Friedman and his *Groupe d'Etudes d'Architecture Mobile* (GEAM) developed a number of schemes called *La ville spatiale* (the Spatial City) in the 1960s, presented as collages showing endless space frame structures floating over European cities or landscapes.[34] These Spatial Cities provided enormous space frameworks, within which inhabitants could build homes according to their needs

5.13
Kenzo Tange, Festival Plaza, 1970. Gigantic ▮ built of space- frame structure▮

5.14
Kenzo Tange, Festival Plaza, 1970. Model

5.15
Yona Friedman▮ Spatial structur▮ above the Sein▮ 1959. Montage

and ideas. Tange's giant roof for Osaka Expo appeared to be a realized version of Friedman's Spatial City. The roof not only sheltered exhibitions and ceremonies on the Festival Plaza, but also had a number of capsules installed within its space frame. Tange must have been fascinated by the space frame structure not only for its capacity of constructing large space, but also for its universal adaptability and infinite extendibility, qualities in accordance with the primary concept of the Festival Plaza – an open and universal space for the gathering of people from throughout the world.

The exhibitions at the Festival Plaza were organized in three sections: Past, Present, and Future. The space under the plaza level housed exhibitions of past civilizations. The plaza level, dedicated to the present and becoming the site of various ceremonies, was dominated by a gigantic sculpture named "Tower of the Sun," a creation of artist Taro Okamoto.[35] The tower took the form of a tapering white column with outstretching arms, adorned by two faces at its midpoint, white and black, front and back, with a golden, concave face at its top. Over seventy meters tall, the sculpture pierced through Tange's mega-roof and became the symbol of the entire site. On the plaza there were also a few large electronic devices operated by robots. These robots, designed by Isozaki, were cybernetically controlled by means of human feedback, showcasing the technology of creating and manipulating spaces based on human activities. The Future section was hung high above in the space frame, only accessible through ramps and escalators within the Tower of the Sun. Visitors could walk through a number of capsules installed within the space frame, suggesting environments of a future aerial city. These capsules were designed by several young architects of Tange's choice, including both Metabolists and Western avant-gardes like Archigram, Hans Hollein, Yona Friedman, Giancarlo de Carlo, and Aleksei

6
ho Kurokawa,
psule at Osaka
oo, 1970

Gutnof. Kurokawa and Kamiya designed a few "Capsules for living;" Archigram presented a "Dissolving City;" and Giancarlo de Carlo created a "City of Participation."[36]

The capsule was the theme of many pavilions in the Osaka Expo, an influence attributable to the 1967 World Exposition in Montreal. The most memorable architectural work in this exposition was Moshe Safdie's experimental collective housing project Habitat '67. This building, stacking numerous prefabricated concrete boxes one upon another to form an extraordinary "hill town," explored the future form of housing. A more substantial idea of capsule architecture, however, came from Archigram. Since its emergence in 1961, this British avant-garde group had developed the design concept of capsule in several projects, drawing inspiration from various areas such as space travel, minimal living, and atypical materials. In particular, Peter Cook's 1964 project "Plug-in City" envisioned mass-prefabricated capsules for dwelling and office clipped on a vast diagonal space frame to form a whole city. Futuristic schemes like this, celebrating flexibility, expandability, and mobility, became enormously influential in the 1960s.

One of the structures that confirmed Archigram's influence at Osaka Expo was the Expo Tower designed by Kikutake. It stood at the south end of the Symbol Zone's main axis and offered views of the entire Expo city. Visitors could ascend in two high-speed lifts that took them to capsules and overlook platforms on different levels. The architect was apparently inspired by Peter Cook's unbuilt project of Montreal Tower submitted to the 1967 World Exposition. Like Montreal Tower, Kikutake's design consisted of a tower-shaped megastructure with a number of capsules attached to the main structure. The capsules on both towers took the form of geodesic spheres, an invention of

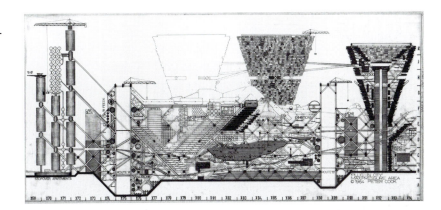

Buckminister Fuller in the late 1940s that had become well known when Fuller used it to build the US Pavilion at Expo '67. While Cook's main structure was a solid tower with Brutalist imprint, Kikutake's tower was a space-frame structure composed of steel pipe struts and cast steel ball joints. This design made the Osaka tower appear lighter and suggestive of the capacity for future extension.

5.20
Kisho Kurokawa, Toshiba IHI Pavilion, 1970

It was Kurokawa who made the capsule his iconic form at the Osaka Expo. In addition to one of the capsule houses suspended over Festival Plaza, Kurokawa designed two corporate pavilions, Toshiba IHI Pavilion and Takara Beautilion. Both of them were based on three-dimensional frameworks used as open structures to organize capsule units. Sponsored jointly by an electrical and a heavy industrial company, Toshiba IHI Pavilion featured a 500-seat dome theatre clad with orange steel panels. The theatre was lifted above ground by an expressive space-frame structure consisting of six giant columns and a gigantic canopy built of 1,500 black metal tetrapods. Underneath the theatre was a reception hall. A 50-meter tower, assembled using the same tetra-pieces, stood on the main approach to the theatre. The other pavilion Takara Beautilion was one of the most successful technological fantasies at the Osaka Expo. It was characterized by a three-dimensional framework

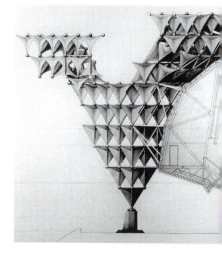

5.21
Kisho Kurokawa, Toshiba IHI Pavilion, 1970. Detail of structure

22
sho Kurokawa,
kara Beautilion,
70

23
isho Kurokawa,
akara Beautilion,
970. Interior

made up of steel pipes that stretched out in all directions. A number of cubic capsules clad with stainless steel, housing displays of the company's beauty products, were installed in the framework with connectors. In both pavilions, the frameworks terminated at opened joints, giving the buildings unusual silhouettes and strongly suggesting incompleteness and expandability. Kurokawa extensively employed the technology of prefabrication, allowing instant assembly of the structure and installation of capsules. In fact, Takara Beautilion was put together on site in only six days. The pavilions could also be dismantled with ease and transported elsewhere for reconstruction.

Kurokawa continued to develop his capsule architecture after the Expo. The Nakagin Capsule Tower, built in 1972, gave this concept its most pronounced form and became arguably the most notable building of the Metabolist movement. The concept of capsule substantiated Metabolism's original idea of distinguishing interchangeable elements from permanent structure. It was also emblematic of Metabolism's somewhat naïve faith in technology in changing the urban formation as well as social structure. The fast-developing and by then readily available industrial technology of prefabrication and standardization seemed to offer a direction for contemporary architecture and urbanism. In reality, however, just like Tange's Yamanashi Press and Broadcasting Center and Safdie's Habitat '67, the Metabolist concept of capsule never became a successful model for the mass-production of living or work spaces. The individual designs built turned out to be heavy, inflexible, and over-deterministic with regard to the megastructure. Overemphasized industrialization made them yield to a culture of consumerism.

Toward an architecture of consumerism

The 1970 Osaka Expo was by many standards a significant event. It drew an astonishing 64 million visitors in just six months, more than double the number expected. The largest single-day population reached 800,000.[37] The Expo boosted Japan's export-oriented industry and gave a final spur to the nation's decade-long double-digit economic growth. It also brought Japanese vanguard architects unprecedented opportunities to test their design concepts, resulting in a number of magnificent structures. Despite these impressive achievements, Osaka Expo failed to make a more lasting impact on modern architecture. The entire site turned out to be a gigantic pleasure machine that left no room for noble ideas. As Wilhelm Klauser criticized, it was not the architecture that afforded a glimpse of this city of the future, but the overwhelming commercial success of this undertaking.[38]

The Expo adopted the theoretical theme of "Progress and Harmony for Mankind," and the pavilions proclaimed similar slogans. However, critics argued that, in regard to architectural forms, its pavilions and facilities bore no relation to the stated themes.[39] Instead of a cultural gathering centered on humanity, the exposition was a chaotic competition driven by national pride and commercial interests. J. M. Richards, then editor of *Architectural Review*, saw in this exposition "the ambiguity of purpose between trade promotion and cultural exposition, ambiguity of design-objective between the serious contribution to architecture and display technique and the attention-catching gimmick."[40] To him, the entire Expo exhibited more of the character of a funfair than serious architectures. The rivalry between individual pavilions had smothered the atmosphere of "harmony for mankind," as the exposition represented little more than a collection of buildings, "each trying to shout louder than its neighbor."[41] Disappointed by what he had observed, Richards boldly declared that the Osaka Expo should be the world's last Expo, because it did not achieve its goal: to be a prototype of the future city and of techniques – of transportation, crowd control and overall landscape design – that could make modern cities more civilized.[42] Instead of showing a vision for the city and human life, the Expo brought a deep feeling of "disillusion."

Beneath the slogan calling for harmonies were the real objectives of the exposition as a whole: stimulating economic growth, elevation of the spirit of nationalism, and promotion of the Kyoto–Osaka–Kobe region. The contradiction between the official slogan and the actual agenda generated feelings of "falsehood, emptiness, and sham" despite all sorts of decorations.[43] This was most evident in the buildings representing commerce and industry. Many of these structures were designed as three-dimensional advertisements erected solely for commercial concerns. The pavilions explored the extent of technology, but their designs were often unrelated to the industries they represented. The purpose, as Klauser noted, was simply "to lend industry a progressive image – an image that in practice was less a vision of the architecture of the future than an amateurish depiction of it."[44] In the end, the lasting impression of the exposition was that of huge masses of people moving about an enormous futuristic stage set, which Klauser called a new "Potemkin city."[45] Architecture that engaged in plotting the vision of a future city became redundant. By succumbing to politics and industrial interests, architecture lost its autonomy and strength and was turned into an object of commercial fantasy.

The Metabolists' works at this Expo were no exception. Although the architects aspired to create a model city devoted to the future age, using a systems approach and prefabrication technology to shape a coherent environment, their ideas could not help but be overwhelmed by the tide of consumerism. In the end, realizing the impossibility of their idealistic attempts, they embraced the commercial culture and adapted their architecture to this irresistible trend to generate a new vitality.[46] The Osaka Expo was thus characterized by the contradictions between idealism and consumerism, between social agendas and commercial propagandas, and between the search for an eternal order and the pursuit of material goods and entertainment. Common in the idealism and the consumerism was an optimistic attitude to technology. The architects believed technology would propel the human society's advance. They were enthusiastic in applying the most up-to-date techniques and materials in their designs without questioning their viability or social meaning. Employment of advanced techniques gave buildings a futuristic look and made a strong impression on visitors to the Expo, which served the industries' desire to advertise. In many cases, the buildings themselves were intended as displays.

The ambivalent role of technology at the Osaka Expo was manifest in Tange's great roof for the Festival Plaza. This structure was to become a final reflection of Metabolism's idealism. With a stupendous space frame covering the entire plaza, it was in every way a magnificent object displaying the power of modernity. The monumental scale and Platonic geometry indicated the architect's ambition of creating a total environment and an emphasis on the symbolic dimension of technology as a universal language. However, it also betrayed the dilemma of architects confronted with commercialist culture. The megastructure appeared to be detached from the programs and activities that took place on the plaza. People were more or less indifferent to its design. Rather, attention was on the variety of entertainments offered in this setting: performances, robots, and futurist capsules. The plaza turned out to be a shelter of pop culture, like Cedric Price's Fun Palace, rather than a noble gathering place for people from throughout the world, as Tange initially suggested it would be.[47] It was telling that after the conclusion of the Expo Tange himself insisted on tearing down this mega-roof, despite popular proposals for making it a permanent structure.[48]

The decline of utopia

The Osaka Expo represented the culmination of the Metabolists' urban utopias. It surpassed all their previous attempts in building a comprehensive environment, although the Expo city only existed for six months. A notion of the progress of modernity virtually dominated its planning and architecture. The introduction of a variety of advanced technologies, such as moving walkways, capsules, architectural lighting, and large-span structures, together with the exhibition of great scientific discoveries and technological innovations, created a totally futurist world.[49]

Paradoxically, instead of calling it a triumph of the Metabolists' long-time pursuit of an ideal city, the Expo represented the bankruptcy of their utopian projects. Immediately after this spectacular festival of modern technology and design, the crisis of architecture was pervasive as the social relevance of megastructure continued to erode. With the rise of postmodernism and its reappraisal of modern assumptions about culture, identity, and history, heroic social ambition no longer had a place in Metabolist designs. Hajime Yatsuka observed:

> The breakdown of Modernism in the Osaka World's Fair seemed to mark the arrival of a new era. But was it really something new in the progressive sense, as was then assumed, or was it not only the appearance of an old problem which had hitherto been ignored? One possible reading is this: just as the technologically oriented rationality of Metabolism failed to achieve a true public realm, so the grandiose void of the festival plaza revealed the limitations of Tange's symbolism and the bankruptcy of his aspiration not only to be an architect but also a leader of the people.[50]

Takabumi Sasaki, a contributor to *Japan Architect* magazine, held a similar opinion. Instead of seeing the Expo as simply a funfair, he criticized the atmosphere, saying it had been "removed from that of the world of humanity, suggesting Dys-topia."[51] He worried that this dystopia, with a sense of reality, "has already come into concrete being."[52] Within about six months, most of the buildings and facilities on the Expo ground were torn down. But in the real world, driven by consumerism, a similar sense of ephemeral existence that disregarded any serious social idea was becoming a characteristic of many buildings.

The dominance of commercialism at the Osaka Expo and the decline of social utopia were certainly due to how the exposition was financed as well as to the increasing power of large corporations in Japanese society. Far from an isolated phenomenon, however, the loss of architectural utopia reflected a worldwide socio-cultural transition that had been underway for years. Some of the significant symptoms of this transition included the 1968 student demonstrations in Europe and the Cultural Revolution in China, both associated with the iconoclastic attempt to overthrow any established institution. Similar student protests were staged in Japan: even the Tower of the Sun at Osaka Expo was once occupied by a young man named Hideo Sato who, wearing a helmet saying "Red Army," climbed into the right eye of the golden face on the top of the sculpture, and encouraged his audience to "crush the Expo."[53] These movements aroused debates throughout the world, reflecting disillusionment over techno-culture that was largely understood as a destructive force in the age of the Vietnam War and the ecology movement. As a result, avant-garde architects were overtaken by revolutionary forms they themselves had created, and architecture transformed itself into a caricature. Two remarkable theoretical works, both published in 1966, reflected this transition in architecture: Robert Venturi's *Complexity and Contradiction in Architecture* and Aldo Rossi's *The Architecture of the City*.[54] Although the authors argued from quite different perspectives, indicating influences of American populism and European neo-rationalism respectively, both were among the first to reject the modernist technological utopias and the validity of a total environment.

In Japan, the architects' optimism about technological and social progress was mainly supported by the nation's continuous economic growth during the 1960s. But when the energy crisis hit the world in 1973, Japan was among the countries that suffered most because of its dependence on imported oil. Although the energy crisis was relieved after a few months, it had triggered an economic recession throughout the world that seriously affected Japan's export-oriented industry. The Japanese became painfully aware of the vulnerability of their country's economy. The energy crisis not only drastically slowed down the momentum of postwar economic growth, but fundamentally changed conceptions of the world and demanded re-evaluation of prevalent approaches to planning and design. Faith in technological and social progress and their perpetual continuation, which previously justified large-scale urban interventions, suddenly became open to doubt. As Klauser argued, Tange's great roof at the Osaka Expo, which had elicited praise from many critics for its dimensions and its symbolism of uniting peoples of the world under one roof, was now viewed by Japanese architects as strangely dated because "its form had evidently been inspired by those very chemical plants, refineries, and shipping lines whose significance was rapidly declining after 1973."[55] On the other side of the Pacific, Tange's 1969 proposal for the redevelopment of Yerba Buena Gardens, featuring a megastructural complex of stadium, convention center, and office skyscrapers in the center of San Francisco, also encountered forceful resistance and was ultimately abandoned.[56] It demonstrated that massive, permanent urban designs was no longer relevant in changes taking place in society.

The decade after Japan's energy crisis was characterized by economic restructuring. In his election campaign of 1972, Kakuei Tanaka, who was to become prime minister, announced the "Plan of Reconstruction of the Japanese Archipelago." Although the statement was not without a technocratic tone, the project nevertheless reflected the general mood of crisis and signified the conservative shift in Japan's national policy. In the economic sector, emphasis was gradually shifted to more energy-sensitive and service-oriented industries. New economic conditions and cultural consciousness in the early 1970s prompted architects to rethink their approaches to urban design. Following the bankruptcy of Metabolism's idealism at the Osaka Expo, architects moved away from previously prevalent utopian projects and reacted in different ways to the changing urban conditions. The common message embodied in their increasingly personal works was clear: the age of large-scale, revolutionary urban schemes based on technocratic utopianism was over. Such schemes were not only highly problematic, but also impossible within the current social, ideological, and cultural climate. In a word, the city was no longer regarded as a subject of design.

In an article published in 1971, Maki criticized the naïve belief in a city's capacity for continuous growth and the lack of concern among architects with human spaces in the city. He wrote: "Until quite recently we, with few exceptions, have not questioned the menace of unlimited expansion of large metropolises . . . but today there is increasing uneasiness and apprehension among us."[57] Realizing that previous super-scale urban interventions were beyond the architect's control, Maki contended: "At what level can we be most effective? I find that architects are most useful and effective in restructuring our physical environment at a scale ranging from, say roughly, a district of several thousand inhabitants to a small neighborhood to a complex of buildings in one block."[58] He implied that the Metabolist visions were too ambitious and that one simply could not design an entire city. He thus urged architects to think small and practice at the scale of what he called "micro-scale planning."

Other architects questioned the notion of urban design with an emphasis on physical structure that had underlay most Metabolist schemes. Moving away from his early concepts of megastructure, Isozaki raised the idea of "invisible city" to remind people of the non-physical aspects of the city. He later recalled:

The city is undeniably in a state of flux. Invisible, it is virtually simulated by the codes that fill it. In my "Invisible City," which alludes to ruins, I foresaw a city filled with unreal codes where the interpretation of the classical structure of cognition is meaningless. I now believe that design and city planning will become impossible using methods that involve only the manipulation of physical actualities. Since coming to this conclusion, although I regard cities as fit objects for consideration, I have ceased to think that they can be designed and hence no longer undertake work of that kind.[59]

Starting with a series of projects in his hometown Oita, Isozaki developed an architectural language characterized by symbolism and historical metaphors, and he became a pioneer of postmodernism.

The new generation of Japanese architects, represented by Kazuo Shinohara, Tadao Ando, and Toyo Ito, denied the possibility or effectiveness of comprehensive intervention in cities. As they retreated from the public realm to the private domain for their practice, they took more personal, non-dogmatic, and irreducible approaches to design. Unlike the Metabolists who aspired to create a universal and collective built environment, the younger architects limited their works to individual buildings, with metaphorically sophisticated and often fragmented imagery. In his 1971 essay entitled "Beyond Symbol Spaces," Shinohara wrote: "It is no longer necessary to disguise one's belief that the house is a kind of spatial creation based on a criticism of civilization."[60] Instead of seeing the city as an extension of architectural logic, these architects treated it as an enveloping, oppressive "alien" presence. They thus rejected direct involvement with the city and, rather, attempted to provide sheltered enclaves where their clients could hide from a hostile environment. Although the architects of the 1970s shared Tange and the Metabolists' concerns about the repressive impact of existing urban conditions, they no longer assumed the responsibility for curing these problems. It thus concluded an era of utopias.

Notes

1   Botond Bognar, *Contemporary Japanese Architecture: Its Development and Challenge* (New York: Van Nostrand Reinhold, 1985), 114.
2   A detailed discussion of MITI's role in Japan's economic growth is provided in Chalmers A. Johnson, *MITI and the Japanese Miracle: The Growth of Industrial Policy, 1925–1975* (San Francisco: Stanford University Press, 2004).
3   *Keiretsu* literally means system or series.
4   Japan's GNP in 1960 was $39.1 billion; W. Germany, $70.7 billion; Britain, $71.9 billion; the United States, $503.8 billion. In 1970, Japan's GNP rose to $203.1 billion; W. Germany, $184.6 billion; Britain, $124.0 billion; the United States, $992.7 billion. Keizai Koho Senta, *Japan: An International Comparison* (Tokyo: Keizai Koho Senta, 1983), 5.
5   Botond Bognar, *Contemporary Japanese Architecture: Its Development and Challenge* (New York: Van Nostrand Reinhold, 1985), 104.
6   Ibid.
7   Wilhelm Klauser, "Introduction: Rules and Identities," in Christopher Knabe and Joerg Rainer Noennig, eds., *Shaking the Foundation: Japanese Architects in Dialogue* (Munich: Prestel, 1999), 10.

8   Kisho Kurokawa, "The Architecture of the Age of Life Principle," *Japan Architect* 18 (Summer 1995): 4–13.

9   Reyner Banham, *Megastructure: Urban Futures of the Recent Past* (New York: Harper & Row, 1976), 47.

10 Kenzo Tange and Terunobu Fujimori, *Kenzo Tange* (Tokyo: Shin Kenchiku Sha, 2002), 345.

11 Klauser, 11 (see note 7).

12 Makoto Kikuchi, ed., *Medeia toshite no kenchiku: Pirannzi kara Expo '70 mate (Architecture as Media: From Roma 1760 to Osaka 1970)* (Tokyo: the University of Tokyo Museum, 2005), 116.

13 David B. Stewart, *The Making of a Modern Japanese Architecture: 1868 to the Present* (Tokyo: Kodansha International, 1987), 182.

14 The structural engineer of the National Gymnasium was Tsuboi Yoshikatsu. It was designed in 1960 and completed in 1964.

15 Historically and geographically, there have been two major urban clusters in Japan: the Kanto region around Tokyo, and the Kansai region around Osaka and metropolises of Kyoto, Kobe, and Nara. Both regions play an important part in Japan's economy.

16 For details of the planning committee of the Osaka Expo, see Kenzo Tange and Fujimori Terunobu, *Kenzo Tange* (Tokyo: Shinkenchiku-sha, 2002), 381–382.

17 Uzo Nishiyama, "A Plan for Kyoto," *Japan Architect* (Feb 1965): 66.

18 Uzo Nishiyama, "Image Planning," in the World Design Conference Organization, *World Design Conference 1960 in Tokyo* (Tokyo: Bujutsu Shuppansha, 1961), 191.

19 Uzo Nishiyama, "A Plan for Kyoto," *Japan Architect* (Feb 1965): 69.

20 *Iepolis* is the combination of *ie*, meaning "home" in Japanese, and the Greek suffix -polis.

21 Uzo Nishiyama et al., "Home City: Future Image of City," *Kindai kenchiku* 14 (Mar. 1961): 52. A discussion of Nishiyama's idea of Home City is included in Andrea Y. F. Urushima, "Genesis and Culmination of Uzo Nishiyama's Proposal of a 'Model Core of a Future City' for the Expo 70 Site," *Planning Perspective* 22 (Oct. 2007): 402–403.

22 Tange and Fujimori, 381–382 (see note 10).

23 In the second issue (1966) of *Exposition Quarterly*, a newsletter published by the Association for the 1970 World Exposition, Nishiyama wrote: "The master plan for the 1970 World Exposition seeks to emphasize the need for 'harmony' that should go hand in hand with 'progress' and to embody this in a 'model of the core of a future city' to be built at the exposition site. . . . The core of a city is the central nerve of a society where information necessary for keeping it going is amassed and dispensed quickly. . . . a 'model core of a future city' incorporating these and other features will be presented in the Symbol Area situated in the centre of the site in the forms of the Festival Plaza, artificial ponds, control centre and moving roads." It is quoted in Urushima, 398 (see note 21).

24 Urushima, 400 (see note 21).

25 Arata Isozaki, *Japan-ness in Architecture* (Cambridge, MA: MIT Press, 2006), 71.

26 Toshi dezain kenkyukai, *Nihon no Toshi Kukan (Japanese Urban Space)* (Tokyo: Shokokusha, 1968); and Isozaki, 66 (see note 25).

27 Isozaki, 71 (see note 25).

28 Urushima, 392 (see note 21).

29 Coverage of the Osaka Expo can be found in *Architectural Review* (Aug. and Oct. 1970), *Architectural Record* (June 1970), *Architectural Design* (June 1970), *Progressive Architecture* (Aug. 1970), *Architectural Forum* (Apr. 1970), *Bauwelt* (May 1970), *Architecture d'aujourd'hui* (Oct./Nov. 1970), *Canadian Architect* (July 1970), *Japan Architect* (Apr. 1969 and May/June 1970), among others.

30 Kenzo Tange and Noboru Kawazoe, "Some Thoughts about Expo '70 ," *Japan Architect* (May/June 1970): 34. *Chugoku* is the westernmost part of the main Japanese island, *Honshu.*

31 Takabumi Sasaki, "A Passage through the Dys-topia of Expo '70 ," *Japan Architect* (May/June 1970): 145.

32 Kenzo Tange, "The Expo '70 Master Plan and Master Design," *Japan Architect* (May/June, 1970): 18.

33 This seminar was considered a significant event in postwar Japanese architecture, igniting young architects' enthusiasm in new building technologies. Hajime Yatsuka and Hideki Yoshimatsu,

Metaborizumu: 1960 nendai no Nihon kenchiku avangaruto (*Metabolism: Japanese Architectural Avant-garde of the 1960s*) (Tokyo: Inax Publishing Co., 1997), 11. For Wachsmann's theory, see Konrad Wachsmann, *The Turning Point of Building: Structure and Design*, trans. Thomas E. Burton (New York, Reinhold, 1961).

34   Friedman founded the Groupe d'Etudes d'Architecture Mobile in 1958 to advocate his idea of mobile architecture. Among its members were David Georges Emmerich, Camille Frieden, Günter Günschel, Oskar Hansen, Jean Pierre Pecquet, Eckhard Schulze-Fielitz, and Werner Ruhnau. For the latest study regarding Friedman and GEAM's works, see Larry Busbea, *Topologies: The Urban Utopias in France, 1960–1970* (Cambridge, MA: MIT Press, 2007).

35   Taro Okamoto created three sculptures for the Festival Plaza: the Tower of the Sun, the Tower of Motherhood, and the Tower of Youth. The Tower of the Sun is the only major piece preserved after the Expo when the site was turned into an Expo Park.

36   Mildred F. Schmertz, "Expo '70," *Architectural Record* (June 1970): 119.

37   Kenzo Tange, "Recollections: Architect Kenzo Tange," *Japan Architect* (Oct. 1985): 9; Rob Gregory, "Lost in Translation" (exhibition review), *Architectural Review* 217 (June 2005): 38.

38   Klauser, 11 (see note 7).

39   Sasaki,143 (see note 31).

40   J. M. Richards, "Expo 70," *Architectural Review* (Aug. 1970): 67.

41   Ibid.

42   Ibid.

43   Sasaki, 143 (see note 31).

44   Klauser, 12 (see note 7).

45   Ibid. The term "Potemkin city" was the title of one of Adolf Loos's famous essays that criticized the falseness of city building in Vienna. Adolf Loos, *Spoken into the Void: Collected Essays, 1897–1900* (Cambridge, MA: MIT Press, 1982), 95–97. Loos borrowed the term from the story about Potemkin villages, the purportedly fake settlements erected in 1787 at the direction of Russian minister Grigori Aleksandrovich Potemkin to fool Empress Catherine II into believing that her conquests in Crimea were valuable.

46   It is notable that some other Japanese architects took a different stance within this social transformation, and intentionally kept their architecture divorced from the dominant consumerist culture, prominently among them Kazuo Shinohara and Seiichi Shirai. For discussion of Shinohara's work, see David B. Stewart, *The Making of a Modern Japanese Architecture: 1868 to the Present* (Tokyo: Kodansha International, 1987). For discussion of Shirai's works, see Hajime Yatsuka, "Architecture in the Urban Desert: A Critical Introduction to Japanese Architecture after Modernism," in *Oppositions* (Winter 1981): 2–35.

47   Yatsuka has argued that Tange's stance was always ambivalent, as his work moved between consumption and anti-consumption. Hajime Yatsuka, "Architecture in the Urban Desert: A Critical Introduction to Japanese Architecture after Modernism," in *Oppositions* (Winter 1981): 3. Cedric Price was regarded as a forerunner of interactive architecture, envisioning a reconfigurable building technology with a potential for interactivity with people. The Fun Palace, an inbuilt project proposed for East London, was intended as a "laboratory of fun," an enormous flexible environment for events, including dancing, music, drama and fireworks. It also adopted a gigantic space-frame structure. In addition to its possible influence on Tange's Festival Plaza, this project also inspired Richard Rogers and Renzo Piano's design of the Centre Georges Pompidou in Paris.

48   Tange argued in a pragmatic manner, citing the difficulties of maintenance. Kenzo Tange, "Recollections: Architect Kenzo Tange, 7" *Japan Architect* 8510: 13.

49   One of the highlights of this exposition was a large moon rock on display in the United States' pavilion. It had been brought back from the moon by Apollo 11 astronauts in 1969.

50   Hajime Yatsuka, "Architecture in the Urban Desert: A Critical Introduction to Japanese Architecture after Modernism," in *Oppositions* (Winter 1981): 8.

51   Sasaki,143 (see note 31).

52   Ibid.

53   Angus Locker, "The Logic of Spectacle *c.*1970," *Art History* 30, no.4 (Sept 2007): 571–589.

54   Robert Venturi, *Complexity and Contradiction in Architecture* (New York: Museum of Modern Art, 1966); Aldo Rossi, *L'architectura della città* (1966), trans. by Diane Ghirardo and Joan Ockman as *The Architecture of the City* (Cambridge, MA: MIT Press, 1982).

55 Wilhelm Klauser, "Introduction: Rules and Identities," in Christopher Knabe and Joerg Rainer Noennig, eds., *Shaking the Foundation: Japanese Architects in Dialogue* (Munich: Prestel, 1999), 12.

56 For the history of Yerba Buena Gardens project, see Kuang Shi, Gary Hack, and Zhongjie Lin, *Urban Design in the Global Perspective* (Beijing: China Architecture and Building Press, 2006), 112–122.

57 Fumihiko Maki, "The Potential of Planning," *Architecture in Australia* 60 (Aug. 1971): 695.

58 Ibid.

59 Arata Isozaki, *The Island Nation Aesthetic* (London: Academy Editions, 1996), 36.

60 Shinohara Kazuo, "Beyond Symbol Spaces: An Introduction to Primary Spaces as Functional Spaces," in *Japan Architect* (April 1971): 81–88.

Chapter 6

Epilogue

The future of the past and its future

In April 2007, a report from *Architectural Record* drew worldwide attention to a building in Japan: Kisho Kurokawa's Nakagin Capsule Tower is scheduled to be demolished.[1] This news astonished many architects and historians because Nakagin Capsule Tower is not only an iconic work of Kurokawa, but has been widely acknowledged as one of the masterpieces of postwar modern architecture in Japan. The possible demolition of the Nakagin Building brought the Metabolist movement back under the spotlight nearly half a century after its inauguration.

Since 1996, Nakagin Capsule Tower has been listed as an architectural heritage by DoCoMoMo, the international organization devoted to the documentation and preservation of modern architecture. Due to the lack of maintenance, however, the interior of the building is falling into disrepair. There is also a growing concern among residents about the health issue of the asbestos used on the capsules as well as the building's ability to withstand earthquake. Under such circumstances, the association of residents at Nakagin Capsule Tower voted to tear it down and build a new fourteen-story tower, which would expand the usable area substantially. Trying to save the Nakagin Building, Kurokawa proposed a renovation plan to replace the capsules with new units, allowing the building to undergo self-renewal as he had originally envisioned. However the building's management remained unconvinced. DoCoMoMo pleaded for the United Nations' heritage arm to protect this landmark, but did not succeed either.

Nakagin Capsule Tower is not an isolated case in which modern architectural landmarks in Japan are jeopardized. Should it be demolished, the Nakagin Building would join a few other Metabolists' works in a long list of modern buildings demolished in recent years. For instance, the Sony Tower in Osaka, another famous capsule building by Kurokawa completed in 1976, was torn down in 2006; Kiyonori Kikutake's Sofitel Tokyo, a 1994 building with a dynamic silhouette and emblematic of the architect's concept of "tree-shaped

6.1
**Kisho Kurokawa
Nakagin Capsule
Tower, 1972**

community," was replaced with a larger residential tower in 2007. The notoriously high land price in major Japanese cities played a big role in these "tragedies," which indicate the dilemmas in preserving modern buildings in the face of the rapid pace of contemporary urbanization. These demolitions or scheduled demolitions also raised several issues particularly related to Metabolism: the ideas of adaptability and replaceability that characterize the design of the Nakagin Building and Metabolist projects in general, the relevance of Metabolist theory to the contemporary practice of architecture and urbanism, and, finally, the historical evaluation of the Metabolist movement.

Death and life of the capsule building

Kurokawa began his exploration of capsule architecture at Expo '70 through the design of Takara Beautilion. This pavilion, as well as most other structures for the

nori Kikutake,
tel Tokyo,
3. Demolished
7

Expo, was demolished after the event which lasted six months, but the Expo effect lingered. Torizo Watanabe, then president of real estate firm Nakagin Co. in Tokyo, visited Osaka Expo and was so intrigued by Takara Beautilion that he decided to retain the architect to design another capsule building, for permanent use. Watanabe conceived of this new development not as a conventional condominium but rather as a new form of work/live space for urban dwellers. A specific sales policy was implemented to target small or medium-size business owners and high-level employees, who already owned a house or apartment and were looking for a space in Tokyo's city center as a studio or for occasional overnight stays. The location of the Nakagin Building in the bustling business district of Ginza justified this purpose.[2] Kurokawa also declared the capsule building as "housing for *homo movens*: people on the move," and used the building to address the emergence of the "urban nomad" and the almost round-the-clock working culture in Japanese society.[3]

This idea of impermanence and moveability originating from the Metabolist urban theory influenced every step of the design and construction of Nakagin Capsule Tower. According to their different "metabolic cycles," Kurokawa divided Nakagin Building into two basic components: the mega-structure (two ferroconcrete shafts connected with bridges every three stories) and the capsules (144 individual living units). They were designed with different

6.3
**Kisho Kurokawa
Nakagin Capsule
Tower, 1972.
Model**

6.4
**Kisho Kurokawa
Nakagin Capsule
Tower, 1972. Plan**

lifespans: the main shafts would last sixty years, while the capsules would be up for replacement in twenty-five to thirty-five years. Kurokawa wrote that the lifespan of capsules was not a mechanical one, but rather a social one, implying that it is the changing human needs and social relationship that necessitated such periodic replacement.[4] The towers, containing circulations and service spaces, serve as vertical "artificial land," upon which the capsules are installed. The towers rise to different heights and the capsules are arranged in a seemingly random pattern, suggesting an ongoing process: the shaft could grow, and more capsules could be piled up. Kurokawa regarded this incomplete look as the "aesthetics of time," referring to Metabolism's central notion of the city as process.[5]

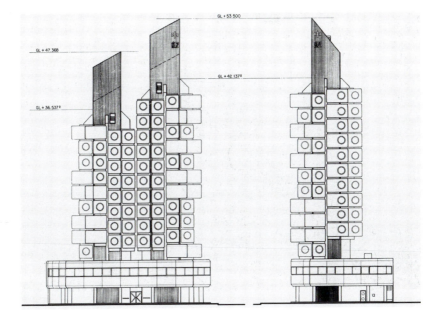

no Kurokawa,
agin Capsule
ver, 1972.
vations

Each capsule measures 2.3 x 3.8 x 2.1 meters, and is built of welded light-weight steel frames – identical to the structure and size of a shipping container. There is a Plexiglas porthole window on the external wall of each capsule – and because of that, Charles Jencks jokingly described the building as "superimposed washing machines."[6] The interior is mechanized and standardized with a variety of installations within a small space. In additional to a plastic integrative bathroom unit, each capsule is preinstalled with a bed, storage cabinets, a color television set, a clock, a kitchen stove, a refrigerator and an air conditioner. The space and the outfitting are minimal to guarantee the basic living conditions and individual freedom of a single person in the industrial society.

Construction took place in separate locations: onsite and off-site. Onsite construction included the two towers and spaces for equipment. The capsules were fabricated and assembled at factories in other cities. After being transported to the building site, they were hoisted by crane and fastened to the concrete shafts, starting from the bottom up. Each capsule was attached independently and cantilevered from the shaft so that, ideally, any capsule could be removed without affecting others. Each capsule was tied to the concrete core with only four high-tension bolts: two each on the upper and lower sides. The entire construction took only a year.

When Nakagin Capsule Tower was completed in 1972, it was a significant event in architecture. *Japan Architect* dedicated an entire issue in October 1972 to Kurokawa's building as well as potential developments of capsule architecture in the future. As the world's first capsule architecture put into actual use, Nakagin Building brought a number of revolutionary ideas in

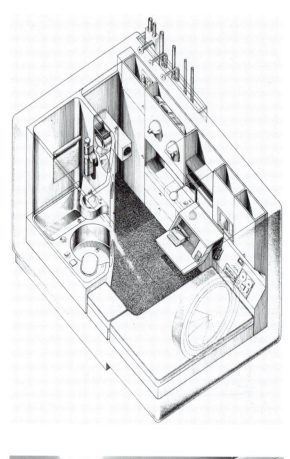

6.6
**Kisho Kurokawa,
Nakagin Capsule
Tower, 1972.
Axonometric of
interior of a
capsule**

6.7
**Kisho Kurokawa,
Nakagin Capsule
Tower, 1972.
Interior of a
capsule**

allation of
sules in 1972

okawa in a
sule

practice. It helped create a new building type, the capsule hotel, with minimum space and supplies for living to provide inner-city accommodation unique to Japanese big cities. Furthermore, some design features of Nakagin Capsule Tower later made their way into industrial products, such as the prefabricated integrative bathroom. For the building as a whole, Kurokawa envisioned it would become a new prototype of urban architecture and stimulate mass production of prefabricated housing. But this dream did not come true.

When designing the building, Kurokawa expected that the capsules would be replaced every twenty-five to thirty-five years. Ironically, a contemporary city like Tokyo is growing and transforming itself so rapidly that it even outpaces the "metabolism" that the Metabolists envisioned, and requires renewals on the scale of entire buildings instead of individual capsules. Hence the plan to tear down the Capsule Tower, following the demolition of the Sony Tower and Sofitel Tokyo. Contributing to these demolitions was a common issue: the escalating land price in major Japanese cities and thus the property owners' desire to maximize the land value. According to Botand Bognar, an average building in a large Japanese city costs only about ten percent of the land on which it sits; this results in more renovation and rebuilding in Japan than in most other

6.10
Kisho Kurokaw
Nakagin Capsul
Tower, 1972.
Detail of capsul

places.[7] Therefore it is difficult to preserve modern architecture. The Metabolist buildings were hit particularly hard. The rigorous megastructure-and-capsules combination in fact provides little flexibility in terms of space usage and structural expansion. In addition, because the Metabolist architects were keen to represent individuality by giving each capsule its expression on the façade, their buildings' floor-area ratios are often below average. In fact, the new fourteen-story building being proposed to replace Nakagin Capsule Tower would generate 60 percent more floor area. These factors have posed difficult problems for the preservation of the Nakagin Building.

Since 1998, Kisho Kurokawa Architects & Associates has been working on a "Nakagin Capsule Tower Renovation Plan." The plan proposes updating service equipment and replacing capsules with new units while keeping the structural shafts intact. Kurokawa argued that replacing the capsules would be more economic than tearing down the towers and building a new one. He thus launched a campaign to save Nakagin Capsule Tower. His appeal was supported by architectural societies in Japan, including the Japan Institute of Architects, as well as architects and designers from throughout the world.[8] The overwhelming support from the profession indicates a general acknowledgement of Nakagin Capsule Tower as an architectural heritage. That the building is at risk of being erased reminded people that it is an important part of the history of modern architecture.

1
ho Kurokawa,
kagin Capsule
wer Renovation
n, 1998–2007

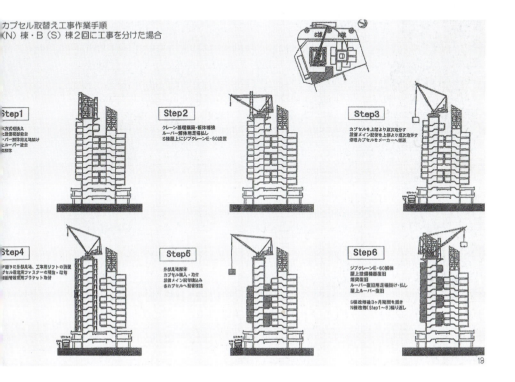

カプセル取替え工事作業手順
（N）棟・B（S）棟2回に工事を分けた場合

| Step1 |
| Step2 |
| Step3 |
| Step4 |
| Step5 |
| Step6 |

18

After Kurokawa died in 2007, the campaign lost some momentum, but attempts are still being made to save the building. In the meantime, interest continues to grow in displaying the design of Nakagin Capsule Tower and the works of Metabolism in general. In summer 2008, an exhibition entitled "Home Delivery: Fabricating the Modern Dwelling" was staged at the Museum of Modern Art (MoMA), which included an original model of the Capsule Tower. The design was characterized as "representing the whole world of architectural thought in the 1960s from the Metabolist group in Japan."[9] Word also came out that the Pompidou Center is preparing an exhibition on Japanese Architecture in 2010, and a real capsule from Nakagin Capsule Tower, should the building be demolished, would be featured at the exhibition.[10] Furthermore, a circular has been distributed for the Twenty-fourth World Congress of Architecture (UIA), to be held in Tokyo in 2011, calling for "reconsideration of the Metabolism model."[11]

Re-assessing metabolism

The wide support for preserving Nakagin Capsule Tower and various interests in exhibiting Metabolism's work confirmed a notable shift in architectural criticism: the attitude toward architectural avant-gardes of the 1950s and 1960s, such as Team 10, Archigram, Super Studio, Yona Friedman, and Metabolism, has changed considerably, if subtly, in recent years. Reyner Banham's 1976 *Megastructure* was the first comprehensive historical account of these avant-garde movements, characterizing their common futuristic approach to urban design.[12] However, Banham held that megastructure was no longer a viable design strategy by the time of writing. He thus added a subtitle to his book: *Urban Futures of the Recent Past*, and called these megastructural projects "dinosaurs of modern movement," referring not only to their "bigness" but anticipating their extinction as a "species."[13] Since Banham's book, mega-structural schemes have often been dismissed as techno-centric and politically naïve ideas, or, more critically, as authoritarian attempts to control the development of architecture and society with a fixed set of design concepts and to introduce urban interventions on an inhuman scale. Moving away from this point of view, recent historic accounts situate these architectural and urban experiments in their respective historic contexts and view these radical ideas and projects as alternatives to both rigid mainstream modernism and nostalgic postmodernism. They are thus treated as relevant precedents to contemporary design practices and social studies.[14]

Although the battle over Nakagin Capsule Tower's future is not yet settled, the debate resulting from its scheduled demolition affords an opportunity to revisit Metabolism, reexamining its design ideas and reconsidering its implication for the urban future, which is the purpose of this study. The Metabolists' ambitious urban projects, when they were proposed, had limited influence on physical planning. They were essentially utopian speculations and polemical schemes that went against what the official master plans stood for. These futuristic plans nevertheless represented a body of powerful urban ideals that continued to inspire bold visions of the modern city. Similarly, the

Metabolists' realized buildings were idealistic in nature. Nakagin Capsule Tower, for instance, was an attempt to invent a new prototype of architecture responding to the transformation of modern society and the continuing growth of modern megalopolises. The solution offered by this architectural experiment was again problematic, but the notion of transformation embodied in the design connects it to contemporary architectural culture.

This book traces the evolution of Metabolism from its inception at the 1960 World Design Conference to its spectacular swansong at the Osaka World Exposition in 1970. The urban reconstruction, economic miracle, and cultural resurgence in Japan since the late 1950s provided an evocative setting for Metabolists' utopian projects. The Metabolists' visionary projects of the city, in turn, represented attempts to reinvent Japanese identity in architecture and address urban issues of an emerging postindustrial society. They stood at the intersection of urbanism and utopianism, reflecting currents of the aesthetic, technological, and ideological changes in postwar Japanese society.

Metabolists held that technological advance, combined with powerful design concepts, could provide the modern society with a new order, directing urban development into a virtuous cycle, enhancing the quality of life, and, paradoxically, guaranteeing individual liberty. Such a technocratic notion was evident in Tange's seminal works during the 1960s, which are examined in this book: the Plan for Tokyo, the Yamanashi Press and Broadcasting Center, and the Plan for Reconstruction of Skopje. Translating Metabolists' ideas into physical environments, these projects combined a structuralist approach to the city, which attempted to regulate urban growth based on predetermined patterns, and a desire for legibility of the urban form by turning megastructure into images and symbols.

Metabolism is known primarily as a megastructural movement, causing another aspect of the Metabolist discourse to often be neglected: Fumihiko Maki's concept of group form, which he articulated in *Investigations in Collective Form*.[15] Although he shared the other Metabolists' notion of the city as process instead of artifact, Maki was critical of the utopian idea of megastructure. Against a rigid comprehensive system, he proposed a design methodology based on generative elements in space. The group form shifts the emphasis of design from physical structure to the more subtle internal order underlying the evolution of the city. Maki's Hillside Terrace project demonstrated the potential of group form to accommodate urban growth and change, notwithstanding the fact that the assembly was still carried out by one architect.

Neither megastructure nor group form had a conspicuous impact on Japanese urban landscapes during the 1960s and 1970s, but their influence has proved to be far-reaching and persistent, inspiring urban developments in the subsequent decades. The magnificent image of Tange's Tokyo Bay plan not only gained credibility for large-scale urban interventions, but also provided a model of systems approach to planning, which called for a spatial organization based on the circulation network rather than the rigid method of zoning. As Banham noted, this project "marks a definitive break with all previous urban design concepts, however vast."[16] Under its influence, a steady stream of mega-projects have been carried out in the Tokyo Bay area, especially during another period of economic expansion and construction boom known as the "Bubble Economy" in the 1980s. Tokyo Teleport Town and Yokohama Minato Mirai 21 are two recent mega-projects of this kind on Tokyo Bay. There is a considerable continuity in both design languages and political implications between the Metabolists' megastructural projects during the Economic Miracle and the large-scale developments during the Bubble Economy.[17] Like the earlier megastructural projects, the recent mega-projects are driven by a strong technological optimism and characterized by integration of infrastructure, architecture, and public space. Their architecture and urban forms embody a strong symbolism, providing visual cues of what cities should be like in the information age.

Since the 1980s, the trend of large-scale development has spread from Japan to other regions in Asia, including Southeast Asia, Korea, China, and most recently the Middle East. The economic restructuring and the impact of globalization in these countries have led to dynamic urbanizations and construction booms. Vast tracts of land are turned into new urban areas at an unprecedented pace, and historic urban centers continue to be renewed. The metamorphoses that the cities are undergoing are so drastic that they surpass the dictates of all plans. Massive projects dominate the skylines of large cities. Megalomania associated with megastructural ambitions in the past resurfaces in the age of economic globalization and consumerist culture. A public appetite for an image nourished an obsession of "bigness" in place making.

In a trajectory similar to that of megastructure, Maki's concept of group form did not gain wide recognition in the 1960s, but it contributed to the formulation of contextualism in the decades that followed. Synthesized in Colin Rowe's *Collage City*, the notion of contextualist urbanism influenced a whole generation of architects and planners to think "small" when intervening in urban development.[18] Arising out of this mentality was a different understanding of "metabolism." Instead of imposing a comprehensive framework to regulate the growth of a city, this new understanding calls for respecting pre-existing urban conditions and stresses a city's inherent process of slow evolution and natural renewal, like the metabolism of an organism.[19]

In fact, the urban landscape of Tokyo, as well as those of many other Asian cities, has been shaped by two competing forces, reflecting the different urban ideas emblematic in megastructure and group form respectively. One comes from planners of mega-projects who tend to make grand plans of the city, and the other represents the natural force of the city that continues to renew itself like an organism, as well as design interventions by architects who are conscious of this process. As a result, cities can no longer be realized as coherent entities. They often appear chaotic, but never lack vitality. In fact, such chaos is a reflection of their urban vitality. As Rem Koolhaas observed in Tokyo, chaos is "not only well documented and understood, but that it has already become an object for consumption."[20]

ato Mirai 21,
ohama,
–present

6.13
Rem Koolhaas
and OMA, CCTV
Building, 2009

Although the practical impact of their planning remained questionable, Tange's and the Metabolists' urban visions represented efforts to introduce a new urbanism to the imminent postindustrial city, channeling its growth both spatially and temporally. The megastructural forms they proposed in the 1960s appear inflexible and dated nowadays, but many themes they broached became astonishingly timely; the participatory strategy of design, adaptability of building, impermanence of urban structure, and the concept of city as process. They confirm the nature of their utopian projects whose value lies not in their relation to the present but to a possible future.

As the twenty-first century continues, the need to shelter a growing world population remains a pressing issue. Metabolist projects were intended as solutions of architectural production serving a mass market. Characterized by a three-dimensional framework organizing a variety of urban components around circulation and infrastructure, the Metabolists' megastructural concept suggests a compact urban form that has made its imprint on several types of high-density developments, such as the large-scale urban complexes centered on a train or subway station often seen in Asian cities. They combine mass transit facilities with commercial, business, and residential uses, and bring remarkable vitality to urban cores. Such compact urban form may inspire the search for a sustainable approach to urbanization, particularly in the developing countries and the world's mega-cities.

Mass production and mass consumption raise another issue in contemporary architecture and culture: the contradiction between massification and individuality. Addressing this challenge, Metabolists envisaged a spatial urbanism allotting inhabitants their own space within the infrastructural framework and allowing them to build their own dwellings. The concepts of modular and capsule also encourage such participatory design and customized construction. Such idealistic concepts were proposed without support of matured technologies, and were not sophisticated enough to cope with the complexity of contemporary social structure. They nevertheless provide a hint about the future development of participatory architecture. The rapid expansion of communication networks powered by the world wide web, particularly the recent development of peer-to-peer networking, has offered new possibilities for participatory design and collective intelligence. However, these communication technologies are carried out in a direct and non-hierarchical manner, rather than as a top-down sequence or the mechanism of an instituting power that Metabolist projects relied on.[21]

Metabolist urban projects, as well as other megastructures, were more about accommodating change than about size. Addressing the rapidly changing conditions of the postindustrial society, their schemes propagated the idea that "we should not try to forecast what will happen, but try to make provision for what cannot be foreseen."[22] The Metabolists therefore proposed buildings and urban structures in unconventional forms, perceiving them as interactive systems adaptable to the volatile social and economic conditions. Although the technical possibilities of adaptability remained unresolved in their projects, the Metabolist idea of distinguishing elements of different life cycles offered a diagrammatic model of construction with a conscious use of industrial technologies and materials to this end. The dichotomy of permanent infra- structure and mobile units to a certain extent responds to the transition from the industrial to the digital era. However, the conflict between the impro- visational construction and the reliance of this strategy on a durable and fixed system has yet to be overcome to address the increasingly flattened world.

Finally, emerging at a time of uncertainty and instability, Metabolists' works reflected a new thinking about the city: rather than understanding the city as an artifact or monument, Metabolists conceived of it as a site of change and impermanence. Italian Futurist Antonio Sant'Elia had articulated such an impermanent nature of the modern city in 1914: "Things will endure less than us. Every generation must build its own city."[23] The Metabolists' notion of urban impermanence, however, differed from Sant'Elia's more radical urbanism in that Metabolist projects paradoxically sought a cultural and social continuity through such urban impermanence, just as the periodic reconstruction of Ise preserves the architectural tradition of Shintoism. Their urban projects attempted to establish patterns that could respond actively to technological advance and

4
ta Isozaki,
mputer-aided
, 1972. Model
w

changing social conditions, and they envisaged an architecture engaging in a cyclical process of construction, dismantling, and reassembly. Ironically the demolition of Metabolist buildings, including Nakagin Capsule Tower, has become a manifestation of the Metabolists' belief in the impermanent nature of the contemporary city.

Underlying the idea of urban impermanence was the Metabolists' faith in continuing technological advance, which they believed was propelling the transformation of cities. Their late projects, such as Isozaki's 1972 Computer-aided City, reconfirmed this consciousness of the role of technology, although in a more subdued form. Technological change in the past few decades has occurred at a pace never before experienced, and its impact has been unprecedented. With the shift from the second industrial age to the digital age, the accelerating flows of population, materials, and information within the global network have fundamentally changed conceptions about "permanence" and "transience." As a result, cities are transforming dramatically as the emphasis of urbanism is shifting from concrete structures to more complex and flexible organizations as well as "soft" (digital and ecological) infrastructures. Networks carrying flows of information now reach every part of the world, creating a virtual but truly unified community.[24] This has caused real revolutions of spatial and social structure in reality, and thus the Metabolist idea of the city as process remains provocative in studying the emerging phenomena of urbanism.

Notes

1 Yuki Solomon, "Kurokawa's Capsule Tower to be Razed," *Architectural Record* 195, n.6 (June 2007): 34. The report first appeared on http://archrecord.construction.com on Apr. 30, 2007.

2 In fact, a surprising number of professionals, including travel agents, accountants and architects, moved in after the building was completed and used the capsule as their business space. Hiroshi Watanabe, *The Architecture of Tokyo* (Stuttgart and London: Edition Axel Menges, 2001), 148.

3 Jin Hidaka, "Nakagin Capsule Tower Building," *UIA 2011 Tokyo* (International Union of Architects 2011 Congress in Tokyo) circular, 2008.

4 Noriaki Kurokawa, "Challenge to the Capsule: Nakagin Capsule Tower Building," *Japan Architect* 47 (Oct. 1972): 17.

5 Botand Bognar, "What Goes Up, Must Come Down: Recent Urban Architecture in Japan," *Harvard Design Magazine* 3 (Fall 1997): 42.

6 Charles Jencks, *The Language of Post-Modern Architecture* (London: Academy Editions, 1977), 40.

7 Bognar, 35 (see note 5).

8 Architectural organizations in Japan, including the Japan Institute of Architects, the Japan Federation of Architects and Building Engineers Associations, and DoCoMoMo Japan, unanimously supported the preservation of the building and Kurokawa's proposal of renovation. Kurokawa also received enormous support from international societies of architects and designers. According to a poll of over 10,000 architects in 100 countries by London-based *World Architecture News*, 95 percent voted to preserve Nakagin Capsule Tower and 75 percent voted to support Kurokawa's idea of replacing the capsules. Kisho Kurokawa, "Recent Situation about Nakagin Capsule Tower," Kisho Kurokawa Architect & Associates, http://www.kisho.co.jp; "Nakagin Tower WAN Poll Result," *World Architecture News*, http://www.worldarchitecture news.com, Sep. 23, 2005.

9 Audio representation of the exhibition "Home Delivery: Fabricating the Modern Dwelling," Museum of Modern Art (MoMA), New York, July 20–Oct. 20, 2008.

10 Blair McBride, "Nakagin Capsule Tower: Architecture of the Future," http://pingmag.jp, Dec. 2008.

11 Hidaka, ibid (see note 3).

12 Reyner Banham, *Megastructure: Urban Futures of the Recent Past* (New York: Harper & Row, 1976).

13 Ibid, 8–9.

14 Several recent historic accounts have demonstrated this trend: Simon Sadler, *Archigram: Architecture without Architecture* (Cambridge, MA: MIT Press, 2005); Max Risselada and Dirk van den Heuvel, eds., *Team 10, 1953–81: In Search of Utopia of the Present* (Rotterdam: NAi Publishers, 2006); Peter Lang and William Menking, eds., *Superstudio: Life Without Objects* (Milan: Skira, 2003); Larry Busbea, *Topologies: The Urban Utopia in France, 1960–1970* (Cambridge, MA: MIT Press, 2007); Hadas Steiner, *Beyond Archigram: The Structure of Circulation* (Abingdon, UK: Routledge, 2008); and Cherie Wendelken, "Putting Metabolism Back in Place: The Making of a Radically Decontextualized Architecture in Japan," in Sarah Williams Goldhagen and Rejean Legault, eds., *Anxious Modernism: Experimentation in Postwar Architectural Culture* (Cambridge, MA: MIT Press, 2000), 279–300.

15 Fumihiko Maki, *Investigations in Collective Form* (St. Louis, MO: Washington University, 1964).

16 Banham, 51 (see note 12).

17 For a comparative study of the megastructural proposals in the 1960s and the ongoing mega-projects of the Tokyo Bay region, see Zhongjie Lin, "From Megastructure to Megalopolis: Formation and Transformation of Mega-projects in Tokyo Bay," *Journal of Urban Design* 12 (Feb 2007): 73–92.

18 *Collage City* does not reject utopianism in urban design; rather it suggests an attitude that accommodates a whole range of utopias in miniature. It does however reject the notion of total planning, and proposes analyzing urban form as the fragmented, incomplete result of every attempt ever made to organize it logically. Colin Rowe and Fred Koetter, *Collage City* (Cambridge, MA: MIT Press, 1978). The aesthetics and economics of "small" developed during the 1970s, accompanied by the emerging environmental movement after the energy crisis. E. F. Schumacher, *Small is Beautiful: Economics as if People Mattered* (New York: Harper & Row, 1975).

19 This understanding of urban "metabolism" can be found in some recent architectural research, which studied the city as an ecosystem. Abel Wolman, "The Metabolism of Cities," *Scientific American* 213 (1965): 156–174; Joel A. Tarr, "The Metabolism of the Industrial City," *Journal of Urban History*, v.28, n.5 (July 2002): 511–545.

20 Koolhaas continued: "There, where intelligence meets masochism, chaos had rapidly become the dominant leitmotif of architecture and urbanism." Rem Koolhaas, "Urbanism after Innocence: Four Projects," *Assemblage* 18 (Aug. 1992): 94.

21 A special issue of *Architectural Design* in the fall of 2006 studies the issue of collective intelligence in design. *Architectural Design* 76 (Sep./Oct. 2006): whole issue.

22 Nicholas Habraken, *Support: An Alternative to Mass Housing* (London: Architectural Press, 1972), 42.

23 Antonio Sant'Elia, "The Manifesto of Futurist Architecture" (1914), in Umbro Apollonio, ed., *Futurist Manifestos* (Boston: Museum of Fine Arts Publications, 2001), 172.

24 A session called "Metaworlds" in a 2000 exhibition at New York Public Library examined how the internet is expanding the notion of utopia. Roland Schaer et al., eds., *Utopia: The Search for the Ideal Society in the Western World* (New York: New York Public Library, Oxford University Press, 2000).

Bibliography

Writings and monographs of Kenzo Tange

Bettinotti, Massimo, ed., *Kenzo Tange 1946–1996*. Milan: Electa, 1996.

Gropius, Walter and Kenzo, Tange. *Katsura: Nihon kenchiku ni okeru dentō to sōzō* (*Katsura: Tradition and Creation in Japanese Architecture*). Tokyo: Zōkeisha, 1960.

Kultermann, Udo, ed., *Kenzo Tange 1946–1969: Architecture and Urban Design*. Artemis Zurich: Verlag für Architektur, 1970.

—— *Kenzo Tange*. Barcelona: G. Gili, 1989.

Kurita, Isamu, ed., *Gendai Nihon Kenchikuka Zenshu 10: Tange Kenzo* (*The Complete Works of Contemporary Japanese Architects 10: Kenzo Tange*). Tokyo: Sanichi Shobo, 1971.

Tange, Kenzo. "Michelangelo shō: Le Corbusier ron he no josetsu toshite" (Ode to Michelangelo: as an Introduction to the Study of Le Corbusier). *Geidai Kenchiku* (Dec. 1939): 36–47.

—— "Kensetsu o meguru sho mondai" (Some Questions Related to Construction). *Kenchiku Zasshi* (*Architectural Journal*) (Jan. 1948).

—— *Chiiki keikaku no riron* (*Theory of Regional Planning*). Tokyo: Bureau of Resources Investigation, 1950.

—— "Ashita ni sonaeru toshizō" (The Urban Form for Tomorrow). *Asashi shinbun* (Feb. 14, 1958): 6.

—— "Gendai kenchiku no sōzō to Nihon kenchiku no dentō" (Contemporary Architectural Creation and the Japanese Architectural Tradition). *Sinkentiku* 31 (1956 June): 25–33.

—— "Geidai daitoshi no chiiki kōzō to kenchiku keitai" (The Regional Structure and Architectural Form of Contemporary Large Cities). Dissertation, University of Tokyo, 1959.

—— "An Approach to Tradition." *Shinkenchiku* (Jan./Feb. 1959): 55–58.

—— "Mobility and Stability." *Kenchiku bunka* (Sep. 1960): 43–46.

—— "The Future City over the Sea: The Realization of a New Plan for Tokyo." *Syūkan Asahi* (Oct. 16, 1960).

—— "Technology and Humanity," *Japan Architect* (Oct. 1960): 11–12.

—— "Aestheticism and Vitalism." *Japan Architect* (Oct. 1960): 8–10.

—— "Tokyo no kōzō kaizo keikaku: Asu no 1000 man toshi ni sonaete" (The Plan of Structural Reorganizing for Tokyo: Preparing for a City of Ten Million). *Asashi jānaru* (Feb. 12, 1961): 15–18.

—— "Toshi keikakuka no hatsuso to genzitsu: Tange Kenzo shi to 'mirai Tokyo'" (The Illusion and Reality of an Urban Planner: Kenzo Tange and the "Future Tokyo"). *Asashi jānaru* (Jan. 7, 1962): 31–33.

—— "Kūkan to shōchō" (Space and Symbol). *Kenchiku bunka* 20 (1965 June): 102–103.

—— "From Architecture to Urban Design." *Japan Architect* (May 1967), 23–27.

—— "Tokaido-Megalopolis: The Japanese Archipelago in the Future." In Udo Kultermann, ed., *Kenzo Tange 1946–1969: Architecture and Urban Design*. Artemis Zurich: Verlag für Architektur, 1970.

—— "Toshi to kenchiku" (City and Architecture). Isamu Kurita, ed., *Gendai Nihon Kenchikuka Zenshu 10: Tange Kenzo* (*The complete Works of Contemporary Japanese Architects 10: Kenzo Tange*). Tokyo: Sanichi Shobo, 1971, 94–108.

—— "Function, Structure, and Symbol." In Udo Kultermann, ed., *Kenzo Tange 1946–1969: Architecture and Urban Design*. Artemis Zurich: Verlag für Architektur, 1970, 240–243.

—— "The Expo '70 Master Plan and Master Design." *Japan Architect* (May/June, 1970): 18–20.

—— "Past Lineage and Future Vector of Urban Design at the Tange Studio." *Japan Architect* (Sep. 1971): 43–50.

—— "Special Issue: Lineage of Urban Design." *Japan Architect* 46 (Sep./Oct. 1971): whole issue.

—— "Images of the Future Urban Environment." In Gwen Bell and Jacquelaine Tyrwhitt, eds, *Human Identity in the Urban Environment*. London: Pelican, 1972.

—— "Development of Design Concept and Methodology." *Japan Architect* (Aug/Sep 1976): 11–14.

—— "My Experience." *Space Design* 8001: 184–190.

—— "Kenzo Tange and Urtec." *Space Design* 8001: whole issue.

—— "Recollections: Architect Kenzo Tange, Part 1" *Japan Architect* (Apr. 1985): 7–12.

—— "Recollections: Architect Kenzo Tange, Part 2" *Japan Architect* (May 1985): 6–12.

—— "Recollections: Architect Kenzo Tange, Part 3" *Japan Architect* (June 1985): 6–14.

—— "Recollections: Architect Kenzo Tange, Part 4" *Japan Architect* (July 1985): 6–15.

—— "Recollections: Architect Kenzo Tange, Part 5" *Japan Architect* (Aug. 1985): 6–12.

—— "Recollections: Architect Kenzo Tange, Part 6" *Japan Architect* (Sep. 1985): 6–15.

—— "Recollections: Architect Kenzo Tange, Part 7" *Japan Architect* (Oct. 1985): 6–14.

—— "A Plan for Tokyo, 1986." *Japan Architect* 367/368 (Nov./Dec. 1987): 8–45.

—— "Creating a Contemporary System of Aesthetics." *Japan Architect* 65, n.1 (Jan. 1990): 8–9.

—— *Tange Kenzo: Ippon no enpitsu kara* (*Kenzo Tange: From a Pencil*). Tokyo: Nihon Tosho Sentā, 1997.

Tange, Kenzo, Marato Otaka, Kiyonori Kikutake and Noriaki Kurokawa. "Metaborizumu o megutsu te: Tange Kenzo tai Metaborizumu gurūpu" (On Metabolism: A Dialogue between Kenzo Tange and the Metabolist Group). *Kindai kenchiku* (Nov. 1960): 67–72.

Tange, Kenzo and Terunobu Fujimori. *Tange Kenzo*. Tokyo: Shinkenchiku-sha, 2002.

Kenzo, Tange and Noboru Kawazoe. *Ise: Prototype of Japanese Architecture*. Cambridge, MA: MIT Press, 1965.

Tange, Kenzo and Noboru Kawazoe. "Some Thoughts about Expo '70." *Japan Architect* (May/June 1970): 29–34.

Tange, Kenzo, Noboru Kawazoe and Yoshio Watanabe. *Ise: Nihon kenchiku no genkei* (*Ise: Prototype of Japanese Architecture*). Tokyo: Asahi Shinbunsha, 1962.

Tange, Kenzo and Kuzuo Shinohara. "After Modernism: a dialogue between Kenzo Tange and Kuzuo Shinohara." *Japan Architect* 58, n.11–12 (Nov./Dec. 1983): 7–12.

Kenzo Tange Associates. *Kenzo Tange: Forty Years of Urbanism and Architecture*. Tokyo: Process Architecture Publishing Co., 1987.

Tange Kenzo Team. "A Plan for Tokyo, 1960: Toward a Structural Reorganization." *Shinkenchiku* (Mar. 1961): 8–38.

—— *A Plan for Tokyo, 1960: Toward a Structural Reorganization*. Tokyo: Shikenchikusha, 1961.

Writings and monographs of the Metabolist members and Arata Isozaki

Isozaki, Arata. "City Demolition Industry, Inc." *Shin Kenchiku* (Nov. 1962). Republished in *Arata Isozaki: Architecture 1960–1990*. Los Angeles: Museum of Contemporary Art, 1991, 49–51.

—— "Theory of Process Planning (1963)." *Arata Isozaki 1959–1978* (GA Architect 6), 30.

—— "On Process Planning." 1965. *Kūkan he* (*Towards Space*). Tokyo: Bijutsu Shuppansha, 1971, 76–97.

—— "Invisible City." In *Architecture Culture, 1943–1968: A Documentary Anthology*, edited by Joan Ockman, 402–407. New York: Rizzoli, 1993.

—— "Sukopio keikaku no kaibō" (The Anatomy of the Plan for Skopje). *Kūkan he* (*Towards Space*). Tokyo: Bijutsu Shuppansha, 1971, 352–379.

—— "Mienai toshi" (The Invisible City). *Kukan-e* (*Towards Space*). Tokyo: Bijutsu Shuppansha, 1971, 380–404.

—— *Kukan-e* (*Towards Space*). Tokyo: Bijutsu Shuppansha, 1971.

——, ed., *Kenchiku no senkyu sanjunendai: Keifu to myakuraku* (*The Architecture in the 1930s: The Origins and Branches*). Tokyo: Kajima Shuppankai, 1978.

—— "Ise: no modoki" (Ise: the Artificial Origin). *Ise Jingu* (*Ise Shrine*). Tokyo: Ishinami shoden, 1995.

Bibliography

—— *The Island Nation Aesthetic*. London: Academy Editions, 1996.

—— *Arata Isozaki: Four Decades of Architecture*. New York: Universal Publications, 1998.

—— *Japan-ness in Architecture*. Cambridge, MA: MIT Press, 2006.

Kawahara, Ichiro and Masato Otaka. "Toward a New Living Space." *Shinkenchiku* (Jan. 1957): 24–25.

Kawazoe, Noboru. "Tange Kenzo no Nihonteki seikaku" (Kenzo Tange's Japanese Personality), *Shinkenchiku* 30, n.1 (Jan. 1955): 62–69.

—— "Toward the Discovery of Tradition and People." *Shin kenchiku* (July 1956): 13–15.

—— "Yōtopia to kenchikuka: Risō toshi ron no josetsu toshite" (Utopia and Architect: As an Introduction to Ideal City). *Kindai kenchiku* 13 (Nov. 1959): 9–11.

—— "A step toward the future." *Japan Architect* 34 (Mar. 1959): 24–31.

—— "Metaborizumu no kiso" (The Foundation of Metabolism). *Kindai kenchiku* (Nov. 1960): 31–37.

—— "Geidai sekai ni yokeru kenchikuka no yakuwari: 1960 nien o kaikoshite" (The Role of Architect in the Contemporary World: Reflections of 1960). *Kindai kenchiku* (Dec. 1960): 9–11.

—— "Dai Tokyo saigo no hi: Tokyo no metsumō gaisetsu" (The Last Day of Greater Tokyo: The Death of Tokyo, Introduction). *Kenchiku bunka* 16, n.1 (Jan. 1961): 5–12.

—— "City of the Future." *Zodiac* 9 (1961): 98–111.

—— "A New Tokyo: In, On, or Above the Sea?" *This is Japan* 9 (1962): 57–65.

—— "Tange Kenzo ron: sono sonzai no geidai no imi" (On Kenzo Tange: the Meaning of his Existing in the Contemporary). *Asashi jānaru* (Mar. 21, 1965): 89–97.

—— *Contemporary Japanese Architecture*. Trans. David Griffith. Tokyo: Japan Cultural Society, 1968.

—— "Metabolism." *Japan Architect* 44 (Dec. 1969): 101–108; 45 (Jan. 1970): 97–101.

—— "Thirty Years of Metabolism." *Thesis, Wissenschaftliche Zeitschrift der Bauhaus-Universität Weimar,* 44 (1998): 146–151.

—— "Metaborizumu 1960–2001: 21 seiki he no zikken" (Metabolism 1960–2001: The Experiment of the 21st Century). *Kikan Obayashi* 48 (Special Issue: Metabolism 2001): 2–19.

—— "Metaborisuto tachi to gakunda toki to ima" ("The Metabolists: From the Years of Learning till Present"). In Masato Otaka and Noboru Kawazoe, eds, *Metabolism and Metabolists*. Tokyo: Bijutsu Shūpansha, 2005.

Kikutake, Kiyonori. "Tower-shaped City." *Kokusai Kenchiku* 26 (Jan. 1959): 12–19.

—— "Marine City." *Kokusai Kenchiku* 26 (Feb. 1959): 36–39.

—— *Taisha kenchiku ron (Theory of Metabolist Architecture)*. Tokyo: Shokokusha Publishing Co., Ltd., 1969.

—— *Komyuniti to toshi (Community Civilization)*. Publisher unknown, 1976.

—— *Kiyonori Kikutake: Concepts and Planning*. Tokyo: Bijutsu Shuppan-sha, 1978.

—— "On the Notion of Replaceability." *World Architecture* 32 (1995): 26–27.

—— "Metabolism and Habitat." *World Architecture* 32 (1995): 28–47.

—— *Kiyonori Kikutake: From Tradition to Utopia*. Milan: L'Arca Edizioni, 1997.

Kikutake, Kiyonori, Noboru Kawazoe, Masato Otaka, Fumihiko Maki and Noriaki Kurokawa. *Metabolism: The Proposals for New Urbanism*. Tokyo: Bijutsu Shūpansha, 1960.

Kurita, Isamu, ed., *Gendai Nihon Kenchikuka Zenshu 18: Otani Sachio, Otaka Masato (The Complete Works of Contemporary Japanese Architects 18: Otani Sachio, Otaka Masato)*. Tokyo: Sanichi Shobo, 1971.

—— *Gendai Nihon Kenchikuka Zenshu 19: Kikutake Kiyonori, Maki Fumihiko (The Complete Works of Contemporary Japanese Architects 19: Kikutake Kiyonori, Maki Fumihiko)*. Tokyo: Sanichi Shobo, 1971.

Kurokawa, Kisho. "Metaborizumu hōhōron" (The Methodology of Metabolism). *Kindai kenchiku* (Nov. 1960): 50–63.

—— "A Method and Development of Metabolism: Two Systems of Metabolism." *Kenchiku bunka* 22 (Nov. 1967): 107–134.

—— "Challenge to the Capsule: Nakagin Capsule Tower Building." *Japan Architect* 47 (Oct. 1972): 17–38.

—— *Metabolism in Architecture*. Boulder, CO: Westview Press, 1977.

—— *From Metabolism to Symbiosis*. London: Academy Editions, 1992.

—— *Kurokawa Kisho Nōto: Shisaku to sōzō no kiato (The Note of Kisho Kurokawa: The track of thinking and creation)*. Tokyo: Dōbunshoin, 1994.

—— "The Architecture of the Age of Life Principle." *Japan Architect* 18 (Summer 1995): 4–13.

—— *Each One a Hero: The Philosophy of Symbiosis.* Tokyo: Kodansha International, 1997.

—— "Recent Situation about Nakagin Capsule Tower." Kisho Kurokawa Architect & Associates. http://www.kisho.co.jp (accessed Mar. 30, 2009).

Maki, Fumihiko. *Investigations in Collective Form.* St. Louis, MO: Washington University, 1964.

—— "The Future of Urban Environment." *Progressive Architecture* 45 (Oct. 1964): 178.

—— "Some Thought on Collective Form." In G. Kepes, ed., *Structure in Art and Science.* New York, 1965.

—— *Movement Systems in the City.* Cambridge, MA: Graduate School of Design, Harvard University, 1965.

—— "The Theory of Group Form." *Japan Architect* (Feb. 1970): 39.

—— "The Potential of Planning." *Architecture in Australia* 60 (Aug. 1971): 695.

—— "Street Space and Urban Scene." *Japan Architect* 49 (Jan. 1974): 42–44.

—— "Notes on Collective Form." *Japan Architect* (Winter 1994): 247–297.

—— *Fumihiko Maki: Buildings and Projects.* New York: Princeton Architectural Press, 1997.

—— "Acceptance Speech at the 1993 Ceremony for Pritzker Architecture Prize." Hyatt Foundation. *The Pritzker Architecture Prize 1993, Presented to Maki Fumihiko.* Los Angeles: Jensen & Walker, 1993.

—— *On Maki Architecture/Maki on Architecture.* Tokyo: Fumihiko Maki Traveling Exhibition Executive Committee, 2001.

Otaka, Masato. "Toshi oyobi kenchiku no kun riron" (Theory on City and Architectural Group). *Kindai kenchiku* (Nov. 1960): 26–30.

Otaka, Masato and Noboru Kawazoe, eds, *Metabolism and the Metabolists.* Tokyo: Bijutsu Shūpansha, 2005.

Stewart, David and Hajime Yatsuka, eds, *Arata Isozaki: Architecture 1960–1990.* Los Angeles: Museum of Contemporary Art, 1991.

Secondary sources

Abercrombie, Patrick. *Greater London Plan 1944.* London: Stationery Office, 1945.

Alberti, Leon Battista. *De re aedificatoria.* 1450. Argentorati: Excudebat M. Lacobus Cammerlander, 1541.

Alexander, Christopher. "A City Is Not a Tree." *Architectural Forum* 122, n.1 (1965): 58–62 and 122, n.2 (1965): 58–61.

—— *The Timeless Way of Building.* New York: Oxford University Press, 1979.

Alexander, Christopher, Sara Ishikawa and Murray Silverstein. *A Pattern Language: Towns, Buildings, Construction.* New York: Oxford University Press, 1977.

Alexander, Peter and Roger Gill, eds, *Utopias.* London: Duckworth, 1984.

Altherr, Alfred, *Three Japanese Architects: Mayekawa, Tange, Sakakura.* Teufen: Verlag Arthur Niggli AG, 1968.

Apter, David E. and Nagayo Sawa. *Against the State: Politics and Social Protest in Japan.* Cambridge, MA: Harvard University Press, 1984.

Asada, Takashi. "Tekiō to soshiki no jidai he" (*Towards an Era of Compatibility and Organization*). Kindai kenchiku (Nov. 1960): 24.

Ashihara, Yoshinobu. *The Hidden Order: Tokyo through the Twentieth Century.* Tokyo: Kodansha International, 1989.

Banham, Reyner. "CIAM." In Gerd Hatje, ed., *Encyclopaedia of Modern Architecture.* London: Thames & Hudson, 1963, 70–73.

—— *The New Brutalism: Ethic or Aesthetic?* London: Architectural Press, 1966.

—— *Megastructure: Urban Futures of the Recent Past.* New York: Harper & Row, 1976.

Banham, Reyner and Hiroyuki Suzuki. *Contemporary Japanese Architecture.* New York: Rizzoli, 1985.

Barnett, Jonathan. *The Elusive City: Five Centuries of Design, Ambition and Miscalculation.* New York: Harper & Row, 1986.

Barshay, Andrew. "Imaging Democracy in Postwar Japan: Reflections on Maruyama Masao and Modernism." *Journal of Japanese Studies* 18 (Summer 1992): 365–406.

Barthes, Roland. *Empire of Signs.* Trans. Richard Howard. New York: Hill & Wang, 1982.

Bibliography

Berns, Toren. "Why Metabolism was Never Modern?" *Architecture et idées* (Summer/Fall 2000): 56–71.

Bognar, Botond. *Contemporary Japanese Architecture: Its Development and Challenge*. New York: Van Nostrand Reinhold, 1985.

—— "Archaeology of a Fragmented Landscape," *Architectural Design* 58 (1988): 15–25.

—— *Tokyo: World Cities*. London: Academy Editions, 1997.

—— "What Goes Up, Must Come Down: Recent Urban Architecture in Japan." *Harvard Design Magazine* 3 (Fall 1997): 33–43.

Boyd, Robin. *Kenzo Tange*. New York: George Braziller, 1962.

—— *New Directions in Japanese Architecture*. New York: George Braziller, 1968.

Bulmer, Kenneth. *City Under the Sea*. New York: Digit Books, 1957.

—— *Beyond the Silver Sky*. New York: Ace Double, 1961.

Burgess, Ernest. "The Growth of the City: An Introduction to a Research Project." In Robert Park, Ernest Burgess and Roderick McKenzie, eds, *The City*. Chicago: University of Chicago Press, 1925. 47–62.

Busbea, Larry. *Topologies: The Urban Utopias in France, 1960–1970*. Cambridge, MA: MIT Press, 2007.

Calza, Gian Carlo. *Hokusai*. New York: Phaidon, 2003.

Chang, Ching-Yu. "Japanese Spatial Conception: A Critical Analysis of its Elements in the Culture and Tradition of Japan and its Post-war Era." Dissertation, University of Pennsylvania, 1982.

Coaldrake, William H. *Architecture and Authority in Japan*. London and New York: Routledge, 1996.

Coleman, Nathaniel. *Inventing an Exemplary Architecture: The Function of Utopia in Architectural Imagination*. Dissertation, University of Pennsylvania, 2000.

—— *Utopias and Architecture*. London: Routledge, 2005.

"Collective Intelligence in Design." *Architectural Design* 76 (Sep/Oct 2006): whole issue.

Collins, George R. "The Linear City." In David N. Lewis, ed., *Pedestrian in the City: Architects' Year Books, V.11*. London: Elek Books. 204–217.

Colquhoun, Alan. *Essays in Architectural Criticism: Modern Architecture and Historical Change*. Cambridge, MA: MIT Press, 1981.

—— "Post-modernism and Structuralism: A Retrospective Glance." In *Modernity and the Classical Tradition, Architectural Essays 1980–1987*, 243–255. Cambridge, MA: MIT Press, 1989.

Committee of the Second Architectural Convention of Japan. *Structure, Space, Mankind, Expo '70: A Photographic Interpreter*. Tokyo: Shinkenchiku-sha, 1970.

Conrads, Ulrich, ed., *Programs and Manifestoes on 20th-century Architecture*. Cambridge, MA: MIT Press, 1971.

Considerant, Victor. *Description du Phalanstére et considerations socials sur l'architectonique*. Paris: Librairie Sociétaire, 1848.

Cook, Peter. *Architecture: Action and Plan*. London: Studio Vista, 1967.

—— *Archigram*. London: Studio Vista, 1972.

—— "Archigram Effect." *Croqui*. 8 (Apr./May, 1989): 4–40.

Crilley, Darrel. "Megastructures and Urban Change: Aesthetics, Ideology and Design." In Knox, Paul L., ed., *The Restless Urban Landscape*. Englewood Cliffs, NJ: Prentice Hall, 1993.

Curtis, William. *Modern Architecture since 1900*. Englewood Cliffs, NJ: Prentice Hall, 1996.

Cybriwsky, Roman. *Tokyo: The Changing Profile of an Urban Giant*. Boston: G. K. Hall & Co., 1991.

Dahinden, Justus. *Urban Structures for the Future*. Trans. Gerald Onn. New York: Praeger, 1972.

Davis, Ian. "Skopje Rebuilt: Reconstruction following the 1963 Earthquake." *Architectural Design* 45 (Nov. 1975): 660–663.

De Long, David G., ed., *Frank Lloyd Wright and the Living City*. Weil am Rhein: Vitra Design Museum, 1998.

Deyong, Sarah. "Planetary Habitat: the origins of a Phantom Movement." *Journal of Architecture* 6 (Summer 2001): 113–128.

"Dialogue: Questions by Mr. Kenzo Tange and Answers by Mr. Antonin Raymond Broadcast on April 27th, 28th and 29th, 1960 in Japanese." *Architectural Design* (Feb. 1961): 56–57.

Dickson, Gordon R. *The Space Swimmers*. New York: Berkley Publishing Corporation, 1963.

Donat, John, ed., *World Architecture*. Vol. 2. New York: Viking Press, 1965.

Dower, John W. "Peace and Democracy in Two Systems: External Policy and Internal Conflict." In Andrew Gordon, ed., *Postwar Japan as History*. Berkeley: University of California Press, 1992.

Doxiadis, C.A. "On Linear Cities." In David N. Lewis, ed., *Urban Structure: Architects' Year Books*, v.12. London: Elek Books, 49–51.

Drew, Philip. *Third Generation: The Changing Meaning of Architecture*. New York: Praeger Publishers, 1972.

Drexler, Arthur. *The Architecture of Japan*. New York: Museum of Modern Art, 1955.

Dreysse, D.W. *May-Siedlungen: Architecturürer durch acht Siedlungen des Neuen Frankfurt, 1926–1930*. Frankfurt am Main: Fricke, 1987.

Eaton, Ruth. *Ideal Cities: Utopianism and the (Un)Built Environment*. London: Thames & Hudson, 2002.

"Editorial." *Japan Architect* (April 1961): 7.

Eto, Jun. *A Nation Reborn: A Short History of Postwar Japan*. Tokyo: International Society for Educational Information, Inc., 1974.

Evenson, Norma. *Le Corbusier: The Machine and the Grand Design*. New York: George Braziller, 1969.

Ferguson, Russell, ed., *At the End of the Century: One Hundred Years of Architecture*. Los Angeles: Museum of Modern Art, 1998.

Fiévé, Nicolas, and Paul Waley, eds, *Japanese Capitals in Historical Perspective: Place, Power and Memory in Kyoto, Edo and Tokyo*. London: RoutledgeCurzon, 2003.

Filarete (Antonio di Piero Averlino). *Trattato di architettura* (1461–64). Milan: Il Polifilo, 1972.

Fisher, Jack C. "The Reconstruction of Skopje." *Journal of American Institute of Planners* 30 (Feb. 1964): 46–48.

Fishman, Robert. *Urban Utopias in the Twentieth Century: Ebenezer Howard, Frank Lloyd Wright, and Le Corbusier*. Cambridge, MA: MIT Press, 1982.

—— "From the Radiant City to Vichy: Le Corbusier's Plans and Politics, 1928–1942." In Russell Walden, ed., *The Open Hand: Essays on Le Corbusier*. Cambridge, MA: MIT Press, 1977, 144–183.

Fourier, Charles. *Description du Phalanstére et considerations socials sur l'architectonique*. Paris: 1848.

Frampton, Kenneth. *Modern Architecture: A Critical History*. New York: Thames & Hudson, 1992.

—— "Notes on Soviet Urbanism, 1917–32." In David N. Lewis, ed., *Urban Structure: Architects' Year Book*. v.12 (1968), 238–252.

—— "The Work and Influence of El Lissitzky." In David N. Lewis, ed., *Urban Structure: Architects' Year Book*. v.12 (1968), 253–268.

——, ed., *A New Wave of Japanese Architecture*. New York: The Institute for Architecture and Urban Studies, 1978.

—— "The Rise and Fall of Mega-architecture: Arata Isozaki and the Crisis of Metabolism, 1952–66." In Kenneth Frampton and Yukio Futagawa, eds, *Arata Isozaki*. Tokyo: A. D. A. Edita, 1991, 8–15.

—— "The Five Voices of Kisho Kurokawa," *Japan Architect* (Summer 1995): 14–19.

—— *Megaform as Urban Landscape: 1999 Raoul Wallenberg Lecture*. Ann Arbor: The University of Michigan, A. Alfred Taubman College of Architecture and Urban Planning, 1999.

Fujimori, Terunobu. "Dentō ronsō" (Tradition Debate). In *Gendai kenchiku no kiseki* (*The Trace of Modern Architecture*). Tokyo: Shinkenchiku, 1995, 16–30.

—— *Nihon no kindai kenchiku* (*Modern Architecture of Japan*). 2 vols. Tokyo: Iwanami Shisho, 1993.

Fujisaki Keiichiro. "Kikutake sensei, ano yoru, Kahn to nanni ga attan desuka?" (Professor Kikutake, how was the meeting with Kahn that evening?), *Casa* (July 2004): 74–76.

Garon, Sheldon. "Rethinking Modernization in Japanese History." *Journal of Asian Studies* 53, n.2 (May 1994): 346–366.

Gayle, Curtis. *Marxist History and Postwar Japanese Nationalism*. London: RoutledgeCurzon, 2003.

Geddes, Patrick. *Cities in Evolution: An Introduction to the Town Planning Movement and to the Study of Civics*. London: William & Norgate, 1915.

Geoghegan, Vincent. *Utopianism and Marxism*. London: Methuen, 1987.

Goldhagen, Sarah W. and Réjean Legault, eds, *Anxious Modernisms: Experimentation in Postwar Architectural Culture*. Cambridge, MA: MIT Press, 2000.

Gordon, Andrew, ed., *Postwar Japan as History*. Berkeley: Univ. of California Press, 1993.

Gordon, David. *Battery Park City: Politics and Planning on the New York Waterfront*. Amsterdam: Gordon & Breach, 1997.

Gottmann, Jean. *Megalopolis: the Urbanized Northeastern Seaboard of the United States*. New York: Twentieth Century Fund, 1961.

Bibliography

Gregory, Rob. "Lost in Translation (Exhibition Review)." *Architectural Review* 217 (June 2005): 38–41.

Guiheux, Alain. *Kisho Kurokawa: Le Métabolisme, 1960–1975*. Paris: Centre Georges Pompidou, 1997.

Habraken, N. J. *Supports: An Alternative to Mass Housing*. 1971. Trans. B. Valkenburg. London: Urban International, 1999.

Hamaguchi, Ryuichi. *Hyumanizumu no kenchiku* (*Architecture of Humanism*). Yokyo: Yukeisha, 1947.

—— "Nihon kokumin kenchiku yōshiki no mondai: Kenchikugaku no tachiba kara" (The Problem of the Style of Japanese Civil Architecture: The Position of Architecture and others), Part 4. *Shinkenchiku* 20, n.20 (Oct. 1944): 270–279.

Harootunian, Harry. "America's Japan/Japan's Japan." In Masao Miyashi and Harry Harootunian, eds, *Japan in the World*. Durham, NC: Duke University Press, 1993, 196–221.

Hein, Carola. "Visionary Plans and Planners." In Nicolas Fiévé and Paul Waley, eds, *Japanese Capitals in Historical Perspective: Place, Power and Memory in Kyoto, Edo and Tokyo*. London: RoutledgeCurzon, 2003, 309–346.

—— "The Transformation of Planning Ideas in Japan and Its Colonies." In Joe Nasr and Mercedes Volait, eds, *Urbanism: Import or Exported?* Chichester: Wiley-Academy, 2003.

Hein, Carola, Jeffrey Diefendorf and Ishida Yorifusa, eds, *Rebuilding Urban Japan after 1945*. London: Palgrave/Macmillan, 2003.

Henshu Tokyo Kokuritsu Hakubutsukan. *Doki no Zokei: Jomon no do, Yayoi no sei* (*The Form of Mud Vessel: The Dynamics of Jomon and the Quietness of Yayoi*). Tokyo: Tokyo Kokuritsu Hakubutsukan, 2001.

Hidaka, Jin. "Nakagin Capsule Tower Building." *UIA 2011 Tokyo* (International Union of Architects 2011 Congress in Tokyo) circular, 2008.

Hirro, Ichikawa. "Reconstructing Tokyo: The Attempt to Transform a Metropolis." In *Rebuilding Urban Japan After 1945*, edited by Carola Hein, Jeffrey Diefendorf and Ishida Yorifusa, 50–67. New York: Palgrave Macmillan, 2003.

Horiguchi, Setemi. "Geijutsu to kenchiku to no kansō" (The Thought on Arts and Architecture). In *Bunriha Kenchikukai sakuhinshū* (*The Architectural Works of Secessionism*), v.2. Tokyo: Iwanami Shoten, 1921.

——, ed., *Architectural Beauty in Japan*. Tokyo: Kokusai Bunka Shinkōkai, 1955.

Howard, Ebenezer. *Garden Cities of To-Morrow*. London: S. Sonnenschein & Co. Ltd., 1902.

Hursch, Erhard. *Tokyo*. Tokyo: Charles E. Tuttle, 1965.

The Hyatt Foundation. *The Pritzker Architecture Prize 1993, Presented to Fumihiko Maki*. Los Angeles: Jensen & Walker, 1993.

"International Competitions, 1965." *UIA: revue de l'Union international des architects* 37 (Feb. 1966): 9–30.

Ishida, Yorifusa. *Tokyo seichō to keikaku 1868–1988* (*Tokyo Growth and Planning 1868–1988*). Tokyo: Toritsu Daigaku Toshi Kenkyūjo, 1988.

—— *Nihon kindai toshi keikaku no hyakunen* (*100 Years of Modern Planning in Japan*). Tokyo: Jichitai Kenkyūsha, 1987.

Ito, Chuta. *Ito Chuta chosakushu: Nihon kenchiku no kenkyu* (*Chuta Ito's Research: Research of Japanese Architecture*). Tokyo: Hara Shobo, 1982.

—— "Shin Nihon kenchiku nit suite" (Towards a New Japanese Architecture). *Kenchiku chishiki* 1, n.1 (Jan. 1935): 1–6.

Ito, Teiji. "Moratorium and Invisibility." *Arata Isozaki: Architecture 1960–1990*. Edited by David Stewart and Hajime Yatsuka. Los Angeles : Museum of Contemporary Art.

Ito, Teiji. "Kenchikukai rokujū nendai no danmen" (The Anatomy of the Architectural Circle in the 60s). *Kenchiku bunka* 16, n.1 (Jan. 1961): 73–80.

Jacobs, Jane. *The Death and Life of Great American Cities*. New York: Random House, 1961.

"Japan World Exposition, Osaka, 1970." *Japan Architect* 45 (May/June 1970): whole issue.

Japanese Illustrated Encyclopedia. *Japanese History: 11 Experts Reflect on the Past*. Tokyo: Kodansha International, 1996.

Jencks, Charles. *The Language of Post-Modern Architecture*. London: Academy Editions, 1977.

Jerome, Mike. "Whatever Happened to the Metabolists?" *Architecture Design* (May 1967): 208–217.

Jinnai, Hidenobu. *Tokyo: A Spatial Anthropology*. Trans. Kimiko Nishimura. Berkeley: University of California Press, 1995.

Johnson, Chalmers A. *MITI and the Japanese Miracle: The Growth of Industrial Policy, 1925–1975*. San Francisco: Stanford University Press, 2004.

Johnson, Eugene J. and Michael J. Lewis. *Drawn from the Source: The Travel Sketches of Louis I. Kahn*. Cambridge, MA: MIT Press, 1996.

Kahn, Louis I. "Toward a Plan for Midtown Philadelphia." (1953). In Alessandra Latour, ed., *Louis I. Kahn: Writings, Lectures, Interviews*. New York: Rizzoli, 1991, 28–52.

—— "Form and Design." (1960). In Alessandra Latour, ed., *Louis I. Kahn: Writings, Lectures, Interviews*. New York: Rizzoli, 1991, 113–116.

—— "New Frontiers in Architecture: CIAM in Otterlo 1959: Talk at the Conclusion of the Otterlo Congress." In Alessandra Latour, ed., *Louis I. Kahn: Writings, Lectures, Interviews*. New York: Rizzoli, 1991, 81–99.

Keizai Koho Senta. *Japan: An International Comparison*. Tokyo: Keizai Koho Senta, 1983.

Kestenbaum, Jacqueline Eve. "Modernism and tradition in Japanese architectural ideology, 1931–1955." Dissertation, Columbia University, 1996.

Kikan Obayashi (*Quarterly of Obayashi*). "Age of Metabolism." *Kikan Obayashi* 48 (Special issue: Metabolism 2001): 96–99.

Kikuchi, Makoto, ed., *Medeia toshite no kenchiku: Pirannzi kara Expo '70 mate* (*Architecture as Media: From Roma 1760 to Osaka 1970*). Tokyo: University of Tokyo Museum, 2005.

Klauser, Wilhelm. "Introduction: Rules and Identities." In Christopher Knabe and Joerg Rainer Noennig, eds, *Shaking the Foundation: Japanese Architects in Dialogue*, Munich: Prestel, 1999. 10–14.

Koolhaas, Rem. "Urbanism after Innocence: Four Projects." *Assemblage* 18 (Aug. 1992): 82–113.

Kopp, Anatole. *Town and Revolution, Soviet Architecture and City Planning, 1917–1935*. New York: G. Braziller, 1970.

Koschmann, J. Victor. "Intellectuals and Politics." In Andrew Gordon, ed., *Postwar Japan as History*. Berkeley: University of California Press, 1992.

Kumar, Krishan. *Utopianism*. Minneapolis: University of Minnesota Press, 1991.

Kural, René. *Architecture of the Information Society: The World City Expressed through the Chaos of Tokyo*. Trans. Kenja Henriksen. Copenhagen: Royal Danish Academy of Fine Arts, 2000.

Lang, Peter and William Menking. *Superstudio: Life Without Objects*. Milan: Skira Editore, 2003.

Laotse. *I Ching*. Translated by Richard Wilhelm. Princeton, NJ: Bollinggen, 1967.

Larson, Kent, ed., *Louis I. Kahn: Unbuilt Masterwork*. New York: Monacelli Press, 2000.

Le Corbusier. *The City of To-morrow and Its Planning*. (1924). Trans. Frederick Etchells. New York: Dover, 1987.

—— *The Radiant City: Elements of a Doctrine of Urbanism to Be Used as the Basis of our Machine-age Civilization*. (1933). New York: Orion Press, 1967.

—— *The Athens Charter*. (1933). Translated by Anthony Eardley. New York: Grossman, 1973.

—— *L'unité d'Habitation de Marseille*. Trans. Geoffrey Sainsbury. *Marseilles Block*. London: Harvill Press, 1953.

—— *Précisions sur un état présente de l'architecture et de l'urbanisme*. (1930). Trans. Edith Schreiber Aujame. *Precisions on the Present State of Architecture and City Planning*. Cambridge, MA: MIT Press, 1991.

Ledoux, Claude-Nicholas. *L'Architecture consideree sous le rapport de l'art, des moeurs, et de la legislation*. Paris: Chez l'auteur, 1804.

Lem, Stanislaw. *Solaris*. New York: Walker, 1962.

Lévi-Strauss, Claude. *Structural Anthropology*. Translated by Claire Jacobson and Brooke Grundfest Schoepf. New York: Basic Books, 1963.

Lin, Zhongjie. "From Megastructure to Megalopolis: Formation and Transformation of Mega-projects in Tokyo Bay." *Journal of Urban Design* 12 (Feb. 2007): 73–92.

Lissitzky, El. "Alte Stadt – Neue Baukorper." *Russland*. Reprinted in *Ullstein Bauwelt Fundamente* 14: 32–38.

—— *Russland*. Trans. Eric Dluhosch. *Russia: An Architecture for World Revolution*. Cambridge, MA: MIT Press, 1970.

Locker, Angus. "The Logic of Spectacle c.1970." *Art History* 30, no.4 (Sep. 2007): 571–589.

Loos, Adolf. *Spoken into the Void: Collected Essays, 1897–1900*. Trans. Jane O. Newman and John H. Smith. Cambridge, MA: MIT Press, 1982.

Bibliography

Lynch, Kevin. *The Image of the City*. Cambridge, MA: Technology Press, 1960.

Mannheim, Karl *Ideology and Utopia*. London: Routledge & Kegan Paul, 1960.

"Marina City, Chicago." *Architectural Record* 134 (Sep. 1963): 193–214.

Marx, Karl and Friedrich Engels. *Communist Manifesto*. Edited by Fredric L. Bender. New York: W. W. Norton, 1988.

McBride, Blair. "Nakagin Capsule Tower: Architecture of the Future." http://pingmag.jp (accessed Dec 2008).

Mcleod, Mary. "Le Corbusier and Algiers." *Oppositions* 19 (Winter/Spring 1980): 54–85.

Meller, Helen E. *The Ideal City*. Leicester: Leicester University Press, 1979.

Meyerson, Martin. "Utopian Traditions and the Planning of Cities." In Lloyd Rodwin, ed., *The Future Metropolis*. New York: G. Braziller, 1961.

Miliutin, N. A. *Sotsgorod: The Problem of Building Socialist Cities*. (1930). Trans. Arthur Sprague. Cambridge, MA: MIT Press, 1974.

Moos, Stanislaus von. *Le Corbusier: Elements of a Synthesis*. Cambridge, MA: MIT Press, 1979.

More, Thomas. *Utopia*. Trans. Clarence H. Miller. New Haven, CT: Yale University Press, 2001.

Mumford, Eric. *The CIAM Discourse on Urbanism: 1928–1960*. Cambridge, MA: MIT Press, 2000.

Mumford, Lewis. "Utopia: The City and the Machine." *Daedalus: Journal of the American Academy of Arts and Sciences*, XCIV, Special Issue "Utopia" (Spring 1965): 271–292. Reprint in Frank E. Manuel. ed., *Utopias and Utopian Thought*. London: Souvenir Press, 1973. 33–44.

—— "Yesterday's City of Tomorrow." *Urban Prospect*. New York: Harcourt, Brace & World, 1968.

—— *Story of Utopias*. New York: P. Smith, 1941.

Muramatsu, Teijiro. *Nihon kindai kenchiku no rekishi* (*History of Japanese Modern Architecture*). Tokyo: Nihon Hōsō Shuppan Kyōkai, 1977.

Museum of Modern Art. *The Changing of the Avant-garde: Visionary Architectural Drawing from the Howard Gilman Collection*. New York: Museum of Modern Art, 2002.

—— "Home Delivery: Fabricating the Modern Dwelling." New York, July 20–Oct. 20, 2008.

"Nakagin Tower WAN Poll Result." *World Architecture News*. http://www.worldarchitecture news.com, Sep. 23, 2005 (Accessed Mar. 30, 2009).

Nevzgodine, Ivan V. "'Press – Fight for Socialist Cities!': Perception and Critique of the Architecture of Novosibirsk, 1920–1940." *Thema* 7 (Jan. 2003).

Newman, Oscar. *New Frontiers in Architecture: CIAM'59 in Otterlo*. New York: Universal Books, 1961.

Nishiyama, Uzo. "Home City: Future Image of City." *Kindai kenchiku* 14 (Mar. 1961): 52–58.

—— "Image Planning." In World Design Conference Organization, ed., *World Design Conference 1960 in Tokyo*. Tokyo: Bijutsu Shūpansha, 1961, 189–191.

—— "A Plan for Kyoto," *Japan Architect* (Feb 1965): 61–80.

—— "Sangaku toshi" (Cities on Mountain Slopes). In Nishiyama Uzo, ed., *Chiiki kūkan ron* (*Reflections on Urban, Regional and National Space*). Tokyo: Keisō Shobō, 1978.

—— *Nihon no sumai* (*Housing in Japan*). 3 vols. Tokyo: Keisō Shobō, 1975, 1976, 1980.

—— *Machizukuri no koso* (*The Idea of City Building*). Tokyo: Toshi Bunkasha, 1990.

Nitschke, Günter. "The Metabolists of Japan." *Architectural Design* 34 (Oct. 1964): 509–524.

—— "Tokyo: 'Olympic Planning' versus 'Dream Planning'," *Architectural Design* 34 (Oct. 1964): 482–508.

—— "'Ma': The Japanese Sense of 'Place' in Old and New Architecture and Planning." *Architectural Design* 36 (Mar. 1966): 116–156.

Noffsinger, James Philip. *Kenzo Tange: Modern Japan's Genius Architect*. Van Bibliographies, Architecture Series, 1980.

Ockman, Joan, ed., *Architecture Culture 1943–1968: A Documentary Anthology*. New York: Rizzoli, 1993.

Okamoto, Taro. *The Rediscovery of Japan – Records of Art of the Land*. Tokyo: Shinchosha, 1958.

Oshima, Ken Tadashi. "Manfredo Tafuri and Japan: An Incomplete Project." *Architectural Theory Review: The Journal of the Department of Architecture, Planning and Allied Arts* 8 (Apr. 2003): 16–29.

Packard, George R. *Protest in Tokyo: The Security Treaty Crisis of 1960*. Princeton, NJ: Princeton Press, 1966.

Raymond, Antonin. *An Autobiography*. Tokyo and Rutland: Charles E. Tuttle, 1973.

—— "Interview with Antonin Raymond." *Architectural Design* (Feb. 1961): 56–57.

Reed, Peter Shedd. *Towards Form: Louis I. Kahn's Urban Designs for Philadelphia, 1939–1962.* Dissertation, University of Pennsylvania, 1989.

Reischauer, Edwin and Albert Craig. *Japan: Tradition and Transformation.* Boston: Houghton Mifflin, 1978.

Reynolds, Jonathan M. "Ise Shrine and a Modernist Construction of Japanese Tradition." *Art Bulletin,* 83 (June 2001): 316–341.

—— *Maekawa Kunio and the Emergence of Japanese Modernist Architecture.* Berkeley: University of California Press, 2001.

Riani, Paolo. *Kenzo Tange.* London: Hamlyn, 1969.

Richards, J. M. "Expo 70." Editorial. *Architectural Review* (Aug. 1970): 67, 70.

Risselada, Max and Dirk van den Heuvel, eds, *Team 10, 1953–81: In Search of Utopia of the Present.* Rotterdam: NAi Publishers, 2006.

Pohl, Frederick and Jack Williamson. *Undersea Quest.* New York: Gnome Press, 1954.

—— *Undersea Fleet.* New York: Gnome Press, 1956.

—— *Undersea City.* New York: Gnome Press, 1958.

Ross, Michael. F. *Beyond Metabolism: The New Japanese Architecture.* New York: Architectural Record, 1977.

Rossi, Aldo. *L'architecture della città.* 1966. Trans. Diane Ghirardo and Joan Ockman. *The Architecture of the City.* Cambridge, MA: MIT Press, 1982.

Rowe, Colin and Fred Koetter. *Collage City.* Cambridge, MA: MIT Press, 1978.

Rudofsky, Bernard. *Architecture without Architects: An Introduction to Nonpedigreed Architecture.* New York: Museum of Modern Art, 1964.

Sabsovich, Leonid. *SSSR cherez 10 let.* Moscow: Gosizdat RSFSR "Moskovskii rabochii," 1930.

Sadler, Simon. *The Situationist City.* Cambridge, MA: MIT Press, 1998.

—— *Archigram: Architecture without Architecture.* Cambridge, MA: MIT Press, 2005.

Sant'Elia, Antonio. "The Manifesto of Futurist Architecture" (1914). In Umbro Apollonio, ed., *Futurist Manifestos.* Boston: Museum of Fine Arts Publications, 2001, 172.

Sasaki, Takabumi. "A Passage through the Dys-topia of Expo '70." *Japan Architect* (May/June 1970): 143–150.

Saussure, Ferdinand de. *Course in General Linguistics.* Translated by Wade Baskin. New York: Philosophical Library, 1959.

Schaer, Roland, Gregory Claeys and Lyman Tower Sargent, eds, *Utopia: The Search for the Ideal Society in the Western World.* New York: New York Public Library, Oxford University Press, 2000.

Schirren, Matthias, ed., *Bruno Taut: Alpine Architektur, eine Utopie.* Munich: Prestel, 2004.

Schumacher, E. F. *Small is Beautiful: Economics as if People Matter*ed., New York: Harper & Row, 1975.

Schmertz, Mildred F. "Expo '70." *Architectural Record* (June 1970): 115–119.

Scott, Felicity. "Architecture or Techno-Utopia." *Grey Room* 1 (Apr. 2001): 112–126.

Scoville, J. G.. "The Taylorization of Vladmir Ilich Lenin." *Industrial Relations* 40 (2001): 620–626.

Serenyi, Peter. "Le Corbusier, Fourier and the Monastery of Ema." *Art Bulletin* 49 (Dec. 1967): 277–286.

Shi, Kuang, Gary Hack and Zhongjie Lin. *Urban Design in the Global Perspective.* Beijing: China Architecture and Building Press, 2006.

Shiga, Shigetaka. *Nihon Fukei-ron (Theory of the Japanese Landscape).*Tokyo: Iwanami Shoten, 1937.

Shinohara, Kazuo. "Beyond Symbol Spaces: An Introduction to Primary Spaces as Functional Spaces." *Japan Architect* (April 1971): 81–88.

Shirai, Sei-ichi. "Jomon no narumono" (The Transformation of Jomon). *Shinkenchiku* (April 1956): 8–9.

Shively, Donald H., ed., *Tradition and Modernization in Japanese Culture.* Princeton, NJ: Princeton University Press, 1971.

Simeoforidis, Yorgos. "Notes for a Cultural History and the Contemporary Urban Condition." In Rem Koolhaas et al., eds, *Mutations: Harvard Project on the City.* Barcelona: Actar, 2001, 414–425.

Smithson, Alison, ed., *Team 10 Primer.* Cambridge, MA: MIT Press, 1968.

Bibliography

——, ed., *Team 10 Meeting: 1953–1984*. New York: Rizzoli, 1991.

Smithson, Alison and Peter Smithson. "The Re-birth of Japanese Architecture." *Architectural Design*, Special Japan Issue (Feb. 1960): 55–81.

—— *Urban Structuring: Studies of Alison and Peter Smithson*. New York: Reinhold Publishing Corporation, 1967.

Smithson, Peter. "Reflections on Tange Kenzo's Tokyo Bay Plan." *Architectural Design* (Oct. 1964): 479–480.

Sorensen, André. *The Making of Urban Japan: Cities and Planning from Edo to the Twenty-first Century*. London and New York: Routledge, 2002.

Soria y Mata, Arturo. *La cité linéaire: conception nouvelle pour l'aménagement des villes*. (1882). Paris: École nationale supérieure des Beaux Arts, 1984.

Steiner, Hadas A. *Beyond Archigram: The Structure of Circulation*. New York: Routldege, 2009.

Stewart, David. *The Making of a Japanese Modern Architecture: 1868 to the Present*. Tokyo: Kodansha International, 1987.

Strauven, Francis. *Aldo van Eyck's Orphanage: a Modern Monument*. New York: NAi Publishers, 1996.

Sussman, Elizabeth, ed., *On the Passage of a Few People through a Rather Brief Moment in Time: The Situationist International, 1957–1972*. Cambridge, MA: MIT Press, 1989.

Suzuki, Hiroyuki. "Tokyo has a Thousand Eyes." *Japan Architect* 57 (Apr. 1982): 10–16.

Suzuki, Hiroyuki, Reyner Banham and Katsuhiro Kobayashi. *Contemporary Architecture of Japan 1958–1984*. New York: Rizzoli, 1985.

Tafuri, Manfredo. *Architecture and Utopia: Design and Capitalist Development*. Cambridge, MA: MIT Press, 1976.

—— *Theories and History of Architecture*. Trans. Giorgio Verrecchia. New York: Harper & Row, 1980.

—— *The Sphere and the Labyrinth: Avant-gardes and Architecture from Piranesi to the 1970s*. Cambridge, MA: MIT Press, 1987.

Tafuri, Manfedo and Francesco Dal Co. *Modern Architecture*. Translated by Robert Erich Wolf. New York: H. N. Abrams, 1979.

Tatayama, Aika. "Datong toshi keikaku oboka" (Memo of the City Planning of Datong). *Geidai kenchiku* 4 (Sep. 1939): 48–57.

"Taraka Beautilion." *Architectural Review* (Aug. 1970): 100.

Tarr, Joel A. "The Metabolism of the Industrial City." *Journal of Urban History*, v.28, n.5 (July 2002): 511–545.

Taut, Bruno. *Alpine Architektur*. Hagen: Folk-Verlag, 1919.

—— *Houses and People of Japan*. Tokyo: Sanseido, 1937.

Taylor, Frederick. *The Principles of Scientific Management*. New York: Harper & Brothers, 1911.

Taylor, Jennifer. *The Architecture of Fumihiko Maki: Space, City, Order and Making*. Basel: Birkhäuser, 2003.

"Tokyo into Venice?" *Architectural Forum* (Sep. 1961): 142–143.

Tokyo Metropolitan Government. *A Hundred Years of Tokyo City Planning*. Tokyo: Tokyo Metropolitan Government Publications, 1994.

Toshi dezain kenkyukai (Urban Design Research Group). "Nihon no Toshi Kukan" (Japanese Urban Space). *Kenchiku bunka* (Dec. 1963): whole issue.

—— *Nihon no Toshi Kukan (Japanese Urban Space)*. Tokyo: Shokokusha, 1968.

Toshi Keikaku Gakkai. *Century of Modern City Planning and Its Perspective*. Tokyo: Shōkokusha, 1988.

Trotsky, Leon. *Literature and Revolution*. (1923). Trans. Rose Stunsky. Ann Arbor: University of Michigan Press, 1960.

Tyrwhitt, Jaqueline, Jose J. Sert and Ernesto Regers, eds, *Heart of the City: Towards the Humanization of Urban Life*. London: Lund Humphries, 1952.

Ulam, Adam. "Socialism and Utopia." *Daedalus: Journal of the American Academy of Arts and Sciences*, XCIV, Special Issue "Utopia" (Spring 1965): 382–400.

Urushima, Andrea Y. F. "Genesis and Culmination of Uzo Nishiyama's Proposal of a 'Model Core of a Future City' for the Expo 70 Site." *Planning Perspective* 22 (Oct. 2007): 391–416.

Veblen, Thorstein. *The Engineers and the Price System*. New York: Viking Press, 1921.

Venturi, Robert. *Complexity and Contradiction in Architecture*. New York: Museum of Modern Art, 1966.

Venturi, Robert, Denise Scott Brown and Steven Izenour. *Learning from Las Vegas: The Forgotten Symbolism of Architectural Form*. Cambridge, MA: MIT Press, 1972.

Wachsmann, Konrad. *The Turning Point of Building: Structure and Design*. Translated by Thomas E. Burton. New York: Reinhold, 1961.

Watanabe, Hiroshi. "Kahn and Japan." *Progressive Architecture* 65 (Dec. 1984): 78–81.

Watanabe, Yoshio. "*Architectural Beauty in Japan.*" Tokyo: Society for International Cultural Relations, 1955.

Welter, Volker M. *Biopolis: Patrick Geddes and the City of Life*. Cambridge, MA: MIT Press, 2002.

Wendelken, Cherie. "Putting Metabolism Back in Place: The Making of a Radically Decontextualized Architecture in Japan." In Sarah Williams Goldhagen and Réjean Legault, eds, *Anxious Modernisms: Experimentation in Postwar Architectural Culture*. Cambridge, MA: MIT Press, 2000.

—— "International Perspectives on Metabolism." *Kenchiku bunka* 55, n. 646 (Aug. 2000): 124–132.

White, Anthony G. *Kenzo Tange: A Selected Bibliography*. Monticello, IL: Vance Bibliographies, 1990.

Wiener, Norbert. *Cybernetics: Or Control and Communication in the Animal and the Machine*. New York: Wiley, 1948.

Wilde, Oscar. "The Soul of Man Under Socialism." (1891). In Hesketh Pearson, ed., *De Profundis and Other Writings*. Harmondsworth: Penguin, 1973.

Wolf, Peter. "City Structuring and Social Sense in 19th and 20th Century Urbanism." *Perspecta* 13/14 (1971): 220–233.

Wolman, Abel. "The Metabolism of Cities." *Scientific American* 213 (1965): 156–174.

The World Design Conference Organization. *World Design Conference 1960 in Tokyo*. Tokyo: Bijutsu Shūpansha, 1961.

Wright, Frank L. *The New Frontier: Broadacre City*. Spring Green, WI: Taliesin Fellowship, 1940.

—— *When Democracy Builds*. Chicago: University of Chicago Press, 1945.

—— *The Living City*. New York: Horizon Press, 1958.

Yatsuka, Hajime, *Shiso toshite no Nihon jindai kenchiku* (*The Intellectual History of Japanese Modern Architecture*). Tokyo: Ishinami shoden, 2005.

—— "Internationalism Versus Regionalism," In Richard Koshalek, Elizabeth Smith et al., eds, *At the End of the Century: One hundred Years of Architecture*. Los Angeles: Moca, 1998, 186–198.

—— "The 1960 Tokyo Bay Project of Kenzo Tange." In Arie Graafland and Deborah Hauptmann, eds, *Cities in Transition*. Rotterdam: 010 Publishers, 2001, 178–191.

—— "Architecture in the Urban Desert: A Critical Introduction to Japanese Architecture after Modernism." *Oppositions* 23 (Winter 1981): 2–35.

—— "Between West and East Part III: What Has – And Has Not Happened in the Japanese Cities?" *Telescope* 8 (Autumn 1992): 86–95.

——"Between West and East Part IV: Nippon Postmodern." *Telescope* 9 (Jan./Feb. 1993): 144–161.

—— "Kindai kenchiku no 'kikai'" (The 'Machine' of Modern Architecture). In Mori Art Museum, ed., *Archilab: New Experiments in Architecture, Art and the City, 1950–2005*. Tokyo: Mori Art Museum, 2005.

—— "Japan, the Object of Dual Aestheticization." *Thesis, Wissenschaftliche Zeitschrift der Bauhaus-Universität Weimar* 44 (1998): 18–27.

Yatsuka, Hajime and Yoshimatsu Hideki. *Metaborizumu: 1960 nendai no Nihon kenchiku avangaruto* (*Metabolism: Japanese Architectural Avant-garde of the 1960s*). Tokyo: Inax Publishing Co., 1997.

Yokohama Minato Mirai 21 Corporation. *Yokohama Minato Mirai 21: A City of Creative Experimentation*. Yokohama: Yokohama Minato Mirai 21 Corporation, 2002.

Young, Louis. *Japan's Total Empire: Manchuria and the Culture of Wartime Imperialism*. Berkeley: University of California Press, 1999.

"Yume o kizuku 'kaijō toshi'" (Building the Dream of a "Marine City"). *Shūkan yomiri* (Jan. 8, 1961): 112–117.

Interviews

Kinya Maruyama – June 22, 2004.
Kisho Kurokawa – June 24, 2004.
Hisao Kohyama – June 25, 2004.
Ryoji Terajima – June 28, 2004.
Hajime Yatsuka – June 30, 2004.
Fumihiko Maki – July 1, 2004.
Toshio Nakamura – July 2, 2004.
David Stewart – Sep. 15, 2005.
Ching-yu Chang – June 22, 2006.
Kiyonori Kikutake – July 23, 2008.
Fumihiko Maki – July 25, 2008.
Mikio Kurokawa – Aug. 6, 2008.
Arata Isozaki – Nov. 12, 2008.

Index